Figures That Speak

Modern Intellectual and Political History of the Middle East
Fred H. Lawson, *Series Editor*

Select Titles in Modern Intellectual and Political History of the Middle East

The Autocratic Parliament: Power and Legitimacy in Egypt, 1866–2011
Irene Weipert-Fenner

Hakibbutz Ha'artzi, Mapam, and the Demise of the Israeli Labor Movement
Tal Elmaliach; Haim Watzman, trans.

Iran's Experiment with Parliamentary Governance: The Second Majles, 1909–1911
Mangol Bayat

National Symbols in Modern Iran: Identity, Ethnicity, and Collective Memory
Menahem Merhavy

Ottoman Rule of Law and the Modern Political Trial: The Yıldız Case
Avi Rubin

Shaykh Yūsuf al-Qaraḍāwī: Spiritual Mentor of Wasaṭī Salafism
Sagi Polka

Watermelon Democracy: Egypt's Turbulent Transition
Joshua Stacher

Why Alliances Fail: Islamist and Leftist Coalitions in North Africa
Matt Buehler

For a full list of titles in this series, visit https://press.syr.edu/supressbook-series/modern-intellectual-and-political-history-of-the-middle-east/.

Figures That Speak

The Vocabulary of Turkish Nationalism

Matthew deTar

Syracuse University Press

First Edition 2022

22 23 24 25 26 27 6 5 4 3 2 1

∞ The paper used in this publication meets the minimum requirements of the American National Standard for Information Sciences—Permanence of Paper for Printed Library Materials, ANSI Z39.48-1992.

For a listing of books published and distributed by Syracuse University Press, visit https://press.syr.edu.

ISBN: 978-0-8156-3740-0 (hardcover)
978-0-8156-3726-4 (paperback)
978-0-8156-5527-5 (e-book)

Library of Congress Cataloging-in-Publication Data

Names: deTar, Matthew, author.
Title: Figures that speak : the vocabulary of Turkish nationalism / Matthew deTar.
Other titles: Vocabulary of Turkish nationalism
Description: Syracuse : Syracuse University Press, [2022] | Series: Modern intellectual and political history of the Middle East | Includes bibliographical references and index. |
Summary: "'Figures That Speak' builds a critical analysis of a vocabulary of 'figures' in Turkish public discourse that structure public thought and define the possibilities of political action: religion, the minority, the founding father (Atatürk), the military, and Europe. This unique focus on processes of representation and their circulation in public culture gives readers a new perspective on the effects of the way that contemporary politicians, journalists, academics, and the public all speak about international politics"— Provided by publisher.
Identifiers: LCCN 2021004570 (print) | LCCN 2021004571 (ebook) |
ISBN 9780815637400 (hardcover) | ISBN 9780815637264 (paperback) |
ISBN 9780815655275 (ebook)
Subjects: LCSH: Nationalism—Turkey. | Communication in politics—Turkey. |
Discourse analysis—Turkey.
Classification: LCC DR477 .D453 2021 (print) | LCC DR477 (ebook) |
DDC 320.5409561—dc23
LC record available at https://lccn.loc.gov/2021004570
LC ebook record available at https://lccn.loc.gov/2021004571

Manufactured in the United States of America

Contents

Illustrations

Acknowledgments

I would not have been able to write this book without the financial support of a number of organizations. I am thankful to the Institute for Turkish Studies at Georgetown University for funding this project when it began. At Northwestern University, the Buffett Center for Global Studies, the Keyman Modern Turkish Studies Program, the Graduate School, and the Department of Communication Studies provided essential funding for initial archival research in Turkey. The Center for Religion, Law, and Democracy at Willamette University provided funding for the final phase of archival research.

Archival research does not happen without librarians, who sometimes pursue your projects like their own. I am indebted to innumerable archival librarians at the Beyazıt Devlet Kütüphanesi and the Atatürk Kitaplığı in Istanbul and to Fabio Vicini for helping me to navigate the latter. These libraries are incredible public resources. In addition, I thank Dillon Peck at the Hatfield Library of Willamette University and Jessica Hagman at the Alden Library of Ohio University.

I am grateful for the support of many generous colleagues and mentors during all stages of this project, and I am pleased to thank them here. I am greatly indebted to the support, criticisms, questions, and interest of Dilip Parameshwar Gaonkar, Elizabeth Shakman Hurd, and Robert Hariman when I began this project. I also appreciate the time and thoughts of Angela Ray, Lisa Wedeen, Rita Koryan, Burhanettin Duran, İpek Yosmaoğlu, Brian Edwards, Rebecca Johnson, and Nilüfer Göle at various points in the development of this book. Güliz Kuruoğlu and Kagan Arik welcomed me into their

Turkish-language classrooms despite my lack of credentials, providing an essential foundation for this book.

I have also benefited from the support of a variety of colleagues and working groups. Members of the Middle East and North Africa Working Group at Northwestern University provided a unique environment for discussing my work across disciplines, locations, and times. My colleagues at Northwestern University in the Rhetoric and Public Culture Writing Group, including Jesse Baldwin-Philippi, Megan Bernard, Patrick Wade, Kim Singletary, Leigh Meredith, Jamie Merchant, and Randall Bush, provided a steady source of encouragement; Sara VanderHaagen, Erik Johnson, Rana Husseini, Brandon Inabinet, and Timothy Barouch were foundational to my thinking about rhetorical theory. Lisa Uddin's encouragement, comments, and collaborative accountability helped me rethink this project while I was at Whitman College, and my community of colleagues at Whitman provided a range of support: Elyse Semerdjian, Jennifer Cohen, Anne Helen Petersen, Krzysztof Piekarski, Adam Gordon, Jamie Warren, and Melissa Salrin. Writing group colleagues at Willamette University Cindy Koenig Richards, Matthew Bost, Maegan Parker Brooks, and Una Kimokeo-Goes offered important comments. Cayla Skillin-Brauchle and JJ Gregg provided a thoughtful, imaginative new perspective and feedback. Members of the International Rhetoric Workshop at Uppsala University in Sweden in 2016, especially Alan Finlayson, provided valuable comments on chapters in this book, and İnan Özdemir Taştan worked on it with me in Istanbul when travel restrictions after the failed coup attempt that year made it impossible for her to join us in Sweden. Christa J. Olson's comments on the entire manuscript were a model of collaborative, critical reviewing that motivated numerous important revisions. The anonymous reviewer for Syracuse University Press also made suggestions that significantly improved the manuscript. Finally, my department colleagues at Ohio University, especially Devika Chawla, have provided a supportive intellectual environment for completing the book. My community at Ohio University and in Athens have made imagining and finishing this project possible, especially Melissa Haviland,

David Colagiovanni, Adam Fuller, Rachel Cooper, Brian Collins, Jennifer Collins, Kate Raney, Jeremy Bessoff, Berkeley Franz, Mark Franz, Susan Burgess, Laura Black, and Sarah Garlington. I am still searching for ways to thank David Colagiovanni for responding in a moment of minor crisis by creating the complete cover design for the book overnight. Ceren Özcan assisted with final research tasks. I thank Jamie Warren for flexible work on indexing.

I love my children, Charlie and Winston, more than I knew was possible. Writing this book could not have happened without others also caring for them, however, and I am grateful to our extended family at Sycamore Run, Sarah Collins, and many others.

My parents, John and Debbie deTar, and my sister, Laura deTar, have always been supportive of my education, interested in my work, and instrumental in helping me make progress. I am lucky to have the family I do. I can still hear my mother feigning a neutral "no pressure" voice when asking when this book would be complete, and I miss her every day.

Most of all, I am grateful for Lucy Schwallie. She is a constant source of intellect, wit, perspective, and ideas for me. No one has heard as many versions of this project, talked through as many issues, or offered as much essential perspective and sanity as Lucy. For these among other reasons, I thank her.

List of Acronyms

AKP	Justice and Development Party (Adalet ve Kalkınma Partisi)
CHP	Republican People's Party (Cumhuriyet Halk Partisi)
CUP	Committee of Union and Progress (İttihad ve Terakki Cemiyeti)
Diyanet	Directorate of Religious Affairs (Diyanet İşleri Müdürlüğü)
DP	Democrat Party (Demokrat Parti)
EEC	European Economic Community
EU	European Union
JP	Justice Party (Adalet Partisi)
MBK	National Unity Committee (Milli Birlik Komitesi)
MGK	National Security Council (Milli Güvenlik Kurulu)
MHP	Nationalist Action Party (Milliyetçi Hareket Partisi)
OYAK	Armed Forces Mutual Assistance Fund (Ordu Yardımlaşma Kurulu)
PKK	Kurdistan Workers' Party (Partiya Karkarên Kurdistan)

Figures That Speak

Introduction

Figural Reasoning

On October 15, 1927, Mustafa Kemal Atatürk began presenting a speech to the Turkish Parliament that he would continue presenting for thirty-six hours over the course of the next six days. Published in 1928 under the title *Nutuk* (*The Speech*), the colossal speech is one of the most famous texts in Turkey. Parts of *Nutuk* continue to be memorized in schools, and different museums memorialize the original object itself and the places of its drafting. *Nutuk* is frequently mentioned, analyzed, and consulted by scholars, circulating as the founding father's firsthand narrative of the birth of the nation and a detailed history of the Turkish nationalist movement and the foundation of the Turkish Republic. Until the 1950s, it served as the only account in Turkey of the Turkish War of Independence from 1919 to 1923 and of the subsequent reforms of the Republic from 1923 to 1927, making it incredibly influential on future written histories.[1] No bookstore in contemporary Turkey is without one of numerous modern editions of *Nutuk*.

Although *Nutuk*'s fame makes it nearly universally known (of) to both Turkish citizens and Turkish studies scholars, scholars have yet to grapple with its form. Part reinterpretation, part documentary archive, part working draft, part explanation, *Nutuk* focuses on the minutiae of events in the decade preceding its presentation in a way that makes a broad historical narrative difficult to discern. Many of its constituent parts work at odds with common forms of historical narration as large portions of the text include only quoted telegrams, meeting minutes, and letters without intervening explanation or interpretation. Although elements of *Nutuk*'s historical account were refined into the historical textbooks used in Turkish classrooms in the twentieth and twenty-first centuries,[2] these classroom histories produce a narrative legibility absent in the original text. *Nutuk* is both impenetrable and indispensable.

Perhaps owing to the text's unique combination of a compulsory nationalist historical perspective and an unreadably dense archive, *Nutuk* was in some ways displaced in favor of more digestible nationalist historical narratives. By 1931, the Turkish Historical Society had begun publishing textbooks that forged ahead with the ambitious project of a nationalist history, and primary-education curriculum on history was tightly controlled.[3] As these narratives have been refined over time but reappear in numerous iterations in school textbooks, *Nutuk* itself has been transformed into a rough draft of nationalist history, an incomplete whole, when the text was in fact produced at the apotheosis of Turkish republican nationalism. Subsequent scholarly analyses of the text reread *Nutuk* for its strategic misrepresentations of Atatürk's political rivals, who are now thoroughly erased from history, or for its careful selection of events that position Atatürk as the singular founding father. These interpretations frequently construct and rely on ideological unity that appears only in later revisions of nationalist history.[4] The limitations of these instrumental interpretations of the text and *Nutuk*'s own inability to stand as a legible founding text of the nation force critics to unify the text in order to interpret it. *Nutuk*'s complexity and ubiquity foreground the fraught process of critical interpretation.

Even a brief consideration of this text frustrates a set of questions that traverse historical inquiry, rhetorical studies, nationalism, and political and public culture. First: What makes the text so influential? That is, what continues to animate its republication, distribution, and reputation? Certainly, answers privileging *Nutuk*'s content are insufficient to account for the way that the speaker's own reputation produced and continues to produce *Nutuk*'s redistribution, but the text itself similarly constitutes this reputation in myriad ways. The text would be relegated to historical irrelevance without its author's fame, but the text is also a primary site of the production of this fame. The complex interaction of content, meaning, circulation, and form is immediately apparent in an initial critical assessment of the text.

Following a different trajectory, one might consider *Nutuk* as one case of a species of national foundation texts that can be compared to other such foundational histories. But if *Nutuk*'s account of the founding of a nation resembles the accounts of other such foundings around the world, how should one explain this resemblance—as influence, coincidence, result, form? This is not simply a "historical" question about which text came first because the question of resemblance is one of interpretation and perspective as well. Turkish nationalist foundation, like all national foundations, relies on its own specificity for its form, and so the question of general resemblance is immediately implicated in paradoxes of the specific. *Nutuk* is both unique and somehow familiar as a type, and any comparison requires a palpable flattening of its particularity.

Perhaps more broadly: What does *Nutuk* do? This could be a question of instrumental purpose, one of internal content, or one of constitutive or linear effect. Yet all of these perspectives yield answers so numerous and divergent as to be untraceable. *Nutuk* may describe former nationalist allies as traitors for the speaker's instrumental benefit, but it also contains content that contradicts identifiable "strategic purposes," while performing and constituting the speaker's authority and ideology in a way that projects onto the nation itself. It is as if *Nutuk* is a kind of filibuster, but one of other forms/styles of speech, other modes of thought, and one that does not present itself as a blockage but as natural. What, then, is the purpose, content, or effect of a nationalist imaginary, of a discursive form (in Michel Foucault's sense), of a style of thought and speech? Surely this latter question is so abstract as to be rhetorical.

These questions animate *Figures That Speak*. If the extreme length of one speech frustrates singular answers to the preceding questions, it also indicates limitations in the structure of basic questions about public culture, political history, and rhetoric. The relationships between form and content, meaning and circulation, instrumental and constitutive discourse involve necessary, foundational paradox rather than linear antagonism. Repositioning *Nutuk* and public discourse more broadly in a way that accounts for these limitations in our understanding of public culture involves rethinking the production, expression, and circulation of social norms in public. It involves coming to terms with the dynamics of linguistic representation that both make speech possible and originate in speech. Finally, it involves a fluid transgression of the boundaries between general and specific, theory and practice, that are the sites of the production of authority in public speech. The irreducible complexity of a text such as *Nutuk* in the face of the questions given earlier invites reimagining the contours and operation of public discourse.

Accordingly, *Figures That Speak* stipulates a mode of analysis that accounts not only for an exceptional text from 1927 but also for the way that theories of circulation and linguistic representation come to bear on the formulation and reformulation of power, norms, and authority. What circulates around and within *Nutuk* is a set of "figures" that constitute a nationalist imaginary in Turkey: Atatürk, religion, the military, the minority, and Europe. These five primary figures in Turkish public discourse are more than just "key topics" in Turkish politics (rhetorical "topoi"), and they operate as more than simply descriptors of institutions, phenomena, or issues to debate in public.[5] Rather, these figures operate as shorthand for complex networks and histories of authority, constituting and presuming ways of knowing Turkish modernity, democracy, and political culture. The relationships between these figures become the sites of invention of new understandings of authority beyond and before *Nutuk*, and the figures themselves are the terrain on which diverse phenomena are organized into governable unities. That is, these figures not only are spoken and discussed in public but also produce the context into which they are projected, in a sense speaking on their own. *Figures That Speak* is about the diverse mobilization and production of history in the primary figures that circulate in public speech about Turkey.

To explore the figures that constitute Turkish national identity, this introduction offers a rhetorically engaged theory of nationalism, discursive form, social norms, and public practice. Accounting for the figures *in* public speech that *make possible* that speech requires an understanding of the circulation and performance of social norms in language. Charting connections between figures within and beyond speech requires an understanding of the broader form of discourse through which figures circulate. Most importantly, analysis of the production and circulation of authority in speech must be attuned to the rhetorical dynamics of figure and form. Based on this theoretical statement, the chapters of this book focus on individual figures or groups of figures at specific moments in the history of the Turkish Republic. This map of vignettes reflects the theoretical argument because the circulation of figures does not proceed as a linear progression of meaning. Detailed analysis of moments of expression of these figures is the only method of connecting public speech to the simultaneous constitution and presumption of authority in political culture. National identity describes a network of relationships that circulate in discourse as simultaneously constitutive and constituted, and *Figures That Speak* marks these moments of simultaneity.

Figure and Style

In English, the word *figure* implies the vast instability of seemingly simple acts of representation. A metaphor is a figure, but a figure is also a precisely calculated arithmetic value: nonliteral and exact. A figure is a vaguely discernible shadow on the wall, or it is a looming, larger-than-life persona: background and foreground. It is both the shape of a human body and the term for all human and nonhuman bodies: specific and general. And these definitions gloss only the noun forms of the word. The theoretical category "figure" itself might be constituted historically through the function of the figures *ploche* and polyptoton, forgotten rhetorical forms of repetition that produce "the impression that a consistent phenomenon is being discussed consistently."[6] Any discussion of figure must acknowledge the term *figure* itself as a kind of Pandora's box of representational uncertainty.

In classical Greek and Roman rhetorical theory, the concept "figure" is immediately consumed by its own theoretical imprecision. As Jeanne Fahnestock has argued, the earliest systematic treatises addressing figures of speech maintain "no consistent principles of sorting" among figures of speech, tropes, and figures of thought.[7] By the time of Quintillian's twelve-volume *Institutio oratoria* on the theory and practice of rhetoric (95 CE), a tacit (perhaps begrudging) acknowledgment of imprecision in the boundaries among figures of speech, tropes, and figures of thought had become a commonplace in rhetorical theories of figure.[8] The most prominent classical text on rhetoric, Aristotle's *Rhetoric* (circa 350 BCE), includes neither a theory of figures nor a general category such as "figure" to taxonomize the discussion of metaphor, antithesis, asyndeton, and simile in book III.[9] Rather, Aristotle addresses these figures in a discussion of style, propriety, and decorum, perhaps implying that an organizational architecture of figures is an impossibility because style results from a contingent blend of situation, culture, and context. Later attempts to produce a "rationalized architecture" of figures presume problematic distinctions between form and content or meaning, figurative and literal language, and ornamented and "normal" language use. As Paul de Man and many others have shown, figures themselves suspend distinctions between form and content, figurative and literal, and call into question an idea of "normal" language use.[10] The supposed "impurity" of early classical definitions of figure becomes the most definitive characteristic of this contingent linguistic category in rhetorical stylistics.

If we approach figures as subcategories of rhetorical style rather than as purely linguistic phenomena, their constitutive relationship with social norms and propriety becomes visible. As Robert Hariman has argued, the concepts of propriety and decorum in rhetorical theory connect the contingent realm of social norms to "relatively uniform" instructions for practice, making decorum "not so much a set of rules as a process of invention." That is, decorum always contains "a more complicated awareness of [its own] instructions as somewhat arbitrary markers of a constantly shifting field of social relations."[11] If decorum and rhetorical stylistics are to be more than a set of adaptive strategies in the face of the unstable and unpredictable terrain of social norms and relations, then we must also understand *how* and *why* the field of social relations "constantly shifts." For Judith Butler, a "norm only persists as a norm to the extent that it is acted out in social practice and reidealized and reinstituted in and through the daily social rituals of bodily life."[12] The performances that decorum and rhetorical style seek to guide are therefore the location of the reproduction or alteration of social norms and relations: performance is what shifts social relations or reinstitutes them. In this way, social norm and rhetorical style are mutually constitutive, and insisting on figures as an element of rhetorical style transforms them into a location of the mutual constitution of performance, social norm, and language use.[13]

Insisting on this status for figures expands the category in ways that depart significantly from the classical tradition, opening the possibility that figures themselves are constituted in performance and repetition. The classical tradition's expansive lists of tropes and figures produced from antiquity through the end of the nineteenth century presume a basic separation between performance and the syntactical and/or ideational character of figures rather than a mutually constitutive relationship between performance, social norms, and language use. Technical lists of figure forms such as metaphor, metonymy, synecdoche, antithesis, and so on aid in the presumption that each figure is an identifiable form absent the content of a specific case. In the classical tradition, figures are abstract, universal linguistic strategies to be molded in performance to the particulars of the situation. If there is a mutually constitutive relationship among performance, social norm, and propriety in rhetorical style, however, then even the form of a figure, its name, and its syntactical/ideational operation would reflect a mutually constitutive and historically located harmony of decorum and word use. Figures would move and shift with historical sedimentations of authority and norms; they would emerge and disperse organically according to the logics of shifting propriety. The connection between propriety and figure is more complex than a choice of fitting ornamentation, and at times propriety is simultaneously constitutive of and circulated through figures. Figures should be thought of as one element of the mutual constitution of performance, social norm, and language use, and as such their function, form, representational operation, and even name should be understood as the product of this mutual constitution.[14]

The classical trend toward cataloging figures as well as some contemporary scholars' emphasis on figures as functional in argumentation can be understood as means of "reining in" a potentially infinite expansion of the concept of figure when it is bound only by the contingent realm of social norm.[15] Quite simply, a theory of figures advocating for a contingent, mutually constitutive relationship among style, social norm, and performance would run into the anti-relativist's rhetorical question "What stops everything from being a figure?" This question proceeds, however, from the presumption that historical contingency and arbitrary choice in the present are the same thing. Social norms are not necessary and universal, but nor are they completely arbitrary: contingent practice sediments historically into ideas of social norm, decorum, style. Furthermore, in Butler's theory of norms, each instance of the performance of a norm also *idealizes* "the norm" as a theoretical, abstract category, something to approximate and imitate.[16] Although performance is the location of the production and reproduction of norms, and although "the norm has no independent ontological status," performance is constrained by previous performances because performance reproduces the very idea that norms exist.[17] Anything or everything can be a figure, then, only in the ahistorical vacuum of abstract theory. In the situated context of practice, only certain concepts become figures, despite the contingent conditions of their formation. History, power, and social norm are the contingent but sedimented limits on the appearance of figures that also define their content and form.[18]

Figures That Speak argues for a sense of figure that expands on the classical tradition but departs from its architecture and formal definitions. It contends that five concepts act as *figures* in modern Turkish political speech: Atatürk, religion, the military, the minority, and Europe. These figures do not displace the existence of something such as metaphor but embody the range of lexical, syntactical, ideational, substitutive, and contiguous processes that the classical tradition describes. To reprise de Man, these concepts are figures because they simultaneously mobilize literal and figurative, description and prescription, transhistorical meaning and contingent authority in a way that blurs the boundary between the two elements of each binary.[19] Similarly, these figures are neither only content nor only form: in many cases (beyond Turkey), one can imagine the military as both an institutional descriptor and a form of patriotism. Figures are not examples that deviate from "normal" use; rather, they make visible the mutually constitutive connections among representation, context, and social norm that are the foundation of meaning and form. Figures are not tools a speaker chooses for persuasion or for constituting audience identity but rather are constitutive of the terrain of speech and performance: speakers are as constituted and constrained by the condensation of social norm in figures as audiences are. Finally, because figures in public speech constitute and reproduce social norms simultaneously, their appropriateness is not a product of speaker choice among options, as it is when figures are conceived as ornaments. Propriety—the power that is fashioned and recirculated through propriety; the institutions, the actors, and the interests authorized by "the proper"—constitutes and is contained in the form and content of figures.[20] To build a rhetorically attuned sense of figure today, we must be attentive to the classical location of figure as a component of style and then reconstruct figure from within contemporary considerations of the contingency of propriety.[21]

Just as the concept of figure developed here extends beyond classical rhetorical theory, it also extends beyond representational complexity to consider how figures mobilize authority through economies of affect. For Sara Ahmed, emotion and affect do not inhere in particular individuals or in particular objects but rather take up residence in subjects and objects as a result of historical contact with them. Words and other signifiers gain affective value as an effect of those signifiers' circulation and repetitive contact with particular affects, making it seem as if a particular emotion inheres or resides in an object or an individual subject.[22] As specific affects circulate in contact with objects or subjects, this contact gains traction, or what Ahmed calls "stickiness," such that particular signifiers become associated with specific affects over time.[23] Beyond this, specific words can circulate with associated "atmospheres" of affect, and Ahmed explains that a word such as *racism* operates in many contexts as an accusation, a disturbance, a way of "stirring things up," and an entire history and context of affect circulate with the word.[24] The figures explored in this book similarly mobilize authority, history, and power not only through representational complexity but also through the affects that circulate with and through them. Figures' authority is atmospheric; their perceptual significance includes historically sedimented affects that "stick" to them and move with them. These figures embody a range of linguistic processes while also transmitting a "sense" that alludes to histories of power, presumptions of knowledge, and contingent institutional formations.

Although the figures traced in this book cannot be contained by a universal architecture or grammar, this does not mean that figures are isolated, irregular, or unbounded in their relationships to one another. Rather, figures are elements of a history; they are the mechanisms for the emergence and sedimentation of authority, and they create their own logics of circulation. In many ways, figures compose a "discourse" in Foucault's sense: not a totalizable matrix of topics or knowledge, not a temporal succession of meanings, not a static procedure of communication but a fluid substrate of relationships of authority that appear in speech, in institutional forms, in presumed knowledge, and in habits of practice. Figures establish moments of order in discourse; they coalesce power; they mark the contours of an incomplete whole. What is appropriate to a theory of figures in discourse is not a compendium of universal definitions, as classical and early-modern rhetorical theorists have attempted, but a located analysis of moments in discourse when certain figures appear, circulate, and dissolve. The chapters of this book constitute these moments, and a broad familiarity with a vocabulary of figures serves as the outline of a discourse.

Figure, Discourse, Nation

Although understanding figures through their performance of propriety helps emphasize their contingent appearance and constitution, figures must still be located within a broader theory of discourse to avoid reverting to their status as ornament.[25] Foucault's explanation of the circular constitution and naturalization of authority through discourse in *The Archaeology of Knowledge* provides a necessary lens for locating figures' circulation of propriety, power, and norms. For Foucault, an analysis of discursive forms should specify the statements, modes of authority, and types of objects mobilized in a discourse rather than seek "an architecture of concepts sufficiently general and abstract to embrace all others and to introduce them into the same deductive structure."[26] Discourses themselves are contingently premised on the particulars of their constituent elements; they shift and mutate rather than remaining a static architecture, and power and authority are discourse-level effects of a constellation of elements within a discourse. Figures avoid a status as ornament because they appear as the necessary bulwark of this contingent architecture rather than as a supplement to it. Discourse describes an incomplete field of power relations that presents itself as a totality whose horizon is not visible, and it operates as a structure founded on the sedimentation of contingent historical accretions of power.

Locating an analysis of figures in Turkish nationalism within this theory of discourse entails particular understandings of speech, statements, and language. For Foucault, a discourse encompasses a far greater number of phenomena than simply linguistic ones, and specifying a discourse involves more than making an outline of the relevant terms used. Rather,

> discourse is characterized not by privileged objects, but by the way in which it forms objects that are in fact highly dispersed. This formation is made possible by a group of relations established between authorities of emergence, delimitation, and specification. One might say, then, that a discursive formation is defined (as far as its objects are concerned, at least) if one can establish such a group; if one can show how any particular object of discourse finds in [discourse] its place and law of emergence; if one can show that it may give birth simultaneously or successively to mutually exclusive objects, without having to modify itself.[27]

A discursive form would organize a "highly dispersed" set of objects or figures (such as religion, Atatürk, etc.), comprising the various relations of authority between those objects and establishing their "laws of emergence" and dispersal. Foucault offers, within or related to each of these objects, the idea of "statements" as the expressions of the "concrete contents" of discourse's "structures and possible unities."[28] Statements are more than the words of a speaking subject and resemble instead a kind of discursive event, a function within discourse. Statements combine linguistic and nonlinguistic phenomena and constitute the trace of a discursive object, a concrete example, the accumulation of which constitutes an object in discourse.[29] Language, then, operates at a different level of existence from the statement;[30] groups of statements serve as the evidence of discursive objects; and the discursive form as a whole organizes these objects and the relations of authority between them.

This understanding of the relations between discourse, objects, statements, and language organizes the selection of cases in and the mode of analysis of *Figures That Speak*. I locate "figures" of Turkish nationalism at the level of discursive objects: their traces are visible in spoken language, but they describe unities that extend beyond language. For example, in order to analyze the figure or object "religion" in contemporary Turkey, I identify various "statements" that work as traces of the object as a whole. The material that comprises these "statements" might include a political speech, a set of responses to that speech or articles in anticipation of it, and a consideration of the speech's historical context. Because this material is textual, and because a statement, for Foucault, extends beyond the words of a speaking subject and, indeed, beyond language itself, I read this textual evidence of a statement not for the way it defines or even uses a particular word, such as *religion*, but to evidence the function of a particular concept, religion, in society and the modes of dispersal and authority that constitute this concept. When, for instance, a prime minister announces a change in the liturgical language of Turkey (as in chapter 2), this announcement is significant not because it shows a secret sympathy for religious belief on the part of that prime minister but because a whole system of historical relations designated by the figure "religion" becomes apparent both in the way some of these relations are negotiated through political speech and in the reference to these historical conditions offered in media accounts of the event. *Figures That Speak* charts systems of authority and the dispersal of objects within a specific discursive form of nationalism.

This analysis also entails a particular understanding of history that similarly structures the theoretical concerns, the mode of analysis, and the choice of objects. In *The Archaeology of Knowledge*, one of Foucault's primary concerns is to distinguish his previous work from the history of ideas, and to this extent he argues, "Discursive formations do not have the same model of historicity as the flow of consciousness or the linearity of language. Discourse . . . is not a consciousness that embodies its project in the external form of language (*langage*); it is not a language (*langue*), plus a subject to speak it. It is a practice that has its own forms of sequence and succession."[31] Discursive forms exist on a plane removed from but related to these models of temporality; they are a "unity and discontinuity in history itself."[32] Therefore, discursive forms cannot be traced temporally, but one can mark broad transformations in discourse according to its own unique logics. Statements, however, as the "concrete contents" of the objects within a discourse, are located strictly within time, and "the analysis of statements, then, is a historical analysis. . . . [I]t questions [statements] as to their mode of existence, what it means to them to have come into existence, to have left traces, and perhaps to remain there, awaiting the moment when they might be of use once more; what it means to them to have appeared when and where they did—they and no others."[33] Although historical context is essential to analysis of a particular statement, analysis of discourse does not attempt a comparison of statements differently located in time in order to trace change because a discursive form does not exist within that same temporality.[34]

Foucault's archaeological method lends itself to the process of contemporary rhetorical criticism because it explicitly avoids presumptions about individual agency and the teleology of exigence.[35] By approaching discourse as "a practice that has its own forms of sequence and succession" rather than as a kind of language or consciousness that progresses linearly through history, we are able to avoid assuming the legibility of exigence because criticism focuses on "forms of sequence and succession" rather than presuming linear connections of influence. An archaeological approach to rhetorical criticism avoids assumptions about the centrality of the speaking agent because discourse "is not a consciousness that embodies its project in the external form of language."[36] In addition, for Dave Tell, Foucault's work is useful for rhetorical studies not because Foucault focuses on discourse (a term that commonly and mistakenly becomes a synonym for *speech*) but because knowledge, for Foucault, is organized around identifiable tropes, such as the metonymy of sexuality produced through confession. According to Tell, Foucault follows Nietzsche to understand rhetoric as a compendium of tropes, but these tropes are the form of knowledge, and they form power: confession's "metonymical function . . . 'implants' origins behind surfaces, 'criminals' behind crimes, 'delinquents' behind offenses, and 'sexualities' behind bodies and pleasures," states Tell.[37] Whereas Tell's account privileges metonymy as the primary (perhaps only?) trope and implies that it structures knowledge in the background rather than appearing in language, I locate figures such as the metonymy of sexuality and the figure of religion both within *and* outside the disorderly world of public speech. In my account, figures extend beyond metonymy and the classical lexicon, and figures are reconnected to the circulation and production of decorum, affect, and power that are the effects of discourse but also performed in speech.

Approaching figures such as religion, Atatürk, the military, the minority, and Europe as objects in discourse locates nationalism itself as a discourse that simultaneously presumes and produces the conditions of its own authority. Ever since Benedict Anderson transformed the field of nationalism studies with his work *Imagined Communities* more than thirty years ago, scholars have struggled with the tension between the "nation" as a theoretical category and the nation's production in everyday practice.[38] Anderson makes nationalism into an ideology elaborated in western Europe and "pirated" by others for its revolutionary and liberatory potential.[39] For Craig Calhoun and others since the publication of Anderson's book, this theory makes nationalism into a formal structure repeated in cookie-cutter fashion globally rather than a tool of local political struggle that constantly alters "nationalism" based on situational factors or local interpretation. Calhoun instead argues that nationalism is a "discursive form" (using Foucault's term) and that a number of thematic elements (language, ethnicity, popular sovereignty, territory, history, etc.) appear in different combinations and slightly altered forms to constitute any national identity.[40] Even the fluidity of Calhoun's theory of nationalism as a discursive form begins from a presumption of the legible consistency of certain terms and ideas (such as "nation") rather than focusing on these concepts through their organic emergence in speech. As Rogers Brubaker has famously warned, "The problem with this . . . treatment of nations as real entities is that it adopts *categories of practice* as *categories of analysis*."[41] Presuming that the "nation" exists (from an analytic perspective) prior to its circulation and constitution in discourse (re)naturalizes the highly rhetorical processes by which nations become authoritative actors with identities, histories, and associated state apparatuses.[42]

The collection of figures that circulate in Turkish nationalist discourse marks precisely the kinds of concepts that emerge organically in public speech to simultaneously produce and rely on a definition of the nation. Nationalist discourse structures itself around collections of figures, nodes of knowledge, law, history, and practice, which constitute relations of authority and produce general understanding of the content of national identity.[43] For Talal Asad, an exploration of transnational, transhistorical terms such as *religion*, *secularism*, and *politics* must develop a "comparison of embedded concepts (representations)" in order to locate "the forms of life that articulate [these concepts], the powers they release or disable."[44] Exploration of similarly transhistorical concepts such as nation and nationalism should specify a number of embedded concepts, a constellation of associated terms, in order to examine the "powers they release or disable" in the service of articulating a particular discursive form of national identity.[45] This kind of work, for Asad, focuses a critic on the reasons why a specific cultural concept "has become hegemonic *as a political goal*, what practical consequences follow from that hegemony, and what social conditions maintain it."[46] Focusing on specific figures that are historically contingent, mobilize social knowledge and presumption, and circulate through public speech, nationalism becomes a fluid discourse that disperses knowledge that itself authorizes nationalist discourse.

The relationships among discourse, history, figures, and authority structure the scope of this book as well as its possible conclusions. I do not attempt a history-of-ideas approach to concepts as indeterminate as the military and religion tracing them through nearly a century of Turkish public discourse. Rather, I examine how each figure appears through momentary statements that describe relations of authority at particular moments in time: for example, religion as seen in laws passed in 1932 and 1950 (chapter 2). Following Foucault, it is not possible to map the historical progression of national identity through the figures that compose it. Similarly, the chapters of this book are singular moments in the emergence and dispersal of nationalist discourse, and they cannot be linearly connected to one another to imply a tidy logic of historical progression or the development of consciousness. The emergence of a concept of the state in 1990 (chapter 3) does not provide a conceptual foundation from which one can build an analysis of certain apparatuses of "the state" in 2005, such as citizenship and the Constitution (chapter 4). Indeed, an approach to nationalism that treats it as a discursive form requires one to abandon an understanding of national identity that follows it through time (even Anderson's "homogeneous, empty time") as if nationalism were the evolving description of an individual.[47] Nationalism as a discursive form exists outside of time altogether as a set of relations of authority and processes of emergence and dispersal that exist simultaneously and appear sporadically within statements or sets of statements. The structure of the discursive form of nationalism outlined in this book is therefore partial, limited by the impossibility of creating a map of discourse as large as the original.

This insistence on the singular operation of discourse at discrete moments in time also significantly influences the analyses in each chapter. Forms of discourse are characterized by their lack of underlying significance, which is discoverable only in analysis, and faithfulness to this lack of deeper meaning requires an attention to the surface of discourse.[48] Chapter 1 focuses on Mustafa Kemal Atatürk's six-day speech in 1927, *Nutuk*, describing the way this speech reflects the operation of nationalist discourse as constituted in 1927. Although this chapter discusses the figure of Atatürk, the textual unity produced by this figure, and the interpretive hegemony of this figure on the text and the history of the Republic, it does not emphasize the strategic intent of *Nutuk*, nor does it emphasize the text as the product of a singular, charismatic speaker. *Nutuk* is a collection of various kinds of documents (telegrams, letters, meeting notes, interpretive narrative), and these documents consistently signal a lack of unity in the text. In order to ask questions about this lack of textual unity or the form of the text itself, it is necessary not to read *Nutuk* as the product of unequaled genius or as a strategic historical narrative meant to provide the nationalist interpretation of the early Republic. An analysis that presumes the agential genius of the speaker who created this text overlooks the way in which the figure of the speaker himself operates in the text, unifying it in ways that have important relations to the production of historical knowledge. The analyses offered in each chapter avoid the external attribution of unity or intent; they resist attempts to uncover the hidden significance of texts, speeches, and events. Instead, this book offers a collection of cases that explore the surface of discourse—the unique modes of authority and legitimation that become mobilized and disperse at various moments in time.

Figure and Representation

Public political speech employs a sophisticated set of figures that simultaneously represent presupposed historical knowledge and refer to contemporary events. *Figures That Speak* maps three overlapping processes of the production of authority in such figures: the layering of linguistic and political representation, the simultaneous production and performance of norms, and the circular codependence of form/content and meaning/circulation. Although the processes of authority contained in figures have lineages corresponding to early statements of the fundamental concerns of rhetorical theory (as discussed earlier through Aristotle), they are also familiar issues in contemporary political theory, cultural studies, and linguistic and rhetorical theory.[49] The figures addressed in individual chapters of this work (Atatürk, religion, the military, the minority, and Europe) name general phenomena while simultaneously indexing specific legal, historical, and popular understandings of these phenomena in Turkey. These figures name institutions or actors that are topics of public debate, and yet their naming produces and reproduces historical conditions of authority between sectors of society. Figures operate between a general level of abstraction and a specific historical context; they operate simultaneously as descriptions and prescriptions of phenomena or as mimetic depictions and proxy representations of phenomena. For the regular circulation, constitution, and naturalization of authority in figures to be understood, figures must be read alongside their analogues in rhetorical history and for the way they reanimate contemporary problems of representation.

Figures in discourse circulate simultaneously as descriptions or proper names of institutions or phenomena, as institutional or political histories, and as affective presumptions of the social significance of the phenomena they name. The complexity of these representational dynamics of figures resituates Gayatri Chakravorty Spivak's widely influential distinction between representation as a political phenomenon and representation as a linguistic phenomenon. For Spivak, representation is either a process of standing in as a proxy or a process of depicting something absent, and the impossibility of "subaltern" speech is the result of a *lack* of distinction between these two modes of representation in scholarly work (specifically that of Foucault and Gilles Deleuze).[50] Confusing these two modes of representation leads scholars to mistake the process of depicting voices of the subaltern class as a process of transparently standing in for (as uninterested proxy) voices of the subaltern class.[51] For Spivak, political, proxy representation is more honest about the translation involved in representation than is depiction or mimesis. The absence of this distinction results in a problematic attribution of authority to scholarship: a blurred line between two modes of representation is what produces authority in certain texts, when one is both "speaking for" and "theorizing about" an "other." Spivak and many others influenced by her work use this distinction to address the (im)possibility of hearing voices that are radically "other" or to imagine forms of self-critique.[52]

Although Spivak's essay is a necessary corrective to the authority produced through representation in scholarship (especially given Foucault's own expanding hegemony over scholarship in the humanities and humanistic social sciences),[53] reversing the critical value she places on her own intervention provides a useful explanation of figures in public speech. Rather than reading Spivak's essay only as a *prescriptive* call to disentangle political representation and aesthetic representation from one another in order to avoid the kind of effacement she describes, her essay should also be read as a *descriptive* account of the layering of forms of representation on top of one another in public speech. That is, the absence of a distinction between two modes of representation describes the operation of overdetermined, imprecise figures that are instrumental in public political speech and that produce authority precisely by blurring these two forms of representation. In both instances—scholarship and public speech—the oscillation between description and prescription, mimesis and proxy, produces authority, but in public speech the blurring of these forms of representation is perhaps unavoidable. Treating the imprecise representational form of figures as a necessary condition of their authority helps explain the way that figures themselves can simultaneously produce and reproduce power.

Building an understanding of different forms of representation into a discourse model of figures is imperative for contemporary understanding of the regularities that shape public culture, historical power, social norms, and rhetoric. Although the relationship between social norms and public speech is a foundational concern of rhetorical theory, the global circulation of nationalism as a discursive form challenges the way traditional theories of rhetoric have presumed an easy or legible circumscription of the collectivities that define social norms.[54] Focusing on figures that traverse Turkish nationalist discourse privileges concept use in a way that emphasizes the simultaneous creation and reliance on social norms rather than attempting to locate norms in previously circumscribed communities. As Judith Butler has stated in numerous ways, "Subjects are constituted through norms which, in their reiteration, produce and shift the terms through which subjects are recognized."[55] In the moment of the "reiteration" of norms that constitute the subject, that is, norms themselves are "produc[ed] and shift[ed]." Analysis of figures that circulate in discourse accounts for the way that uses of a figure in the present "produce and shift the terms" of representation of figures in the present. It is in the moment of representation that the means of representing are produced. It is in this moment that the interests of the present are articulated. Figures therefore become the mode of expression of social norms in public speech while simultaneously constituting these norms, and the circulation of a vocabulary of figures conditions the possibilities for political action.

Although layered processes of representation and the simultaneity of performance and constitution of norm produce the forms of authority mobilized by figures in a discourse, the very circulation of these figures is also essential to the production of their authority. Yet as Brian Edwards argues, trans- and intranational circuits of circulation do not produce meaning or authority independent of the content that traverses them, and accounting for the effect of circulating content must also remain attuned to the motivating influence of this content over its own circulation.[56] When, for instance, a founding father's six-day speech is republished in mass quantity over the course of nearly a century, the meaning of such an artifact is no longer locatable only in the words on the page, but nor is it wholly attributable to mass redistribution. Rather, the meaning of this text and the figures that circulate through it are simultaneously produced and reproduced through the interaction of content and its circulation. Similar questions about the location of meaning and the origin of authority animate Catherine Chaput's description of the affective energy of rhetorical circulation, which demonstrates the necessity of both circulation and *expanding* circulation to the value of content.[57] Focusing on the effect of circulation on figures in discourse enables an account of recurring concepts that avoids naturalizing the authority of these concepts that results in part from circulation. It is only in circulation that prescription blurs into description, that norms are repeated and constituted, and therefore the fact of figures' own repetition across time and space is one necessary condition of their power and effect.

Although figures animate some of the most enduring paradoxes in theories of representation, their constitution in social norms and their circulation thoroughly situates them on a foundation of contingency. *Figures That Speak* argues that five primary figures in Turkish public speech operate as abbreviations for complex networks and histories of authority and that the processes of representation mobilized in these figures produce Turkish political culture. The articulation of Turkish modernity, like the articulation of modernities across the globe, does not always or primarily correspond to abstract theoretical principles or general, formalized models of development. Rather, the articulation of Turkish modernity produces its own "figures" that oscillate somewhere between general, abstract theory and specific, local experience. These figures circulate widely, structure public thought, and define networks of authority. When these concepts circulate in public address, they reconstitute complex institutional and national histories, thus in turn producing and limiting ways of knowing Turkish modernity, democracy, and political culture. Despite the fact that figures mark regularities in discourse that define possibilities in the present with reference to histories of authority, a structure of the operation of figures cannot be formally identified outside of their appearance in discourse, and therefore figures themselves are products of their own moments of emergence.[58]

Moments of Discourse

The subsequent chapters of this book focus on individual figures or groups of figures at specific moments in the history of the Turkish Republic: Atatürk, religion, and the military in 1927; religion in 1932 and 1950; the military in 1990; the minority in 2004–6; and Europe in 1963 and 2005. The organization of the chapters constitutes part of the book's argument. By focusing on one or two instances of the expression of a figure in public speech, each chapter provides detailed analyses of the moment of expression while resisting a history-of-ideas approach to the study of these concepts that would trace a progression of meanings through time. The theory of figures that structures this book emphasizes the segmented, momentary nature of each instance of expression of a figure, where the significance of that figure at two distinct times can indicate intervening periods of forgetting, misremembering, or general imprecision rather than a linear progression of signification. In addition, analyzing the circulation of specific figures in public speech at distinct moments in time enables analysis of the way historical narratives are represented, signified, and circulated in popular discourse. This analytic approach is especially important to the examination of the production of history in Turkey, where ideological, nationalist histories that emphasize development and modernization narratives hold hegemonic sway over understandings of Turkish politics. Because representation of the past in the public address of the present produces the possibilities of political action in the present, a strategy for analyzing figures through vignettes is necessary to the rethinking of Turkish history.[59]

Chapter 1 outlines a constellation of concepts as they influence the meaning and content of one of the foundational texts of the Turkish Republic, Mustafa Kemal Atatürk's famous six-day speech of 1927. As a text that purports to both record and evaluate certain documents in the past, *Nutuk* contains two different modes of speaking. On the one hand, it reflects a specific nationalist way of speaking about the Republic that took shape in the years following the end of the Ottoman Empire and was extremely prominent by 1927. On the other hand, *Nutuk* is a vast archive of documents that predate the Republic, many of which were not authored by Kemal but which are read at length or in their entirety in the speech. Although this group of historical documents cannot be said to speak with a unified voice, a number of features of the primary nationalist discourse of Turkey in 1927 become visible through assertions about the presumed meaning of these historical documents in *Nutuk*. This chapter argues that the visible discrepancy between the archival material and the voice of the narration in 1927 marks the absence of a moment of birth of the Turkish Republic, a moment that is effaced and then rhetorically reproduced in the text through a constellation of concepts that circulate in the text: religion, the military, and Atatürk.

Religion is perhaps one of the most popular topics in scholarship on Turkey and in Turkish public discourse, but this concept has emerged in distinct forms throughout the history of the Republic. Chapter 2 challenges the transhistorical unity of the concept "religion" in Turkey. Focusing on a set of legislative changes regarding the language of the call to prayer in Turkey, this chapter argues that the unity of the concept “religion” has a different character, function, and effect at different moments in Turkish history, and the unity of this concept both reflects and helps constitute the relationships of authority in which it emerges. In 1932, the Ministry of Religious Affairs required all mosques to recite the call to prayer in Turkish rather than in Arabic, and public discussion of and justifications for this reform marked a complex delineation between legitimate and illegitimate expressions of religious belief. Following the first free and contested elections in Turkey in 1950, the newly elected Democrat Party announced that the ban on the Arabic call to prayer would end on the first day of Ramadan that year. Whereas discussion of the concept of religion in 1932 was closely tied to the past goals of the revolution and the ideal future nation, discourse surrounding the legislative change in 1950 was anchored by concerns about the propriety and efficiency of action in the present, including electoral procedure, economic growth, and other modes of population management. In 1950, the concept of religion helped organize numerous events and ideas into a single category of governance and helped articulate a continuous process of properly balancing the foundational principles with the social landscape of the present. Through an analysis of public discourse surrounding legislation of the language of the call to prayer in 1932 and 1950, chapter 2 argues that the concepts of religion that emerged at different moments in the history of Turkey reflected and produced different arrangements of authority rather than marking a consistent, transhistorical experience or phenomenon named “religion.”

In a country with universal male conscription and a history of military coups, the authority of the military in the history of Turkey is somewhat self-evident. However, this authority is not simply the result of omnipresence and force but the product of the way the figure of the military circulates alongside a number of other terms in public speech. Chapter 3 accounts for the relational significance of the figure of the military alongside the concepts “state,” “nation,” and “government,” arguing that these concepts produce the meaning, legitimacy, and influence of one another in Turkish politics. In order to detail the relational significance of these concepts, this chapter analyzes a revision of the political legacy of former prime minister Adnan Menderes that took place from 1986 to 1990. On May 27, 1960, Menderes was deposed in the first military coup in modern Turkey's history, and he and two of his colleagues were executed the following year and buried in unmarked graves on a military prison island. Thirty years later, in 1990, Menderes and his colleagues were posthumously exonerated, exhumed, and reburied in Istanbul in a purpose-built mausoleum amid a large state ceremony. During public debate about the reburial, ideas of the military, the state, the nation, and the government emerged as mutually constitutive terms that were essential to understanding the meaning and symbolism of the proposed reburial ceremony. But debate about the form of this reburial occurred within palpable, unspoken limits on appropriate public discussion of the military, given the military's continuing direct control of government offices and the recent and violent military coup in 1980. The meaning of the terms most essential to understanding the reburial was contingent on resignification and a matrix of authority in the present, and the reburial became a contested site of this resignification and authority. By analyzing the simultaneous production of and reliance on the concepts "state," "nation," "government," and "military" in the event of the reburial, chapter 3 argues that the reburial refashioned the authority of the military at the moment this authority helped constitute the meaning of the reburial.

Chapter 4 maps the fluid arrangement of exteriority that constitutes the idea of "the minority" in Turkey, focusing on a series of criminal cases in the mid-2000s in which authors and journalists were accused of "insulting Turkishness." Numerous high-profile cases brought under Article 301 of the Turkish Penal Code corresponded with negotiations to begin European Union accession talks, and the chapter specifically considers the trial of the Armenian-Turkish journalist Hrant Dink in 2004–5, the trial of the Turkish novelist Orhan Pamuk in 2005–6, and the trial of the Turkish novelist Elif Şafak in 2006. Media coverage of these cases and criticism of the defendants mobilized a figure of the minority that fluctuated, sometimes appearing as ethnicity, sometimes as noncitizen, sometimes as enemy of the state, sometimes as a location in a modernization narrative. Chapter 4 argues that a diffuse network of law, history, and norm have defined appropriate action and given content to the figure of the minority, thereby producing variable limits on expression about "Turkishness" referenced in Article 301. Focusing on the circulating figure of the minority in Dink's, Pamuk's, and Şafak's cases, this chapter argues that norms of appropriate speech are expressed in law but that these norms also produce laws regarding expression. Norm and law simultaneously authorize one another in these cases.

Situated at the edge of continental Europe, Turkey has a long history of discussion about its relationship to an ideal of European modernity and civilization. Chapter 5 explores the unique way in which a Turkish nationalist discourse constitutes a figure of Europe that in turn positions Turkey as marginal. From the legal, military, and cultural reforms of the eighteenth- and nineteenth-century Ottoman Empire to the "modernizing" and "civilizing" reforms of the Turkish nationalist movement, Turkey has frequently gauged its own modernity against a perceived Europeanness. This chapter focuses on the historical echoes of perceived Europeanness in two formal instances of Turkey's measurement against an ideal of Europe: the Ankara Agreement of 1963, which formally outlined the terms of Turkish accession to the European Economic Community; and the beginning of formal accession negotiations between Turkey and the European Union in 2005. This chapter argues that the figure of Europe circulates in domestic Turkish political speech as a means to produce understanding of elements of Turkish political life as "transitional." Although Turkey's liminal status implies movement and corresponds to numerous transhistorical narratives of post-Enlightenment development and modernization, the figure of Europe circulates in Turkey to make the status of movement static. In public discourse regarding Turkey's integration into the European Economic Community in 1963 and accession to the European Union in 2005, the figure of Europe emerges as the name of Turkish liminality, the measure of Turkey's status as "in-between."

Although the cases that compose these chapters indicate the circulation of figures at given moments in time, they are not exceptional or ideal-typical instances of these figures' appearance. These cases are simultaneously complex and commonly known; they are the subject of both scholarship and contemporary popular knowledge. In some instances, the material analyzed in a chapter emerged historically to consume media discourse at the time but has significantly faded from collective attention in the present (as in chapters 2 and 3); in some instances, it circulates with the presumption of significance (as in chapters 1 and 5); and in some instances, it becomes significant in circulation (as in chapter 4). I could have chosen other moments in Turkish history to be the material of analysis in this book, and different operational attributes of these figures would likely have emerged in those cases. The chapters of this book do not assert transhistorical definitions of each figure based on a single, specific case but instead ask what it means for these cases "to have come into existence, to have left traces, and perhaps to remain there, awaiting the moment when they might be of use once more; what it means to them to have appeared when and where they did—they and no others."[60] A strictly prescriptive justification of case selection undermines each figure's ability to speak in the moment of its appearance: these cases are not cases of a type; they are not exceptional; they were not even intentionally chosen to cover a certain time span. The particular collection of cases emerged in this work out of a study of Turkish history, and although the analysis demonstrates the operation of a vocabulary of figures in Turkish nationalism, honesty about contingency must recognize that other moments, other figures, and other forms of these figures were and are possible.

Propriety, Discourse, Performance

In developing a theory of figures that accounts for overlapping processes of the production of authority, *Figures That Speak* responds to a set of basic questions of rhetorical analysis when these questions run up against the massive complexity of a six-day speech. But the methods required for addressing *Nutuk* speak to a mode of rhetorical analysis relevant for a diverse array of contemporary and historical political practices. As discussed earlier, the relationships between persuasion and propriety, invention and decorum, are foundational concerns of classical and contemporary rhetorical theory.[61] But public speech embodies and performs the social norms that define propriety. Within speech, the world of social norms becomes visible, but this world of norms also exceeds any one speech and perhaps all speeches. Yet social norms are not an indexable mass of regulations, some of which are relevant to a speaker's situation and the whole of which exists independently of speech.[62] Judith Butler's numerous statements on the relations between norms and performance require abandoning the commonplace belief in rhetorical theory that social norms have an independent existence as a yardstick against which persuasiveness, effect, meaning, and other elements of rhetorical performance can be judged. The universe of social norms is something presumed in performance, and in performance "the norm cannot be reduced to any of its instances, but . . . neither can the norm be fully extricated from its instantiations."[63] A theory of figures that accounts for the layers of political and linguistic representation, for circulation through discourse, and for the performance and constitution of norms thus reframes basic components of rhetorical theory with broad implications for the study of public speech.

In addition to advocating this revised approach to rhetorical study, this book calls for expanded rhetorical studies of nationalism, both because nationalism is a deeply rhetorical practice and because it is an area of theory that cannot overlook its own implication in practice. As argued earlier, distinctions between theory and practice produce authority in certain situations, and these distinctions have been the subject of rhetorical theory since its founding. If romanticism in the eighteenth and nineteenth centuries displaced the traditional study of rhetoric by emphasizing radical originality and dispersing literary production into local vernaculars rather than unified languages and bodies, then the nationalisms that developed at the same time were perhaps the location for resituating the constitutive authority of a distinction between theory and practice. In fact, Don Paul Abbott argues that the simultaneity of the romance displacement of rhetoric and nationalism makes nationalism the location par excellence of the modern history of rhetoric.[64] That is, with this dispersal of cultural production into vernacular languages, rhetoric underwent a profound transformation, and this transformation is evident in the unique production and distribution of nationalism as a discourse. With this argument in mind, inattention to the phenomenon of nationalism, then, seems to correspond to or continue the project of the romance, which dispersed the concerns of rhetoric into increasingly specialized disciplines and relegated rhetorical studies to a cataloging of tropes subordinated to the truth of the symbol.[65] In order to investigate the history of rhetoric, then, it is important for rhetoric scholars to account for the profoundly rhetorical discourses of nationalism and for the way that a globally circulating form of discourse is the product of both complex local history and transnational resemblance. The complexity of meaning and authority in one long speech becomes a touchstone for investigating the history of rhetoric and its possible analytic mode.

Bringing overlapping processes of the production of authority to bear on the study of Turkey is especially important as the means of foregrounding rather than naturalizing Turkey's location in complex geopolitical historical relations. As Yael Navaro-Yashin has argued, "'Turkish Culture,' as such, does not exist."[66] In studying and writing about Turkish politics, history, and language use, one necessarily makes arguments and assessments that are political, "entangled in a history of multiple constructions," beholden to representational categories tied to networks of power.[67] Many clichés about Turkey participate in reproducing these networks of power, as when commentators discuss the "Turkish model" of democracy or position Turkey as a "bridge" between East and West (see chapter 5). As Mehmet Döşemeci argues, the politicization of knowledge production regarding Turkey is apparent in the marginalization of recent Turkish-language analyses of the neoimperialist tendency of European Union policy, which are frequently labeled as "not objective."[68]

The criteria of objectivity themselves are the product of European standards, however, and the marginalization of studies of Turkey informed by postcolonial theory therefore paradoxically presumes the authority of the criteria that this marginalization actually produces.[69] A theory of figures that relies on poststructuralist theory and on a constitutive account of authority in representation allows international relations of power to be the topic of analysis rather than to be presumed as a basis of analysis. Clichés, categories of representation, and academic short-hand concepts (such as "Turkish Culture") traffic in a vocabulary with a long history of circulation in domestic and international political speech about Turkey. *Figures That Speak* is motivated both by Turkish studies scholarship concerned with representational power as well as by interdisciplinary literatures on meaning, form, and authority. *Figures That Speak* introduces a rhetorical mode of analysis directly attuned to networks of power recirculated in common topics in Turkish studies: Europe, religion, minorities, the military, Atatürk.[70]

This book opens a new perspective for approaching Turkish historiography. Historical and political scholarship in Turkish studies often trends toward a few perspectives on the relationship between the state and the people. First, important critical work has expanded on a traditional focus on the state and its policies of nation building or development, what Hale Yılmaz refers to as a "macro" perspective on Turkish studies.[71] Second, in contrast to this perspective, scholars have emphasized "micro," local, or "bottom-up" responses to and experiences of state policies imagined in Ankara, sometimes comparing these responses and experiences with the perspective of nationalist elites.[72] Important departures from both the "top-down" and "bottom-up" analyses of state policies of nation building have explored the relationship of universalizing and Orientalist narratives of modernity and development to Turkish national identity.[73] By envisioning nationalism as a discourse organized by a set of figures, however, *Figures That Speak* retheorizes nationalism from the perspective of Turkish rhetorical circulation. Although it analyzes moments of policy and state-level action, its perspective on these events emphasizes the rhetorical impact of broadly circulating figures in speech for making meaning at these moments. Figures function as a kind of interpretive control on meaning at any given time, thus generating policy as much as do individual actors who pursue policy or local residents who reinterpret or resist policy. Agency is thus considered to be distributed in figures that are the locus of a nationalist worldview, which is a marked departure from the presumptions of agency that characterize both "top-down" and "bottom-up" analyses of Turkish nationalism.

If this book's perspective enables a critical reappraisal of the politics of analytic form, topic, and emphasis, then it is also important to mark a limitation in this project's account of nationalist discourse. As E. Fuat Keyman notes, the discourse of Turkish nationalism operates simultaneously as an identity discourse and "as a hegemonic and state-centric discourse of society."[74] Numerous scholars, such as Keyman, are justifiably interested in producing scholarship that analyzes communal or national practices within Turkey that do not fit neatly into the hegemonic account of national identity. This kind of scholarship is aimed at locating the limits of official discourse and offering alternative imaginings of identity in Turkey. One important motivation for scholarship such as Keyman's is the prevalence and continued production of academic research in Turkey and abroad that reinforces official nationalist discourse in a way that marginalizes communities in the present. One species of contemporary academic scholarship that reinforces official nationalist discourse presents itself as historical accounts of the Armenian Genocide of 1915 that underestimate the number of Armenian deaths, deny the existence of a policy of extermination, and/or emphasize Armenian atrocities against Muslims.[75] The need for alternative research on Turkey like Keyman's is even more necessary after the failed coup attempt in 2016 and the subsequent vast restrictions of academic and press freedom. Although this book explores the figures that structure and circulate in nationalist discourse, I avoid reproducing the frequently unspoken authority of this discourse in analysis by asking the following questions: What sort of knowledge does official discourse legitimate, and how is this discourse reinforced and reproduced? By exploring the forms of knowledge that official Turkish nationalist discourse "releases or disables," *Figures That Speak* explains the continued hegemony of specific forms of thought in contemporary Turkey.[76]

1

Figures of Nationalist Discourse in Atatürk's *Nutuk*

> I shall confine myself to an outline of the general events and indicate the tendency underlying them. I desire to make the task of the historian easier by pointing out the successive stages of the Revolution. I consider it to be my duty to undertake this more in my capacity as a leader of our republican organization than because during the course of these events I have been, and still am, President of the Grand National Assembly of Turkey and its Government, Commander-in-Chief and President of the Republic.
>
> —Mustafa Kemal, *Nutuk*

On Monday, October 15, 1927, Mustafa Kemal (later Atatürk) opened the third session of Turkey's Grand National Assembly with a speech that he delivered in six-hour increments every day for the rest of the week.[1] Known simply as *Nutuk* (*The Speech*) or *Büyük nutuk* (*The Great Speech*), the thirty-six-and-a-half-hour address presents a history of the Turkish nationalist movement, the War of Independence, and the legislative reforms of the new Turkish Republic from 1919 through 1927, centering around the activities of Kemal.[2] The text includes hundreds of documents written by prominent figures

A preliminary version of parts of this chapter previously appeared in Matthew deTar, "Figures of Nationalist Speech in Atatürk's *Great Speech*," in *History, Politics, and Foreign Policy in Turkey*, ed. Kılıç Buğra Kanat, Kadir Üstün, and Nuh Yılmaz (Ankara: SETA Foundation, 2012), 3–26. The revision included here is printed with permission.

of the late Ottoman Empire and the Turkish nationalist movement, offering an insider's perspective on the military campaigns, negotiations, and legislative debates of the early Republic. Kemal's arrival in Ankara to deliver this six-day speech in October 1927 marked the end of a two-year period of intense political power consolidation during which all of Kemal's opponents in the Grand National Assembly and the press were exiled, jailed, or executed, and Kemal presented the speech to a Parliament composed entirely of handpicked representatives.[3] For twenty-five years after its presentation, *Nutuk* remained the only source of historical information about the independence movement available in Turkey, and even when alternative accounts of the period appeared in the 1950s, they had very little influence on the histories taught in primary and secondary classrooms.[4] *Nutuk* has maintained a near-complete hegemony over early Turkish history until relatively recently.

Perhaps the most striking feature of the text is its form. Although *Nutuk* was delivered by Kemal in 1927, it is a vast archive of documents (telegrams, letters, meeting minutes, etc.) composed primarily between 1919 and 1923, many of which were not authored by Kemal and which were read at length or in their entirety in the speech. The collection of documents in *Nutuk* is so extensive that contemporary printed versions include a volume of numbered transcriptions of all of the documents referenced or quoted in the main text of the speech so that readers can follow along (and be further drawn in by the text as documentary archive).[5] This collage of documents makes the speech very difficult to follow for a reader, not simply because he or she is confronted with a complex alternation of voices, allusions, and tones but also because long sections of the speech contain nothing but quoted exchanges of telegrams or letters with almost no intervening interpretation or substantive narrative. The thin narrative trajectory discernible from the chronology of the documents has a tendency to fade to the background of an otherwise impenetrable text. Although popular memory of *Nutuk* characterizes it as the founding father's history of the birth of the nation, as his magnum opus,[6] or as a nationalist history par excellence, the unique form of the text resists these characterizations.

Scholars analyzing *Nutuk* have tended to draw overly clear interpretive lines through the text that emphasize Kemal's instrumental or ideological purposes, treating *Nutuk* as a treatise rather than as a speech. For instance, scholars have shown how the text marginalizes and condemns specific political opponents of Kemal, establishes Kemal as the only legitimate representative of the nation, and constructs an official history reliant on strategically flexible conceptions of "national will" and "internal enemies."[7] These interpretations offer important insights into the text and its later uses, thus challenging both nationalist myths about Turkey's foundation as well as dangerously malleable characterizations of political dissent that continue to circulate in Turkish politics to define enemies of the state. Emphasizing *Nutuk*'s instrumental and ideological purposes tends to exaggerate the regularity or consistency of the speech's content, however, and to downplay the amount of scholarly reconstruction required to make sense of the narration. Particularity, complexity, irregularity, and (perhaps) messiness are fundamental ways that *Nutuk*—as a speech—differs markedly from a treatise or ideological nationalist history. Overlooking these aspects of the text's form thus isolates *Nutuk* from the ways that it is deeply embedded in and representative of the thought patterns of its moment.

This chapter asks different questions to build on prior critical impulses toward *Nutuk* while maintaining the complex form of the text. For instance, Erik Zürcher and others have shown that much of the Turkish nationalist political philosophy evident in *Nutuk* can trace its origins to Ottoman intellectual trends of 1908 or earlier rather than to a "radical break" with the Ottoman past.[8] Building on this understanding of continuity and the contingency of history, this chapter asks: When and how did it become possible to imagine the year 1923 as a radical breaking point where the "new" Turkish Republic emerged from the ashes of the Ottoman Empire? A central presumption of this chapter is that history must acquire narrative form in order for it to mean anything (a presumption Kemalist reformers acted on to produce official history).[9] But this means that in 1923 the year 1923 did not have the status it came to have in 1927, the year *Nutuk* was issued, or in 1931, the year the Turkish Historical Society (Türk Tarih Kurumu) began publishing primary- and secondary-school textbooks.[10] In 1927, *Nutuk* began to outline what the events that it narrates *will have meant. Nutuk* is a transitional text, not fully representative of the condensed form Kemalism was able to take by the early 1930s but not unrelated, either, to that later ideological condensation. This chapter seeks to preserve *Nutuk*'s embeddedness in its moment of presentation, focusing on the juxtaposition of the archival content of the text with the form of the speech in 1927.

As a text that purports both to record and to evaluate certain moments in the past, *Nutuk* contains two different modes of speaking, two different forms of discourse. First, *Nutuk* originated out of the specific historical and political moment of Turkey in 1927. As such, it is a reflection of what Foucault calls "the historical *a priori*," or the background of "unthought" principles, assumptions, and social knowledge that structures forms of discourse and provides the conditions of possibility for what can be explicitly said or thought.[11] *Nutuk*, then, reflects a particular way of speaking about the Republic, a whole form of discourse located in nationalist, republican Turkey that took shape in the years following the end of the Ottoman Empire. This primary form of discourse present in *Nutuk* becomes visible in its interaction with a second form of discourse contained in the text: the quoted historical documents, which for the most part predate the Turkish Republic. Although the quoted historical documents do not speak in a unified voice, features of the primary nationalist discourse of the Turkey of 1927 become visible through *Nutuk*'s attempt to colonize voices heterogeneous with its own. Kemal's speech brought these documents within the political discourse of the Turkey of 1927, and in this juxtaposition of voices some unique features of Turkish nationalist discourse of 1927 become apparent.

This chapter argues that *Nutuk* is a founding document of the nation that disavows its role as founding document. Any declaration of independence names itself as the moment of foundation of a nation and in so doing contains a paradox: declarations of independence must assert their authority to represent a (national) people even though that people cannot exist until after the document names them. The people named in a declaration of independence are paradoxically the product of and prior to the text.[12] *Nutuk* names events prior to itself as the founding moments of the nation and in turn contains a different paradox of authority. In order for *Nutuk* to function as a nationalist history rather than as a declaration of independence, it must obscure the naming function that it performs, pointing out—or constituting—the foundational moments of national history while presuming that these moments were already understood as foundational. In the rhetorical world of the text, this presumption makes the date of the foundation of Turkey into something prior to *Nutuk* but that remains imprecise. In some cases, *Nutuk* even includes historical documents that indicate prior, wholly rhetorical constructions of a national "people." As a founding document and a history of foundations, *Nutuk* both newly constitutes the nation and rhetorically obscures its role in that constitution.

This chapter specifies how three broad "figures" of the discourse of the Turkey of 1927 interact with the historical documents quoted in the text to perform this constitution and obfuscation of constitution.[13] The speech both relies on and helps develop a number of *attitudes*, if not explicit arguments, regarding three figures essential to the nationalist history of Turkey: religion, the military, and Atatürk. It is these attitudes, or the general character of each of these figures, that become visible as Kemal incorporates historical documents into the speech. For instance, although the telegrams quoted in *Nutuk* detail a complex and historically contingent legal and political struggle that preceded the dissolution of the Ottoman Caliphate, the speech also situates "religion" as a generally suspicious figure, which influences audience interpretation and understanding of the detailed historical documentation. Each figure evident in the speech locates the foundational moments of Turkish history and situates these moments as if they were already understood as foundational. As *Nutuk* pronounces and gives meaning to the foundational moments of the Turkish Republic, these figures help obscure *Nutuk*'s constitutive, interpretive work and instead locate the foundation of Turkey outside of and prior to *Nutuk*.

The Figure of Religion

Although Kemal delivered *Nutuk* to loyal delegates and in a political atmosphere in which opposition was forbidden, *Nutuk* indexes and responds to a number of prevailing concerns about his government's relationship to Ottoman religious institutions and Islam more generally. For instance, since at least the Young Turk Revolution of 1908, Kemal's critics worried that any limitation to the power of the sultan-caliph would severely weaken or destroy the state, create a worldwide catastrophe within Islam, and leave Muslim areas open to occupation by Western armies.[14] Anxiety about Kemal's intentions toward the Caliphate became more acute during the Independence War (1919–23), as the *şeyhülislam* (head of the Ottoman religious hierarchy, an official office) issued a fatwa against the nationalist army (declaring the latter anti-Islamic), and many people believed that the nationalist movement meant to install Kemal as a new sultan. Anxiety about the future of Islam in the post-Ottoman state continued even after the declaration of a republic in 1923, when the very short-lived opposition Progressive Republican Party (Terakkiperver Cumhuriyet Fırkası) was outlawed for, among other things, having a platform that stated the party "respects religious thoughts and religious doctrines."[15] The nationalist movement was historically suffused with anxiety about its relationship to religion, and a discursive figure of religion emerges in the speech to manage these anxieties.

The speech recounts the abolition of the Caliphate as the result of a series of contingent events and practical political choices rather than as the result of Kemal's visionary secularization (which is the official memory of these events). This series of events begins with a distinction between the sultan and his cabinet of ministers, a distinction that helps Kemal characterize tension with the Istanbul government as strictly political rather than as designed to threaten the sultan-caliph or Islam. For example, Kemal reads a strongly worded telegram sent from the nationalist General Assembly to the Istanbul cabinet in 1919, which states, "[Because] the Cabinet continues to prevent any communication between the people and their beloved Sovereign and stands in the way of expressing their desires, and as they also persevere in their malicious schemes, the nation has decided to break off all official relations with the Government."[16] According to *Nutuk*, at this point Kemal's nationalist movement ("the nation") breaks off relations with the cabinet rather than with the sultan because the cabinet prevents the sultan from communicating effectively with the "people" (more precisely with the nationalist movement leaders, such as Kemal).[17] The distinction between sultan and cabinet allows Kemal to argue that the cabinet isolated the sultan politically, decreasing the sultan's ability to maintain the sovereignty of the empire and forcing the sultan to collaborate with foreign governments to ensure his own political power.[18] The distinction between cabinet and sultan even enables Kemal to portray the nationalist movement as motivated by a desire to defend the caliph.[19] The distinction removes "religion" from the domestic political tension of the post–World War I era, helps bolster the authority of the nationalist movement, and helps manage any remaining anxieties in 1927 about the recent past.

At this point in the speech, when the cabinet is deemed traitorous and the sultan an isolated figurehead, Kemal emphasizes the sacred and indivisible nature of the "nation," which must be defended at all costs.[20] In a summary of the weaknesses of the cabinet and its ministers, Kemal argues, "They were unable to appreciate that the only factor of salvation was the very nation itself and that it ever would be so. They were stupid enough to imagine that great aims could be attained simply by bowing down before the throne, by trying to gain the favor of foreigners by suave and conciliatory behavior."[21] Capitulation to the terms of the treaties drawn up by the Allies after World

War I, then, results from the "stupidity" and weakness of people who do not have the interests of the "nation" at heart. The nationalist organization, in contrast, sought to uphold the "sacred cause" of the nation, "a cause whose aim is the safeguarding of the country from disintegration and partition, and the security and independence of the State and Nation."[22] According to Kemal, the nationalist movement with Kemal as its leader is the only body removed from the partisan maneuvering that set the cabinet at odds with the sultan and set both on a path to completely undermining the nation's territorial sovereignty and interests.[23]

By emphasizing the "nation" as the sole foundation of political legitimacy, *Nutuk* prefigures the Ottoman imperial government as impossible to maintain. For Kemal, the nationalist movement can defend the nation's interests only by focusing exclusively on the political affairs of the Turkish population. In the discussion of political theory that begins the second volume of *Nutuk*, Kemal explains: "To unite different nations under one common name, to give these different elements equal rights, subject them to the same conditions and thus to found a mighty State is a brilliant and attractive political ideal; but it is a misleading one. It is an unrealizable aim to attempt to unite in one tribe the various races existing on the earth, thereby abolishing all boundaries. . . . The political system that we regard as clear and fully realizable is national policy."[24] The organization of the Ottoman Empire, which spanned modern Turkey as well as the Arabian Peninsula, Syria, Jordan, Lebanon, Israel/Palestine, Iraq, and parts of Greece prior to World War I, was based on this "brilliant and attractive political ideal" that was no longer tenable after the empire's defeat in the war.[25] In pursuing a "national policy" at this point in the narrative, Kemal signals a recognition of the limits of the national army's ability to secure territory and the limits of its interest in securing "non-Turkish" territory, and he presents these limits as coterminous with a realizable and legitimate project to claim "national" (i.e., Turkish) sovereignty.[26]

By emphasizing this "national policy" above all else, Kemal also shifts the relationship of authority between the sultan-caliph and the nationalist movement. Building from the tensions between Istanbul and the nationalist movement from 1919, Kemal quotes his own telegrams from 1920 arguing for a stronger suspicion of the way the Ottoman monarch might manipulate the people. Given Turkish Muslims' affective attachment to the leader of Islam, "if the nation considers him in the light of Caliph and Sultan, it will be obliged to obey his orders and thereby realize the enemy's plans and designs" because the sultan has become a "tool of the enemy employed against our country and our nation."[27] Kemal begins to frame the sultan-caliph as using religion to gain allegiance that would undermine the nation's interests. With an ever-increasing emphasis on the authority of the "nation" above all else, and with the establishment of a bureaucratic body that represents this authority, Kemal subverts the sovereignty of the sultan to the popular sovereignty of the nation.[28]

Once Kemal has completed this series of argumentative maneuvers (separating cabinet and Caliphate, reinforcing the sanctity of the nation, and subverting the authority of the caliph to that of the nation and the Grand National Assembly), a simple political contradiction necessitates rejecting the Caliphate altogether. In November 1922, with the nationalist army in control of much of contemporary Turkey and publicly announcing its intention to abolish the sultanate, Mehmet VI abdicated the throne and fled via a British warship to Malta.[29] In the wake of these events, the Assembly formally separated the Caliphate from the sultanate, abolished the latter, and elected the crown prince, Abdülmecid II, as caliph.[30] The idea of an elected caliph contradicts nationalist ideas of political representation, however, and in recognition of this contradiction Kemal quotes himself from Assembly debates in 1922: "This Assembly is the Assembly of the Turkish people. Your powers and authority can only extend to the Turkish people and our Turkish country and can only be effective in so far as the question concerns their lives and their destiny. Our Assembly, Gentlemen, cannot attribute to themselves powers that comprise the whole of the Islamic world."[31] Since the Grand National Assembly's representational authority extends only to the Turkish nation, electing a caliph for the whole of Islam would overstep the

Assembly's authority.[32] For Kemal, "neither common sense nor reason will ever admit that any individual Muslim State will confer on any man the authority of guiding and administering the affairs of the whole of the Muslim world."[33] In *Nutuk*, the abolition of the sultanate and two years later the Caliphate becomes the necessary, unavoidable result of the way contingent historical events unfolded.

Alongside this detailed history of contingent events, *Nutuk* also suggests a broader conflict between religion and politics that partially constitutes the *figure* of religion in the nationalist discourse of 1927. It is the figure of religion that enables the consolidation of a post hoc narrative characterizing the abolition of the Ottoman monarchy as part of Kemal's visionary, premeditated, modernizing reforms. Late in the speech, Kemal emphasizes the nationalist movement's foresight, reminding his audience, "The enlightened republican sons of Turkey . . . will easily understand that it was impossible to maintain a form of government which, after having proclaimed itself a republic, would have undertaken the obligation of preserving under the title of Caliph at its head a rotten dynasty, and this in a manner which would never have made its removal possible."[34] In this transition to a more evaluative tone, two things become apparent. First, Kemal expects his audience of "enlightened republican sons of Turkey" to easily understand the preceding account of contingent historical events in the same way Kemal does: the abolition of the Ottoman government was obviously the best outcome from the perspective of the Turkey of 1927, no matter the means by which it was achieved. Second, the Republic, on the one hand, and the caliph and the "rotten dynasty," on the other, come into relief as wholly opposed forces. This binary creates an environment where memory of the nationalist movement's work to save the Caliphate and perhaps to establish a British-style constitutional monarchy is inadmissible. Opposing Ottoman/religious institutions to the republicanism of the new Turkey helps to transform the reality of 1927 into the nationalist movement's intentional goal all along.

The loose opposition between these two kinds of governmental systems is distilled even further in the later sections of the speech, establishing an attitude toward religion as a broad figure. For Kemal, abolishing the Caliphate protects the Republic from the institutions of monarchy, but abolishing the Caliphate also "is indispensable in order to secure the revival of the Islamic Faith [and] to disengage it from the condition of being a political instrument, which it has been for centuries through habit."[35] This secularizing description of the separate spheres of religion and politics evidences a major shift in *Nutuk*, where the narrative no longer describes contingently necessitated political changes but rather describes a revolution in philosophy and form of government. In addition, Kemal's assertion that Islam needs to be removed from the political realm for Islam's own sake constitutes a massive departure from the Ottoman perspective since the late nineteenth century, which sought to distinguish religious and political authority through sporadic reforms of Ottoman government institutions.[36] The figure of religion in the discourse of nationalism in 1927 distinguishes between Ottoman and republican institutions as well as between Islam and politics more generally.

An attitude toward religion that presumes that politics and religion *should be* separate renders suspicious any statement perceived to suggest the harmony of religion and politics. In the final hours of presenting *Nutuk*, probably in the afternoon of the sixth day of the speech, Kemal begins to describe the association of religion and politics as dangerous.[37] Moving rapidly through the events of 1925–26, when Kemal used the emergency Law for the Maintenance of Order (Takrir-i Sükûn Kanunu) to exile, jail, or execute numerous political opponents, *Nutuk* justifies the prohibition on the Progressive Republican Party by quoting from the party platform: "Could any sincerity be expected from people who had adopted the following principle: 'The Party respects religious thoughts and religious doctrines'? Was not this principle the standard of all those who pursued personal aims whilst they allured and deceived the ignorant, fanatical, and superstitious people? Has not the Turkish nation for centuries been dragged into the endless suffering and into the pestilential swamps of obscurity under this banner, rescue only being possible through great sacrifices?"[38] At the end of *Nutuk*, then, when republican government and secular Turkish nationalism are the only admissible political positions, the mixture of religion and politics is portrayed as the cause of "endless suffering" during the Ottoman Empire. Political parties or individuals in the modern Republic who might imply such a mixture become deceitful and probably dangerous enemies of the nation. The figure of religion in the discourse of Turkish nationalism in 1927 emerges to organize government institutions, separate Islam from politics, and eventually indict political party platforms that mention religion.

Nutuk, then, offers two accounts of the nationalist movement's relationship to Ottoman religious institutions, which help situate the Turkish Republic of 1927 as the visionary telos of all of Kemal's prior action. On the one hand, circumstantial and practical political decisions result in the abolition of the Caliphate. These decisions develop out of a desire to defend the interests of the nation rather than out of any suspicion of religion (and perhaps even develop from a desire to save Islam from politics). On the other hand, there is a clearly implied suspicion of religion *in 1927* that manifests in condemnation of opposition political parties, the "religious" governmental institutions of the Ottoman Empire, and sometimes Islam more generally. Although these two accounts are not necessarily mutually exclusive, the figure of religion in 1927 looms over the content of the speech to become the hegemonic interpretation of the events documented in *Nutuk*.[39] When Kemal poses the rhetorical questions quoted earlier, it is precisely a transposition of the figure of religion of 1927 into the past that allows Kemal to be clearly understood: "Could any sincerity be expected from people who had adopted the following principle: 'The Party respects religious thoughts and religious doctrines'?" The social knowledge of Turkey in 1927 constitutes a figure of "religion," which is implied to have always guided Kemal's actions, structuring this rhetorical question and those that follow as harsh and obvious censure of the opposition Progressive Republican Party. The figure of religion in the Turkish nationalist discourse of 1927 implies a supposed continuity of purpose for Kemal's actions since 1919.

The Figure of Atatürk

As distinct from the figure of religion, the figure of Atatürk as the founding father, nationalist visionary, powerful general, and adept statesman maintains a constantly visible presence in *Nutuk*. This figure significantly contributes to the text's narrative continuity and mitigates criticism of Kemal's authority that appears in the historical documents quoted in the speech.[40] The figure of Atatürk is apparent from the famous first line of the speech, marking the shared beginning of Kemal's personal story and the national history: "Gentlemen, I landed at Samsun on the 19th [of] May, 1919."[41] As Hülya Adak has argued, from the first line the "unified nation and the unified self are presented in *Nutuk* as interchangeable and intertwined; in general, the nation is denied an autonomous existence extricated from the I of the narrative."[42] In contrast to the conjoining of the figure of Atatürk with the history of the nation, the documents quoted in *Nutuk* present two important challenges to Kemal's historical authority. First, the documents detail a confusion both internal and external to the nationalist movement regarding Kemal's future role in any government that might follow the ouster of the sultan as well as confusion about Kemal's goals for the nationalist movement. Second, a very long passage at the end of the speech presents myriad evidence of a lively, thoughtful public sphere engaged in the process of imagining a new Turkey, yet Kemal presents this passage as a justification for silencing the press for treasonous debate in 1925–26. The figure of Atatürk implicitly frames these kinds of episodes as treasonous by situating them within the incipient form of nationalist discourse emerging from within the Turkey of 1927.

Many documents collected in the speech imply critical uncertainty about Kemal's status in the nationalist movement and the position he might hold in any post-Ottoman governmental structure. Many early telegrams suggest that the nationalist movement meant to protect the seat of the Caliphate and the Ottoman government from foreign invasion.[43] Based on this idea of the nationalist movement's purpose, prominent figures within the movement ask questions or offer comments about Kemal's future role in a post-Ottoman government.[44] Near the end of the speech, Kemal quotes Rauf Orbay (a leader in the nationalist movement sentenced to execution in 1925) at length in a passage meant to present unquestionable evidence of Orbay's treason in comments he made in the Assembly in 1923:

> "We have been commissioned by the nation to establish an administration which is founded without restriction and reserve on the national sovereignty; to create the foundations of a popular administration that is called a democracy. A number of comrades who have been thinking differently [i.e., Kemal and others] have followed a direction which must lead to depriving the Assembly of this national right, and of granting the right of dissolving the Assembly and . . . vetoing their resolutions to some other authority. It is this fact which I have opposed. . . . I am neither an adherent of the Sultanate nor of the Caliphate. My opposition is directed against any authority [namely, Kemal] which would attempt to seize the right of these dignities."[45]

When interpreted outside the context of 1927, Orbay's statement might sound like a common refrain about popular sovereignty, the threatened authority of Parliament, and a consolidation that resembles the authoritarian role of the former sultan. Because this criticism expressed in 1923 was directed at Kemal, however, it appears in 1927 as a threat to the structure of the state that has since been consolidated around Kemal.[46]

Not only people inside the nationalist movement but also members of the Ottoman government were confused about or critical of the role of Kemal in a successor government to the Ottoman state. After Kemal describes the separation of the sultanate from the Caliphate and the abolition of the former, he quotes a series of telegrams between him and the future caliph, Abdülmecid II, that suggest the caliph's own confusion about (or perhaps resistance to) the proposed balance of power in a new constitutional monarchy. In the first telegram in this passage, Kemal instructs Abdülmecid about the precise language Abdülmecid must use when he accepts his appointment as caliph by Kemal and the Grand National Assembly in 1922.[47] After summarizing Abdülmecid's response to this instruction, Kemal complains in the telegram that Abdülmecid must be constantly reminded "that the reply to our [i.e., Kemal's] telegram informing him of his election as Caliph must be addressed to the Presidency of the Grand National Assembly and not to me personally."[48] That is, the future caliph's telegraphic addresses suggest he is perhaps not entirely clear about (or willing to assent to) the new governmental form and sees Kemal himself as a kind of secular sultan with absolute control over the Parliament rather than as president elected by that Parliament. As Zürcher has argued, widespread confusion about Kemal's early role in the government perhaps stemmed from the fact that a purely religious caliph was a foreign concept for many Ottoman elites, and many felt an emotional bond with Abdülmecid once Kemal declared him the new caliph.[49] The historical documents in *Nutuk* suggest uncertainty, anxiety, and critique about the new governmental form and Kemal's political power in this government as it emerged from 1920 to 1923 because no true clarity about the future form of government existed until 1924, with the abolition of the Caliphate.

From the perspective of 1927, however, the figure of Atatürk exerts an interpretive hegemony over the content of these historical documents that denies space for this uncertainty. Because the figure of Atatürk coincides with the nation as a whole, Abdülmecid's subtle changes to the instructions about his first public announcement as caliph become in 1927 an uncooperative gesture, one that suggests a wholesale resistance to the nationalist movement. Addressing a telegram to Kemal rather than to the president of the Assembly becomes evidence that the caliph is unwilling to assume a subordinate position in a new national order conjoined with the figure of Atatürk. Similarly, Rauf Orbay's suggestion that Kemal "would attempt to seize the rights" of the sultan and caliph now becomes evidence of Orbay's nostalgia for the Ottoman regime and lack of support for the Republic. The Republic as embodied by Atatürk in 1927 circulates as the complete opposite of the Ottoman government, and the nuance of Orbay's critique doesn't translate to the discursive world of the Turkey of 1927. By 1927, the figure of Atatürk has begun to develop into a powerful representation of the successes of the nationalist movement and the strength of the Republic, and statements out of step with this figure are understood as dangerous to the nation as a whole. Orbay's and Abdülmecid's statements suggesting uncertainty about Kemal's role in the Turkish nation, then, come into tension with this figure in *Nutuk* and are interpreted as treasonous lapses of loyalty to the Turkish nation.

Perhaps the strongest challenge to the interpretive control of the figure of Atatürk is discussed at the end of the speech in a long passage that extensively quotes newspaper editorials written in early November 1923, days after the Parliament declared Turkey a republic. In *Nutuk*, Kemal justifies the restriction of press freedoms in 1925–26 by arguing that some newspapers' criticisms of his domestic policies in 1925 were not sincere or productive rational debate because these same newspapers also published criticisms of the declaration of the republic in 1923. The peculiar nature of Kemal's argument is visible in an extended quotation:

> After [the journalist] supported his thesis by quotations from my [Kemal's] speeches[,] he related how Washington, the hero of American Independence, had retired to his farm, and he observed that the American Parliament, without regard to personality and only thinking of the general good, had worked out the Constitution in a period of six years in order to elect Washington President afterwards. The journalist disapproved of my having been the promoter of the alteration of our Constitutional Law to its present form.
>
> We should be very simple minded if we believed that this journalist and his like were sincere in the criticisms to which they abandoned themselves for the purpose of emphasizing the defects which they believed to have discovered either in the way the Republic was proclaimed or in the law settling the principles which referred to the Republic.
>
> If these journalists had loyally accepted the Republic on the day of its proclamation instead of beginning with their alarm, if

> they had published articles which were aimed at not driving public opinion into uncertainty, but rather at inculcating the idea that the Republic was useful and that its proclamation was a wise measure, they would have been able to maintain the sincerity of their later criticisms.[50]

In the simplicity of the transition from the first to the second paragraphs in this passage, the hegemonic interpretive influence of the figure of Atatürk becomes apparent. Shifting from an analogy between the American and Turkish constitutional processes that seems to condemn the totality of Kemal's control over government, the passage reminds the audience that "we should be very simple minded" if we do not recognize this treasonous analogy for what it truly is: a journalist's attempt to drive "public opinion into uncertainty" and undermine the Turkish Republic. Atatürk looms over the text as a figure maintaining an unwavering fortitude of purpose in supporting the Republic and representing the will of the nation, whereas the journalist seems to be a kind of polemicist, even criticizing the process that led to the birth of the modern Turkish Republic. Under the influence of this static figure of Atatürk in 1927, a figure that embodies the moral strength of the Turkish nation as a whole, this journalist's condemnation of Kemal appears as ethically inconsistent as the "Boy Who Cried, 'Wolf'!"[51]

It is important to note here that the figure of Atatürk in the Turkish nationalist discourse of 1927 exerts an influence over the interpretation of *Nutuk*'s content that exceeds the momentarily persuasive influence of a charismatic and powerful leader. The structure of political discourse in 1927 is such that the condemnation of a journalist for criticizing the leaders of the Republic makes intuitive sense, and the figure of Atatürk helps structure that discourse in at least two ways. First, the figure contains a sense of visionary purpose that is evident in the speech, which describes the founding father's secret plan all along to modernize Turkey and transform its governmental structure into a secular republic.[52] By 1927, then, the figure of Atatürk is intimately bound to a teleological history of the foundation of Turkey that emphasizes a decisive break with the Ottoman past and the liberation of the Turkish nation, and any critic of Kemal focused on single moments in a debate thus seems to be out of step with the grand march of Turkish history.[53] Second, the visionary trajectory and moral fortitude of the figure of Atatürk enables a slippage in other, related terminology, allowing the abstract governmental form *cumhuriyet*, "republic," to be easily equated with the official name of the nation in 1927, Türkiye Cumhuriyeti, the Republic of Turkey. When Kemal quotes editorials from 1923 that criticize the process leading to the declaration of the Republic, then, the historical trajectory that is bound up with the figure of Atatürk allows this criticism also to sound as if it is aimed at the Turkish Republic as it exists in 1927 rather than at an abstract governmental form. As a figure of discourse, "Atatürk" structures an understanding of history and fixes the interpretation of Kemal's critics to such an extent that *Nutuk* hardly needs to provide a drawn-out explanation of how certain newspaper editors needed to be silenced.

The figure of Atatürk in *Nutuk* transforms questions regarding Kemal's authority presented by the historical documents in the text, but it also helps obscure one of the most salient features of any official nationalist history: the necessarily retroactive nature of the account. In each encounter between historical documents in *Nutuk* and the Turkish nationalist discourse of 1927, Kemal interprets events from the perspective of a successful nationalist movement and governmental transition. In concept, discussion of a visionary plan to abolish the Ottoman Empire and establish a Turkish Republic makes sense only retroactively, when the visionary can be proven to be correct instead of crazy. Because the figure of Atatürk presents itself in *Nutuk* as a continuous, stable presence from Kemal's arrival at Samsun on May 19, 1919, through the delivery of *Nutuk* in 1927, it becomes difficult to recognize *Nutuk* as simply a retelling of events in 1927—Hasn't Kemal always been the figure Atatürk of 1927? The content of this figure is static, and as Adak has argued, *Nutuk* situates Kemal within a cyclical rather than a linear chronology.[54] The idea of a retroactive account of events in 1927 requires a temporal orientation missing from the figure of Atatürk itself. Historical documents instead become juxtaposed with the reality of an existing Turkish Republic and its concomitant nationalist discourse in 1927, and they come to mean something new or something additional in that environment. This new or additional meaning tends to overshadow other possible interpretations still contained in the documents. The figure of Atatürk structures an understanding of the historical documents presented in *Nutuk* that therefore exceeds a simple retroactive reinterpretation or instrumental distortion of the past by a politically powerful Kemal and helps to establish a perspective in Turkish nationalist discourse of 1927 that cannot conceive of *Nutuk* as a purposeful retelling of events.

The Figure of the Military

The military institution of Turkey in 1927 was vastly different from the array of groups that constituted the "nationalist forces" of 1919–21. By 1927, the Turkish Armed Forces (Türk Silahlı Kuvvetleri) exhibited an integrated ideological and bureaucratic form that associated the military with a history that stretched back to the Independence War. This institution was organized into a clear hierarchy of inspectorates and army commands under the administration of a military council.[55] Nearly universal one- or two-year conscription of male citizens made the armed forces a powerful "school of the people," a means of educating the population about nationalist ideals and the Independence War.[56] Less than ten years earlier, the "nationalist forces" were an unorganized, volatile association of elements joined in their opposition to foreign (primarily Greek) occupation. Although nearly the entire command structure of the Ottoman military continued to obey Kemal after he resigned from Ottoman service, Ottoman troop demobilization after World War I left no troops in central and western Anatolia to receive orders.[57] From 1919 through 1921, the Western front of what became a "Turkish independence struggle" (against the Greeks) consisted of irregular groups of armed bandits and slightly more organized guerrilla forces, almost none of which answered to the commands of the former Ottoman generals (such as Kemal) leading the nationalist movement.[58]

Although historical documents collected in *Nutuk* suggest a discrepancy between the state of the military in 1919 and its state in 1927, the speech both articulates and relies on a figure of the military as a unified, determined force throughout history. Quoting a telegram he sent in July 1919, Kemal articulates the figure of the military that runs throughout the speech: "The national forces, which are formed and organized for the preservation of our independence, are protected against any kind of attack or interference. The national will is sovereign in regard to the guidance of the fate of the State and the people. The Army is the willing servant of the national will."[59] The army serves and expresses a lofty, singular purpose: to defend the sovereignty of the state, the people, and the "national will." The quotation of Kemal's early assertions of the army's unity makes other generals' telegrams predicting desertions at all ranks sound like support for the sultan in contrast to support for the nation.[60] A static, ahistorical discursive figure of the military enables an imagined consistency between the structured military institution that existed in 1927 and the group of irregular guerilla bands, appropriated Ottoman troops, and deserting (and sometimes skeptical) Ottoman officers that constituted the "national forces" in 1919. In *Nutuk*, "the military" becomes an expression of Kemal's singular, eternal will to defend the nation transposed onto the form of the military institution of 1927, which itself also becomes eternal.

The static nature of the figure of the military in *Nutuk* rhetorically negotiates two important problems of constitution associated with the birth of the Turkish Republic: the existence of the people and the location of a national land area.[61] First, following the Ottoman defeat in World War I and the sultan's capitulation to the terms of the Treaty of Sèvres, it was not entirely clear *for whom* an independence struggle could be waged.[62] Insofar as an independence struggle could be fought for a people, this people needed to be constituted as a unified entity. The figure of the military thus helps produce "the people" as a transhistorical essence rather than as a newly constituted polity, despite suggestions about the newness of this people that are clearly visible in the historical documents quoted in *Nutuk*. Second and closely aligned with this first problem, the proper land area of a state that would replace the Ottoman Empire was neither apparent nor unoccupied by foreign troops. The multiethnic empire that existed before World War I had broken into a host of states and protectorates, and the independent "Ottoman lands" consisted of only a small part of central and northern Anatolia and parts of the Black Sea Coast.[63] The idea of the military as a continuous institution of defense in 1927 helps naturalize and nationalize the borders of contemporary Turkey as a preexisting Fatherland rather than as something contingently established through military campaigns. The timelessness of the figure of the military as it circulates in *Nutuk*, then, helps mitigate some of the paradoxes of constitution in the Turkish Republic.

The Problem of a People

In *Nutuk*, the challenge of locating a people who would support or constitute a nationalist movement is evident from the beginning of the speech. From his perspective in 1927, Kemal explains that when the Greek army crossed the Aegean in 1919 to occupy Izmir, "there had been no public manifestation of indignation and protest against this dastardly blow that had been aimed at [the] national independence" because "the people had not been fully informed about . . . the severity and ill-treatment that was being inflicted."[64] Arguing that it was therefore necessary "to arouse [the people] and force them to take action," Kemal quotes from a telegram he sent in 1919 in which he orders numerous local governors and army leaders to "raise the people to hold great and imposing meetings, appealing to justice and demanding the intervention of all the civilized nations and the Great Powers to put an end to this intolerable state of affairs."[65] After the Greeks invaded Izmir and western Anatolia, an armed reaction by

Kemal faced a problem of legitimacy because the sultan had relented to the invasion and no body of people seemed upset about it. Thus, Kemal orders his subordinates to engineer a reaction among "the people," making sure to emphasize that demonstrations should be peaceful and therefore legitimate to Western observers by avoiding "hostile demonstrations against the Christian population."[66] From the beginning of *Nutuk*, the historical documents suggest an effort to constitute a legitimate Turkish national people who would support the armed activities of Kemal's troops.[67]

Although *Nutuk* includes historical instructions for the deliberate manufacture of a "people" to support the nationalist movement, the historical documents also simply assert the unity and dedication of the national people. Kemal quotes a telegram from the governor of Kastamonu Province in 1919 expressing anxiety about public support for the nationalist movement in his district and asking "whether the public opinion of the other vilayets [Ottoman provinces] is favorable to us or not."[68] Kemal summarizes his response: "The national movement, full of energy and glowing with enthusiasm, is actively going on even in the remotest parts of the country. The inhabitants, even of the smallest villages, and the Army, down to the smallest units, are responding loyally to our efforts and cheerfully follow our instructions in complete unity."[69] That is, although *Nutuk* quotes a telegram from the Kastamonu provincial governor expressing concern about the disunity of the people as they exist in Kastamonu, in 1927 Kemal asserts the opposite, describing a national unity of the people "even of the smallest villages."[70] Kemal's assertion about the unity of the national people, then, begins to resemble the paradoxical interpellative statements that frequently attend political foundations anywhere—the "We the People" of the American Constitution, for instance.[71] By insisting on the unity of the nation when addressing members of that nation who seem hesitant, Kemal constitutes the unity he describes, signaling a moment that both creates a people and paradoxically implies their prior existence.

Although the historical documents quoted in *Nutuk* mark moments of the constitution of the Turkish people, the newness of this people is mitigated by the constancy of the figure of the military. In Kemal's delivery of *Nutuk* to the Grand National Assembly in 1927, he repeatedly emphasizes the proud history of the Turkish army, drawing seemingly natural connections between the institution of 1927, the forces that fought in 1919, and the will of the nation. For instance, after describing the battles that drove the Greek army out of Anatolia in 1922, Kemal tells the Assembly,

> These operations, which had been developing for a long period of time, which were prepared in all their details and carried out in such a way that they were crowned with success, constituted a sublime action which once again in history proves and confirms the strength and the heroism of the Turkish army, Turkish officers and their commanders. This action is an immortal monument to the spirit of freedom and independence of the Turkish Nation. I am proud and am ever happy to be the son of a nation and the commander of an army that can perform such deeds.[72]

In a concise statement on the figure of the military, Kemal marks the heroic past of this institution, its immortal significance, and its present, suggesting the placement of this figure outside any point in a linear or contingent history. As the "monument to the spirit of freedom and independence of the Turkish Nation," the figure of the military requires an understanding of the Turkish people as a group that predates the activities of the military in 1919 because the military's accomplishments at that time represent via synecdoche that people's "spirit of freedom and independence." Furthermore, as Kemal emphasizes his own continuous relationship to the nation and the army, the constancy of the figure of Atatürk itself (as discussed earlier) helps reinforce the presumed continuity of the military as well as the ancient origins of the Turkish national people because Kemal was born into this "nation."[73] Although the historical documents quoted in *Nutuk* seem to mark the very moment of the constitution of the Turkish people, the timelessness of the figure of the military in the speech obscures the particular moments of constitution.

Problem of National Land Area

The challenge of constructing a Turkish national people is accompanied by an ambiguity about the precise borders of the new nation's land area. Although Kemal states the army's objective that "not an inch of the country should be abandoned until it [is] drenched with the blood of its citizens," the documents in the speech also demonstrate wide uncertainty about the extent of the land area to be defended in this manner.[74] Kemal quotes a long telegram from a nationalist leader in Edirne (a former Ottoman capital, located just within Turkey's contemporary borders with Greece and Bulgaria) in 1920, who reports a lack of Bulgarian defenses across the border in northwestern Thrace and urges Kemal to reclaim all of Thrace for Turkey.[75] Seemingly on the basis of realpolitik, in his response to the telegram Kemal dismisses the suggestion that Turkish nationalists occupy all of Thrace because "to speak of united Western and Eastern Thrace is bad policy." He tells the nationalist leader in Edirne: "Eastern Thrace is incontestably an integral part of our country. As for Western Thrace, this territory had once been ceded by Treaty. Eastern Thrace can, at best, serve as a base of operations for those who are struggling for the liberation of Western Thrace. If we insist on claiming a united Eastern and Western Thrace, this may give rise to certain other claims on Eastern Thrace. . . . It must be remembered that the Bulgarians, too, are demanding an economic exit to the Aegean Sea."[76] Kemal indicates that occupying Thrace in 1920 would draw Bulgaria into war at a time when the only nationalist troops within two hundred miles were guerrillas or other semi-independent militias. Thrace may have been commonly understood to be Turkish territory, and Turkish Thracians may have understood all of Thrace to be part of the Turkish homeland, but the geopolitical arrangement in 1920 required Kemal to declare only eastern Thrace incontestably integral. The edges of the nation's borders seem to correspond to the location of and threat posed by foreign troops.[77]

Not only does *Nutuk* suggest moments when the future physical borders of Turkey were uncertain, but it also signals the need for the nationalist movement to develop the people's affective and historical attachments to the physical space of the state.[78] Early in the speech, Kemal describes the Sivas Congress of September 1919, where all of the prominent nationalist leaders met to revisit the mission of the resistance movement as established at Erzurum in July 1919.[79] During the meeting, leaders discussed amendments to earlier resolutions, and Kemal compares the text of one resolution to its amendment at Sivas:

> [The original resolution reads:] In the event of the Ottoman Government being pressured by foreign states to cede and abandon these places [*buralar*] (namely the Eastern provinces), [the Congress will] decide upon the attitude to be adopted in regard to administration, politics, and military power and determine a provisional administration regarding this question.
>
> In the text of the resolutions passed by the Sivas Congress, the expression "these places [*buralar*]" was amended by the more general phrase "to cede or abandon any part of our homeland [*memleketimizin herhangi bir parçasını*]."[80]

The phrase "to cede or abandon any part of our homeland [*memleketimizin herhangi bir parçasını*]" implies the affective significance of "home" and national belonging, replacing the neutral designation of location, "these places [*buralar*]." The amendments at Sivas suggest both an expansion of the area defended by the resistance movement (beyond eastern Anatolia to all of Anatolia and parts of Thrace) and a redefinition of the whole area as a uniquely national "homeland." Far from a simple procedural amendment, the activities of the Sivas Congress seem to mark a moment of origin of an idea of the Turkish homeland, an inviolable national space to be defended "with the blood of its citizens."

Although moments in the historical documents in *Nutuk* might suggest a new set of boundaries affectively imagined as a homeland for the first time, the figure of the military in the speech naturalizes this land area as ancient and organic. In the narrative of *Nutuk* presented in 1927, Kemal emphasizes the fundamental connection between a people, a land area, and the military. He explains, "Armies have been known in history to have heroically and honorably defended a whole country against superior hostile forces, inch by inch to the last inch of their territory and, in spite of all, have been able to preserve their existence. Such is the character of the Turkish Army."[81] For Kemal, all armies, including the Turkish army, have a fundamental connection to territory that they heroically and tenaciously defend, and so an armed force attempting to establish a new state is beyond the imaginative scope of Kemal's definition here. Kemal builds this understanding of the Turkish army throughout *Nutuk*, reminding his audience in 1927: "You are well aware that speaking of war does not mean two armies fighting against one another but two nations who are both risking their existence and who summon for the fight all their resources, all their possessions, and all their material and moral forces."[82] The military is a representation of the nation as a whole, an armed personification of it, a tool by which a nation risks everything to defend itself. This existential connection between military, nation, and territory explains why the military cannot give up defense of a nation's territory until that territory is "drenched with the blood" of the people who belong to that territory: "*its* citizens."[83] The land area is as much the nation as the people. The figure of the military in 1927 fluidly connects people, military, land area, and nation, presuming the physical area of the Turkish state to be a preexisting and perhaps even ancient national homeland.

Kemal's physical control of telegraph wires in Anatolia served as an important additional means of naturalizing and producing both the national people and the national land area. In 1919, the communications system of the Ottoman Empire consisted primarily of wired telegraph lines, with a main line that ran over land from Istanbul through Izmit, Ankara, Sivas, and Diyarbakır to Mosul and Bagdad.[84] Branching off from this main artery, other lines connected to other Anatolian cities in such a way that all telegraph traffic would have to route through a mainline repeater station to reach Istanbul.[85] By controlling a main repeater station (at Izmit or Ankara or Sivas), Kemal could control all telegraphic communication to or from Istanbul traveling through that repeater station.[86] Control of telegraph lines allowed Kemal to assert both a deep knowledge of the desires of the people and a literal, wired connection to the farthest reaches of the national land area.[87] If his references to the geographical extent of the nation sound overly ideological to contemporary readers, then his consistent reminders to his audience in 1927 of his telegraphic connections with the nation help mitigate these statements.[88] Kemal's physical control of the communication network in Anatolia after 1919 lends an air of descriptive accuracy to seemingly ideological assertions about the people, the nation, and the land area because all of them are connected by a communications infrastructure Kemal dominated.

Authority between Atatürk and the Military

The figure of the military stands in tension with the figure of Atatürk at times in *Nutuk* because a complete erasure of Kemal's role in establishing a nation, people, and land area for the new Turkish state would undermine the significance of his figure as founding father. In the opening pages of *Nutuk*, Kemal emphasizes the challenges facing him in 1919:

> Only one important part of the country, affording protection to a mere handful of Turks, still remained, and it was now suggested also to divide this.
>
> Such expressions as: the Ottoman Empire, Independence, Padishah-Caliph, Government—all of them were mere meaningless words.
>
> Therefore, whose existence was it essential to save? and with whose help? and how? But how could these questions be solved at such a time as this?
>
> In these circumstances, one resolution alone was possible[:] namely, to create a New Turkish State, the sovereignty and independence of which would be unreservedly recognized by the whole world.

> This was the resolution we adopted before we left Constantinople and which we began to put into execution immediately we set foot on Anatolian soil.[89]

This opening passage suggests that Kemal himself created an army, a people, and a land area for the "New Turkish State" seemingly out of nothing, especially given the "meaninglessness" of the expressions "Ottoman Empire, Independence, Padishah-Caliph, Government" and given questions such as "Whose existence was it essential to save? and with whose help?" This passage implies that Turkey might have begun as a "peopleless state" (to reverse Hannah Arendt's formulation), an individual possessed of the singular resolve to assert the sovereignty of a state but with no clear connection to a people—a constitutive paradox that could not "be solved at such a time as this."[90] If the figure of the military naturalizes a national people with a preexisting claim to a specific land area, then this figure does not obscure Kemal's visionary defense of this area in the face of immense challenges.

Although the figure of the military and the figure of Atatürk demonstrate tension at times, these same lines of tension also reinforce each figure in the discourse of Turkish nationalism of 1927. Atatürk's ability to conjure a nation from nothing can appear as the organizational skill of a visionary leader deeply in tune with the people rather than as the power of the leader of a "peopleless state." As Kemal summarizes the speech's introductory remarks, including the passage quoted earlier, he states, "I may add that it was incumbent upon me to develop our entire social organization, step by step, until it corresponded to the great capability of progress which I perceived in the soul and in the future of the nation and which I kept to myself in my own consciousness as a national secret."[91] In *Nutuk*, Atatürk's role in the nationalist movement becomes organizational and even visionary, but the nation also preexists his role in the movement. The national people may even predate the Ottoman Empire, making the military into a necessary entity for the defense of the nation's natural rights. To this effect, Kemal asserts that he stood on a bench in Parliament in 1922 during debates about the future of the sultanate and Caliphate and "in a loud voice" declared: "Sovereignty is acquired by force, by power, and by violence. It was by violence that the sons of Osman [the Ottomans] acquired the power to rule over the Turkish nation and to maintain their rule for more than six centuries. It is now the nation that revolts against these usurpers, puts them in their right place and actually carries on their sovereignty."[92] Here the figures of the military and Atatürk work in tandem as the military defends the ancient, pre-Ottoman sovereignty of the Turkish nation, which Atatürk has organized and led on a path toward progress. As the figure of the military transforms the people and land area of the Turkish nation into an ancient, natural phenomenon, the figure of Atatürk reinforces its own legitimacy as the representation of the "soul of the nation."

Conclusion

This chapter argues that three figures in the discourse of Turkish nationalism in 1927 allow *Nutuk* to locate and name the foundational moments of national formation while simultaneously obscuring the speech's constitutive role in forming the nation. The figure of religion situates the reality of the Turkey of 1927 as the nationalists' intentional goal in 1919. This figure transforms a history of contingent events into a visionary plan, even when the narrative already frames these contingent events as decisions made in the "interests of the nation." The figure of Atatürk in *Nutuk* operates as a static, continuous entity coterminous with the nation as a whole, transporting into the past the state apparatus of 1927 centered on Kemal's authority. This amalgam of temporal reference points in a figure embodied by the speaker himself makes historical voices who question Kemal sound threatening to the nation (of 1927) and obscures the retroactive nature of the whole of *Nutuk*. Finally, the military emerges as an ahistorical figure fusing the people, land area, and nation into an indivisible, ancient whole, overshadowing those moments in the text that indicate that establishing the people and land area resulted from the nationalists' work. These figures reinforce and find tension with one another at different moments in the text, offering a glimpse of Turkish nationalist discourse of 1927 as a whole and obscuring the way *Nutuk* constitutes the Turkish nation rather than simply recounting its history.

It is perhaps tempting to understand the figures evident in *Nutuk* as the purposeful constructions of a powerful and charismatic speaker—as complex rhetorical maneuvers that obscure the "truth" of the historical documents. To avoid this characterization, it would be useful to consider the context of *Nutuk*'s composition. When Kemal began to deliver *Nutuk*, the entire text was incomplete. Although he had likely already selected the historical documents he quotes, decisions about what to say about these documents still lingered. During the week of the text's presentation, Kemal wrote the narrative of the speech in the evening after the delivery of the speech during the day, working alongside a close group of friends and with a team of secretaries.[93] The final product is more a glimpse of the discourse of Turkish nationalism that subsumes Kemal, *Nutuk*, and his audience in 1927—a glimpse of a way of thinking—rather than a careful reframing of specific historical details according to a complex logic of figures and discourse. The archive of documents contained in *Nutuk* do not tell the real, historical truth, which is then manipulated by an ideological narrative. This archive is a strategic selection of documents that best fit the nascent nationalist discourse of 1927. By juxtaposing the historical documents with a nationalist discourse that emerged with and after *Nutuk*, it is the figures of that nationalist discourse of 1927, rather than the "real truth" of history, that become visible.

To treat the historical documents in *Nutuk* as a complete, truthful archive also runs the risk of reinforcing the authority and legitimacy of *Nutuk* as documentary source. As Adak mentions, part of the reason why *Nutuk* maintained hegemony over histories of the early Republic until the 1990s relates to the text's quotation of so many historical documents.[94] The simple fact of extensive citation produces public *and scholarly* perception of historical accuracy in the text, but this perception in turn *produces* the authority of *Nutuk* as the complete history of the birth of the Turkish Republic.[95] As this chapter has shown, however, *Nutuk* structures itself and is structured by the perspective of Turkish nationalism of 1927, and so the text's authority also relies on a specific interpretation of the quoted historical documents because the content of the cited documents frequently undermines the very authority *Nutuk* seeks to construct for itself. The contemporary authority of *Nutuk*, then, relies on a paradoxically circular pattern of interpretation and origin: the official nationalist account of history is legitimate because *Nutuk* offers so much historical evidence, but this historical evidence must first be shaped by figures of nationalist discourse in order to legitimate that discourse.[96] The circularity of *Nutuk*'s authority results from the speech's form: simultaneously a proto-nationalist statement, the foundational text of the nation, and a history of the Republic. As archive, declaration, and historiography, *Nutuk* simultaneously contains, constitutes, and effaces the moments of national origin.

2

The Figure of Religion in the Transition to Multiparty Democracy

On June 16, 1950, the first night of Ramadan, the newly elected Democrat Party (Demokrat Parti, DP) changed the law regulating the language of the call to prayer in Turkey to allow the call to be recited in Arabic in the mosques in Turkey for the first time in eighteen years. Beginning in 1932, as part of a vast series of language reforms, the Turkish government had required all muezzins to recite the call to prayer (*ezan*) in Turkish, following a version recorded in Istanbul and circulated to mosques nationwide.[1] Muezzins who continued to recite the *ezan* in Arabic could be arrested and jailed for up to three months.[2] As originally conceived, a ban on the use of Arabic in Turkish mosques would have included all aspects of mosque practice, including readings from the Koran, delivery of the sermon, and even individual prayer. Proposed regulations on language use inside the mosque were abandoned by 1933, however, because of the inability or impracticality of enforcing these regulations.[3] Only the ban on the Arabic *ezan*, the most public part of mosque practice, remained.

The ban on the Arabic *ezan* was highly controversial in Turkey because it affected both personal religious practice and theology. This reform significantly altered a ritualized, everyday practice in a way that announced itself frequently because many people kept time by and experienced their day as divided by the call to prayer. More importantly, Arabic itself occupies a sacred place in Islam as the language in which Allah communicated the Koran to the Prophet (the Koran is the literal word of Allah rather than a prophet's account of Allah's message), and state mandates about the language of worship thus appeared as mandates about belief.[4] One of the most jarring and symbolic effects of the ban on Arabic in the *ezan* was the translation of "Allah," the Arabic *proper name* of God, to "Tanrı," the "pure" Turkish word for God or a god.[5] The controversial nature of the reform led to numerous arrests during the eighteen-year ban, either of muezzins who continued to recite in Arabic or of people gathered to attack officers who arrested muezzins or even of protesters who recited the Arabic *ezan* at demonstrations to perform a resistance to the law.[6] When in 1950 an amendment to the law made the Turkish *ezan* optional rather than required, every mosque in the country changed back to the Arabic *ezan* seemingly overnight, and newspapers across the political spectrum reported on the public displays of enthusiasm for the new policy (see figure 1).[7] With a simple legal amendment, then, this consistent source of tension between the state and the people disappeared.

The year 1950 is frequently understood as a moment of "relaxation" of restrictions on religion in Turkish history, but it instead marks the beginning of a more total expansion of the state into the institutions of religious worship.[8] In the 1920s and 1930s, reforms of religious institutions indeed restricted some of the most minute parts of everyday life. Mustafa Kemal Atatürk and his Republican People's Party (Cumhuriyet Halk Partisi, CHP) abolished religious education and sharia courts, closed dervish brotherhood lodges and many religious shrines, outlawed Arabic, required a new alphabet of Latin letters (rather than Arabic) for the Turkish language, restricted "religious" clothing for men, replaced the Ottoman calendars and *alaturka* timekeeping with Gregorian calendar system and the international clock, and eliminated the constitutional clause designating Islam as the official religion, among a wide array of other social, political, and legal policies.[9] Although many of these new policies affected extremely specific aspects of individuals' daily lives, they also at times took the form of decreased state funding and a removal

Arabça ezan dün kabul edildi

Kanun, bu sabahtan itibaren yurdun her tarafında meriyete girmiş bulunuyor

Ankara: 16 (Telefonla) — Büyük Millet Meclisi bugün saat 15 de Fuat Hulûsi Demirellinin başkanlığında toplandı ve din dilile ezan meselesini görüştü.

Celse açılınca kürsüye gelen Başbakan Adnan Menderes; Arapça ezan hakkında Demokrat Parti Meclis Grupunun aldığı kararın gazetelerle ve radyo ile yayınlandığını ve bunun neticesinde Arapça ezan okumak gibi hâdiselerin artacağını ve bu hususta bir ka-

(Devamı Sa. 5 Sü. 1 de)

Anıt-kabir arazisine dair soru

23 Haziranda Meclis'te cevaplandırılacak

Ankara: 16 (Telefonla) — Bugünkü Mecliste din dilile ezanın okunmasından sonra verilen kısa bir tatili müteakip gündemde bulunan sözlü sorular görüşüldü.

Sinan Tekelioğlunun, Toprak

1. "Arabça ezan dün kabul edildi: Kanun, bu sabahtan itibaren yurdun her tarafında meriyete girmiş bulunuyor" [Arabic call to prayer approved yesterday: Beginning this morning, the law came into force everywhere in the country], *Yeni Sabah*, June 17, 1950. The words in the image mean "welcome."

of the state apparatus from involvement in religious institutions. Some of these policies, such as the ban on the Arabic *ezan*, had minimal or poorly defined mechanisms of enforcement.[10] Despite the vast restrictions of the 1920s and 1930s, by 1945 the Turkish state's role in religious education, practice, and commemoration was very small. By contrast, the "relaxation" of restrictions on the *ezan* in 1950 corresponded to increased state funding for and involvement in a variety of religious institutions and a more thorough insinuation of the state into these institutions.

Amendment to the law prohibiting the Arabic *ezan* also marks a broad restructuring of the figure of religion and its forms of authority as they circulated at the level of public speech. The authoritarian implementation of reforms in the 1930s was broadly justified by a grand narrative of modernization in Turkey's continuing nationalist revolution. These policies were repetitively correlated in political speech with the goals of the revolutionary nationalist movement, thus anchoring legitimate state action in an external, absolute national will, history, or right. For instance, after the change from Arabic script to the Latin alphabet in 1928, from 1932 to 1950 the Turkish language underwent a "purification" to remove Arabic and Persian elements. Both of these reforms were situated within the context of the Sun-Language Theory (Güneş-Dil Teorisi), which posited the Central Asian and Turkic origin of all human language, and thus the republican language reforms became an attempt to resuscitate national heritage and save the Turkish language.[11] Yet by 1950, when the new government lifted the prohibition on the Arabic *ezan*, public speech no longer justified state action on an idea of the absolute national will. Rather, the change in the law regulating the *ezan* was framed by a more bureaucratic speaking style that emphasized government concern for the proper management of its population, the expediency of regulations, and the practical concerns of the citizens. This chapter explores the distinction between these two moments in the public speech of Turkish national politics.

The shift from a discursive style anchored by a revolutionary/reformist mandate to a discursive style that emphasized the proper administration of the minutiae of everyday life resembles a shift from what Hannah Arendt has called the "revolutionary moment" to what Michel Foucault refers to as "governmentality." For Arendt, the revolutionary moment encompasses both armed rebellion and subsequent constitution making, wherein "the end of rebellion is liberation, while the end of revolution is the foundation of freedom."[12] Although Arendt's work focuses more on the historical conditions of the production of strong "foundations of freedom," her description of the proper "end of revolution" suggests the important temporal orientation of the discursive style of a revolutionary moment. This style of speech frames policy as directed toward the ideal future state or as realizing the expectations of the past rebellion. Foucault describes in contrast to this revolutionary style the emergence of a modern "art of government," which, "instead of seeking to found itself in transcendental rules, a cosmological model or philosophico-moral ideal, must find the principles of its rationality in that which constitutes the specific reality of the state." For Foucault, these "principles of rationality" of the art of government develop through the concept of population, the management of which "comes to appear above all else as the ultimate end of government."[13] According to this idea of government, then, the anchoring purpose for the act of governing is internal to the governing state itself: the proper management of a population. In contrast to the revolutionary style's more transcendental focus on the ideal future government or the purity of the past, the style of governmentality is marked by a bureaucratic concern for the proper present administration of the people.[14]

This chapter explores the shift between these two moments in discourse in Turkey, focusing on the way that the figure of religion articulates different styles of national political speech in 1932 and 1950. The shift between a revolutionary style and a style of governmental rationality in discourse spans an array of political, legal, economic, and social processes. By focusing on the figure of religion, this chapter articulates a succinct vignette of a massive shift in the location of legitimacy in public speech. Although the *policies* of the 1920s and 1930s at times targeted the minutia of individual behavior in a way that parallels the logic of governmentality, *speech about* and justifications for these policies anchored themselves in a transcendental idea of the nation. The legitimacy of these policies was therefore rooted in their relationship to the visionary leadership of Atatürk and the story of the nationalist movement. The policies of 1950 similarly targeted the minutia of individual behavior, but speech about these policies was rooted in arguments about proper management of the population. The circulation of ideas of legitimacy in public speech was transformed between 1932 and 1950, and this chapter outlines the shift from a revolutionary to a governmental style of discourse in political speech about the legislation of the Arabic *ezan* in 1932 and 1950.

Policy in the Early Republic and the Prohibition of the Arabic *Ezan*

The law passed in 1932 that required muezzins to recite the call to prayer in Turkish developed out of a series of reforms in religious institutions and policy that spanned the first decade of the Republic. Eight years prior to the ban on the Arabic *ezan*, in 1924, the new government of the Turkish Republic instituted a vast reorganization of state institutions concerned with religion, abolishing the Caliphate, the *şeyhülislam*, and the Ministry of Religious Affairs and Pious Foundations (Şeriye ve Evkaf Vekaleti) and dividing these offices' administrative duties among three new cabinet-level departments under the direction of the prime minister.[15] First, the new Directorate of Religious Affairs (Diyanet İşleri Müdürlüğü, Diyanet) was responsible for employing imams in Turkey and developing policy regarding religious practice.[16] The establishment of this directorate with an extremely small budget led to the forced retirement or replacement of much of the ulema.[17] Second, the Directorate-General of Pious Foundations (Evkaf Umum Müdürlüğü) would oversee the upkeep of religious shrines and sites and was financed through public donations and an endowment.[18] Third, under the direction of the Ministry of Education (Maarif Vekâleti), primary and secondary religious education was incorporated into the national school system, and a new Faculty of Divinity at Istanbul University replaced all institutions of religious higher education in Turkey.[19] Following this first stage of institutional reform, by the end of 1925 dervish lodges, prayer houses, and religious shrines and tombs were closed (and their maintenance suspended), and the *şeriat* (religious law) courts were abolished, their judges required to retire, and their jurisdiction transferred to the secular state courts.[20] Most importantly, with its founding in 1924, the Diyanet began efforts to nationalize the content of the Friday sermon and develop entire sermons in Turkish, leading to the publication of a book of Turkish sermons in 1927.[21] In the first two years of the Republic, then, reformers completely overhauled the major Ottoman institutional religious apparatus, reframing these institutions within the administrative structure of the Turkish Republic.

By 1928, after the preliminary years of reform in the Republic, most of the momentum for social reform focused on language policies that promoted Turkish and sought various revisions of the language. The most significant state language reform mandated a change in the alphabet from Arabic script to Latin letters. This topic was broached in May 1928; a research committee was formed in June to assess feasibility; and on November 1 Parliament passed the law prohibiting use of Arabic script in a phased process to begin immediately.[22] Although the alphabet reform marked a substantial state intervention in the republic's language, it is rivaled in its impact by the purification reforms developed by the Turkish Language Society (Türk Dil Kurumu) that followed throughout the 1930s and 1940s.[23] The Turkish Language Society focused on removing all Persian and Arabic vocabulary and grammatical elements from Ottoman Turkish, replacing them either with older "pure" Turkish words or with neologisms, and radically intensifying language-reform policies that had been in effect since the Tanzimat (1839–76).[24] These reforms were motivated by a number of factors, including the desire to make the written language look "comprehensible" to Western eyes, to align the written language with vernacular Turkish (Ottoman Turkish was primarily a bureaucratic language by 1928), and to nationalize the language.[25] The extent of the language-purification efforts achieved an alteration of the Turkish language so vast that texts such as Atatürk's *Nutuk* (1927) have gone through numerous "translations" into modern Turkish every few decades.[26] By 1928, then, reformers of the early Turkish Republic had embarked on a series of legislative actions that profoundly altered the language of the new state.

The years following the alphabet reform, from 1928 through about 1938, constitute the heyday of Kemalist and republican ideology in the Turkish Republic, and the atmosphere of ideologically driven reform influenced a wide range of cultural practices. For instance, beginning in 1928 a number of social groups supported the state-mandated language reform that paralleled similar fascist mobilizations in Europe, most notably the Citizen, Speak Turkish! (Vatandaş, Türkçe Konuş!) campaign. These campaigns aimed to discourage use of languages other than Turkish in public and included a widespread adult-education campaign, propaganda efforts, ad hoc committees tasked with correcting public signs and promoting Turkish, and frequently vigilante intimidation and violence.[27] In 1929, these reforms were further supported by the Ministry of Education's decision to stop offering Persian and Arabic classes in public schools.[28] The atmosphere promoting nationalist reform was so widespread that it influenced the direction of myriad academic disciplines outside of linguistics, including history, geography, archaeology, music, art, and even the natural sciences.[29] For instance, beginning in 1926 with the foundation of the Fine Arts Academy (Güzel Sanatlar Akademisi), Turkish folk music was "classicized and classified to suit the modernist predilections of republican orthodoxy," including the fixation of this music in Western notation, the adoption of European instructional techniques, and the clear separation of training in the newly categorized "classical" music from religious musical education (the latter was not part of the Fine Arts Academy curriculum).[30] Although most contemporary scholarship on the republican period focuses on state reform policies regarding religion and language, the 1930s in Turkey were characterized by a climate of reform that extended well beyond the state's activities to permeate numerous areas of social and cultural life, and the scope of the nationalist reform agenda frequently operated without any connection to state officials.[31]

It is in this atmosphere of wide-ranging experiments in the nationalization of society and culture that trends in linguistic, religious, and artistic (musical) reform overlap in the regulations banning the use of Arabic in religious services. Prior to the official change in the language of the call to prayer in 1928, the newly organized Faculty of Divinity at Istanbul University recommended a number of policies for the "modernization" of Islam in Turkey, including a change to worship in the vernacular.[32] Despite these recommendations, and despite the nationalist credentials of the leaders of the Diyanet, in the late 1920s and early 1930s the Diyanet maintained its position against worship in Turkish.[33] In December 1931, however, Mustafa Kemal Atatürk began to take interest in the idea of "Turkifying" Islam, and he invited a number of prominent *hafız*es to discuss the issue of translating mosque ceremonies into Turkish, including the *ezan*, ritual readings of the Koran, and individual prayer.[34] By January 1932, Atatürk arranged a number of ceremonies in Turkish at mosques in Istanbul to correspond with Ramadan that year, including a widely publicized reading of the Turkish Koran at the Ayasofya (Hagia Sophia) on February 3, which was broadcast over state radio and at which newspapers reported seventy thousand people in attendance.[35] By the end of 1932 and in a partial reversal of policy, the Diyanet issued an edict to mosques nationwide that contained the text of the new Turkish *ezan*, began training muezzins in the new *ezan*, and instituted penalties (in February 1933) on muezzins who hesitated to recite the *ezan* in Turkish, although none of the other efforts to translate worship was pursued further.[36] Despite these new regulations on the form of religious service, in 1933 the Istanbul University Faculty of Divinity closed, and the vocational İmam-Hatip Schools (Preacher and Prayer Leader Schools) closed owing to declining enrollment that stemmed from inadequate secondary religious instruction in Turkey, leaving the "very elementary" government Koran courses (Hafız and Koran Courses [Hafız ve Koran Kursları]) as the only institutions dedicated to religious training in Turkey.[37] Thus, the ban on the Arabic *ezan* developed out of overlapping trends in the nationalization of the spheres of culture, religion, and language policy, which simultaneously created institutional obstacles to the development of more complex religious policy.

Political Speech and the Prohibition of the Arabic *Ezan*

In the period preceding the ban on the Arabic *ezan* in 1932, Kemalist political speech began to develop a valuation of religion as a general category that structured discourse regarding political, legal, and cultural reform. In the previous chapter, I outlined a figure of religion in the discourse of the Turkey of 1927 and in Mustafa Kemal's *Nutuk* that implied a suspicion or hostility toward the concept of religion in general. In the years following *Nutuk*, this suspicion became more nuanced, and the new secularist discourse of the republican elite was structured by particular definitions of "good" and "bad" religion. For instance, Necmettin Sadık Sadak, cofounder of the daily *Akşam* and member of Parliament, argued in an editorial in mid-1929, "Intolerance in the civilized world today has become characteristic of the priestly class only, which lives like a parasite on the edge of society."[38] According to this commonly held position, religion was not in danger from the state, nor was it in danger from the state's "modernizing" or "civilizing" policies, and religious leaders who suggested otherwise were insincere and financially motivated (because decreasing funding for religious institutions threatened the livelihood of the ulema). In fact, as Umut Azak argues, the Kemalist discourse of this period relied on a construction of the "rationality of 'true' Islam[,] . . . which was adaptable to the needs of modern society," and therefore reforms that "modernized" religious practice were in harmony with this "true" Islam.[39] Sadak's *Akşam* article articulates a familiar statement about the financial motivations of the ulema and the harmony of religion with republican reform that implies a distinction between "good" and "bad" religion. In these characterizations, the clerical class's supposedly self-interested, "parasitical" practices to maintain legal or institutional structures were deemed illegitimate uses of religion.

The distinction between legitimate and illegitimate religion became more precise in discussions of "freedom of conscience" and reactionary Islam during this period as Kemalist political speech expanded on the idea of "true" Islam and the state's role in defending faith. For instance, in March 1929 Prime Minister İsmet İnönü announced that Parliament would not renew the Law for the Maintenance of Order, which had forbidden the "political" use of religion in 1925 and had led to the closure of both numerous newspapers and the opposition Progressive Republican Party.[40] İnönü explained that the law was no longer necessary because it had achieved "the removal of religion from the state and politics," and citizens were now "free in their beliefs and consciences, and their pure and clean faith was freed from the complex affairs of this world."[41] This speech outlines the important role of the Kemalist state in securing an individual's "freedom of conscience" (*vicdan hürriyeti*), a phrase that during this period referred to the individual's ability to develop a relationship with God unmitigated by institutional authorities but also designated the inside of a person's head as the only legitimate location of religion or religious expression.[42] This explanation of the state's role in guaranteeing the purity of religion became one of the defining features of the figure of religion in the political discourse of this era, and critics of Kemalist reform of religious institutions were considered intolerant and reactionary or were accused of "bigotry and fanaticism."[43] The official discourse of the late 1920s and 1930s, then, asserted clear boundaries between "good" and "bad" religion, where legitimate religion is located in the individual's conscience, is protected by the state, and is silent in public and where any resistance to the Kemalist reform agenda or expression of religion in public is deemed illegitimate, bigoted fanaticism.[44]

This distinction between legitimate and illegitimate practice and expression of religion provides an important touchstone for justifications of the ban on the Arabic *ezan* in 1932. According to official discourse regarding the ban on Arabic, the state's role in protecting individuals' freedom of conscience almost necessitated a change in the language of worship because it would allow individual Muslims to better understand the weekly sermons and therefore develop a stronger faith and a closer contact with God.[45] For Yunus Nadi, the founder of *Cumhuriyet*, the Koran "is more effective in Turkish because those who are repeating it are repeating it knowing what it means, and those who are listening are aware of what they are listening to."[46] More importantly for Nadi, perhaps, was the argument that in translating the Koran and altering aspects of worship, "Turks are far ahead of their time in being able to practice their religion in their own language. . . . The understanding [of the Koran] is perfect, the faith is solid and even the core language that expresses it is very poignant."[47] In this characterization, not only are Turks able to be better Muslims, but also Turkish Islam becomes an innovative leader in worship. The previous definition of legitimate religious practice combines with this account of innovative revision of worship to produce a circular self-authorization of state discourse, tying the distinction between "good" and "bad" religion to the narrative of the revolutionary nationalist movement. In 1941, the law that finally codified specific penalties for violating the ban on the Arabic *ezan* further reinforced these connections, explaining the need "to rescue the people from the influence of the Arabic language attaching them to old mentalities and old traditions."[48] The ban on the Arabic *ezan*, then, became an essential step in the progression toward modernization and westernization in Turkey, a step that helped fulfill the goals of the revolutionary nationalist movement by distancing new Turkey from the Ottoman past. The distinction between legitimate and illegitimate religious expression helped ground the ban on the Arabic *ezan* in a broad discourse of the nation's progress.

Although it is important to recognize the specific contours of the idea of legitimate religion circulating prior to the ban on the Arabic *ezan*, the significance of Kemalist political speech at this time also lies in the way that the figure of religion in discourse allowed various changes in law and episodes of protest or criticism to be lumped together as a single set of phenomena anchored to the revolution. The idea of religion being in danger, being a danger to the state, or even being wrested from the hands of its enemies relied on a unified conception of religion as an object, a figure in discourse, something in flux in a variety of situations connected through their relation to this figure. As Gavin Brockett has argued, Kemalist political discourse and even historiography of republican Turkey grouped together a number of legislative changes (such as the abolition of the Caliphate and the ban on the Arabic *ezan*) with a number of events and protests (such as the Şeyh Said Rebellion in 1925, the Menemen Incident in 1930, the Bursa protest of 1933) as being "about religion" or evidencing a conflict between Kemalism and religion, despite the complexity and uniqueness of each of these events.[49] Similarly, political speech in the late 1920s and early 1930s emphasized a unified figure of religion in discourse, a figure that marked out legitimate modes of worship and belief but that was also intricately linked to a vast overlapping set of elements connected to the revolution. For instance, the elements that anchored the discourse of this period in a "revolutionary moment" became visible in the self-authorization of Istanbul University's Faculty of Divinity, which states, "The Turkish Revolution by creating this Theology Department has recognized" the need that "religious life . . . must be reformed on scientific lines."[50] This statement not only suggests a legitimate mode of religious practice (one "reformed on scientific lines") but also anchors the need for this legitimate religion in the project of the Turkish Revolution, a continuing mission that coordinates diverse aspects of political and cultural life. The unified figure of religion that operates in the political discourse of Turkey surrounding the ban on the Arabic *ezan*, then, helps mark the contours of a revolutionary moment in Turkish nationalist discourse, a moment characterized by an emphasis on a transcendental, extragovernmental justification of action, such as the purity of the revolutionary mission or the goal of establishing an ideal future state.

Turkey in the 1940s and the Amendment of the *Ezan* Law

Mustafa Kemal Atatürk's death in 1938 marks a moment of significant transition in the structure of Turkish political discourse. As mentioned in the previous chapter, a static figure of Atatürk in nationalist discourse helped unify an account of the birth of the Turkish Republic and the subsequent reforms of state institutions as revolutionary steps toward modernization. Although the figure of Atatürk in discourse exceeds the action or biography of the individual, this figure was nevertheless intimately associated with the person of Mustafa Kemal during his lifetime, and his death in 1938 led to a kind of unmooring of the figure of Atatürk. As John VanderLippe has argued, one consequence of Atatürk's death on political discourse in Turkey was the development of a problem in the justification of the policies promulgated by Atatürk's immediate successor, İsmet İnönü. That is, prominent members of the CHP began to disagree about what policies best represented Atatürk's ideals and specifically about the form of statism best suited to Turkey, especially as İnönü developed new economic policy during and after World War II.[51] Although the spectrum of allowable political dissent in the 1940s consisted only of disagreements about the precise content of properly Kemalist policies, and although these disagreements just continued a debate that had begun during Atatürk's lifetime between two of Atatürk's closest associates, İnönü and Celal Bayar, the fact of public disagreement about policy within the CHP constituted an extraordinary development in Turkish politics. With the death of Atatürk, his figure began to truly float in discourse, to be talked about and debated without being anchored to a living representative of the ideals of the revolution, and therefore the political discourse of Turkey in the 1940s began to subtly shift from one that justified all state action in the revolution to one that debated the best continuation of the revolution's legacy.

The discussion about economic policy that defined the new atmosphere of political debate in Turkey in the early 1940s centered on three policies enacted by İnönü's government that eventually led to a split in the CHP and the beginning of multiparty democracy in 1945. The first of these reforms was the Wealth Tax (Varlık Vergisi) of November 1942, a poorly defined punitive tax that was officially intended to curb the fortunes of "war profiteers," semiofficially aimed at having non-Muslims (who were exempted from military service) share the burdens of war, and unofficially intended to force non-Muslim minorities from their position of economic prominence in Istanbul.[52] Because enforcement of this law almost exclusively targeted Greek and Armenian businessmen (many of whom were jailed when they couldn't pay the arbitrarily assessed penalties), opposition to the law in official discourse and in Parliament was minimal given the complete lack of representation for this population in Turkish politics at the time.[53] Under American pressure, however, the Wealth Tax was canceled in 1943 and replaced by the second of İnönü's major economic laws, the Land Products Tax (Toprak Mahsulleri Vergisi). This tax was similarly punitive, but this time it was assessed against all landholders regardless of religion or property size in order to prevent grain hording during the increasingly fragile economic situation of World War II.[54] Because the Land Products Tax was also levied against Muslims, it proved to be much more controversial, but the net effect of the law was the consolidation of land ownership among large landholders, and thus only moderate opposition to this economic policy surfaced in Parliament (where large landholders had influence).[55] These first two major economic policies of İnönü's presidency resulted in increasing debate about the proper administration of statist economic policies and the best way to preserve Atatürk's legacy.

The third of İnönü's major economic reforms, the Land Reform Law (Çiftçiyi Topraklandırma Kanunu) of May 1945, proposed a vast redistribution of public and private land, which would have entirely eliminated the large landholding class in Turkey.[56] According to Feroz Ahmad, since the 1920s the coalition of Anatolian landholders and republican reformers that composed the CHP had operated according to an unspoken agreement that allowed for radical legal, political, and cultural reform as long as this reform did not significantly effect agricultural activity or the economic and social structure of the countryside.[57] The Land Reform Law upset this unspoken agreement, and three weeks after the law was proposed, in June 1945, Celal Bayar, Adnan Menderes, Fuat Köprülü, and Refik Koraltan officially registered their discontent with İnönü's policies by presenting a note known as the Memorandum of the Four (Dörtlü Takrir) to the CHP Parliamentary Group.[58] The carefully worded memorandum argued for the removal of restrictions on civil liberties in Turkey and for changes in the structure of the CHP to encourage a democratic process, although noting that restrictions on speech and control of the party had been necessary in the past, especially during World War II.[59] After the Parliamentary Group rejected the memorandum on jurisdictional grounds, Menderes and Köprülü criticized the CHP's "undemocratic" policies in the press and then were expelled from the party in September 1945, followed by Koraltan for his criticism of this decision to expel his colleagues.[60] When former prime minister and Independence War hero Celal Bayar resigned from the party in December 1945, it became clear the dispute regarding the Land Reform Law had produced a consolidated opposition from within the CHP, and this group announced the formation of the Democrat Party on January 6 the following year.[61]

These debates about the proper management of the economy characterize the beginnings of multiparty democracy in Turkey in 1945, and similarly procedural concerns about proper electoral policy animated the political campaigns during the years leading up to 1950. After the formation of the DP, the CHP decided to hold municipal elections a year early, in the summer of 1946, ostensibly in order to test the mechanism of the new election law ahead of the general election of 1947 but more likely in order to hold elections before the DP could organize.[62] When the DP announced it would boycott these municipal elections, the general elections were also rescheduled for 1946, and the DP had no choice but to participate, winning sixty-six seats in Parliament amid accusations by Bayar that the results had been fixed by the CHP and that İnönü had offered him sixty to sixty-two seats prior to the election.[63] For the most part, political discourse of the next few years focused on democratic procedure, with the DP boycotting elections in 1948 and 1949 and threatening to boycott the election of May 1950 until the CHP finally passed a significant change in election law three months before the elections.[64] This new emphasis on electoral procedure and the strength of Turkish democracy in political debates even led İnönü to attempt to define his role as president as extrapolitical, having "equal responsibility to all parties" to guarantee the impartial functioning of Turkish democracy.[65] Although there were clearly established, unspoken limits to the Turkish state's impartiality toward its burgeoning democracy (prominent socialists were arrested in 1946 and 1948; newspaper editors were arrested for transgressing the bounds of acceptable speech through 1950), the political speech of both the DP and the CHP during this time emphasized the establishment of appropriate electoral procedure, and the primary struggles over policy during the years 1946–49 focused on democracy and election law.[66]

Electoral procedure and economic policy were not the only topics of public political debate, and by late 1947 discussion of government policy on religious expression began seriously to enter official political discourse. A split in the DP in November 1947 led to a much stronger and more vocal third party, the Nation Party (Millet Partisi), which emphasized popular discontent with the government's religious policies (specifically the *ezan* law and the ban on turbans and fezzes) and the lack of discernable difference between the CHP's and DP's policy platforms.[67] Although the themes of discontent expressed by the Nation Party were not new, the articulation of discontent over religious policy in the public sphere by a party led by Marshal Fevzi Çakmak, a hero of the War of Independence, a close associate of Atatürk and İnönü, and a former chief of the General Staff of the Turkish Armed Forces, marked the growing visibility of this discontent.[68] In an apparent effort to appease public criticism of its policies on religious expression, the CHP implemented numerous incremental policy changes from 1948 to 1950, beginning with the establishment of a Faculty of Divinity at Ankara University; the implementation of optional, after-hours religious instruction in primary and secondary schools; and the development of accelerated İmam-Hatip vocational schools.[69] These proposals responded not only to growing public expression of discontent regarding government policy on religion but to a marked dearth of trained religious leaders in the countryside who could administer religious rites such as wedding ceremonies and funerals.[70] By the time the campaign for the general election of 1950 began, then, appropriate religious education and the management of religious institutions were common features of political debate.

Beyond these incremental developments in CHP policy on religion, three events in the years preceding the general election in 1950 emphasized the issue of the state's relationship to religion in public and, in particular, the issue of the language of the *ezan*. First, in 1948 the Diyanet issued revised regulations on the use of Arabic in religious services, allowing the use of Arabic in certain parts of the service or on religious holidays but maintaining the prohibition on the Arabic *ezan* at all times.[71] Although numerous scholars argue that these new regulations indicate a gradual relaxation of restrictions on religion prior to the DP's amendment of the *ezan* law in 1950, the Diyanet's revised policies at this time also suggest a very peculiar institutional identity for the government agency that employs all imams in Turkey. The Diyanet's decision to allow Arabic on the special occasions of religious holidays seems to suggest a continuing belief in the privileged place of Arabic in Islam because, according to the new regulations, Arabic should be employed in particularly significant parts of the service or on particularly significant days.[72] At the same time, however, the very limited introduction of Arabic back into mosque practice suggests a kind of amnesia about the Diyanet's own quasi-theological justifications for the ban on Arabic in 1932, which had emphasized the Hanafi school's belief in the acceptability of Koranic translations while practitioners learned Arabic as well as the importance of fostering a relationship between practitioners and God that was unmitigated by institutional authorities. Because nearly all Arabic-language instruction had ended around the same time the ban on the Arabic *ezan* was introduced, practitioners could not have progressed in their knowledge of the language, and because the Diyanet's oddly limited introduction of Arabic into the mosque accentuated the government's regulation of worship, practitioners were further reminded of an institutional intermediary in religious practice.[73] Although this inattention to the justification for regulating the *ezan* in 1932 may seem like the unremarkable self-contradiction of a government agency over time, it also suggests the development of the distinctively secular character of the Diyanet by 1948, a group of government officials developing regulations of religious practice based more on the knowledges of state rather than on the study of theology.[74]

Two other events of the years preceding the election in 1950 brought the relationship between the state and religion into public focus: a protest in Parliament in 1949 and the death of a prominent official in 1950. In February 1949, two men who had been previously arrested for reciting the Arabic *ezan* gained access to the Parliament building and began to recite the Arabic *ezan* while Parliament was in session.[75] If public discontent with CHP policy toward religion was not apparent to members of Parliament by 1949, this protest brought it directly to the party's attention. Ensuing media coverage of the event clearly articulated the tense climate regarding the *ezan* as opponents of the ban on Arabic argued that the ban represented an "unjust intervention in the freedom of conscience," whereas an editorial in the official newspaper of the CHP, *Ulus*, argued that "if reactionaries are allowed to chant in Arabic today, they would ask for religious law [*şeriat*] and the Caliphate tomorrow."[76] This increasingly public tension regarding religion became more acute in the month prior to the general election in May when the leader of the Nation Party, Marshal Fevzi Çakmak, died. Because of Çakmak's military status and reputation as a national hero, the CHP held an elaborate state funeral ceremony for him in Istanbul, but because of Çakmak's strong personal faith, his family and political supporters argued that he should be buried in a religious ceremony.[77] After protesters demonstrated outside Çakmak's state funeral, both İnönü and Bayar accused the Nation Party of using religion for political gain and urged a more cautious attitude toward religion in the public sphere.[78] By the time of the general election in May, then, public discussion of the state's relationship to religion became common in newspapers, and the DP's perceived support for an amendment of the ban on the Arabic *ezan* gave it an advantage in the election over the CHP's glacial pace of reform.[79]

The political discourse that developed during the 1940s and continued into the multiparty era in Turkey, then, is characterized by a wide range of discussions about effective management of society and the proper activity of the state. After Atatürk's death in 1938, the efficient organization of the economy and the correct adaptation of the Kemalist principle of "statism" to contemporary Turkey became the primary sites of political debate. By the beginning of the multiparty era in 1945, an emphasis on minute differences in economic policy transitioned into a concern for electoral procedure and alterations in the system of counting votes in Turkey. As the political campaigns leading up to the election began to include concerns about the functioning of religious institutions and the state's relationship to religious practice, then, these issues emerged in a national discourse that was thoroughly focused on the state's present activity and the proper management of society. In turn, public discontent regarding religious issues in the late 1940s nearly always emphasized the practical effects of state policy or the minutiae of specific, limited state actions, such as the lack of imams in the countryside or the funeral of a single former general.[80] This emphasis on good management of the country in the political discourse of this period constituted a marked shift from the political discourse of the 1930s, which emphasized a kind of epic struggle between the state and religion. Although there were still elements of this struggle in the discourse of the multiparty era in Turkey, discussion of reform of religious institutions and regulations was also significantly more focused on the management of religion best suited to the Turkish people. The moment in discourse that corresponds to the amendment of the *ezan* law, then, is characterized by topics of management, procedure, and the present daily activity of the state.

Political Speech and the Amendment of the *Ezan* Law

The surprise upset of the CHP in the general elections on May 14, 1950, placed the Democrat Party in the undefined role of the first opposition party in Turkey's history to gain control of the Parliament, and the response of DP leaders Celal Bayar and Adnan Menderes to their victory was correspondingly restrained.[81] After the formal transference of power, on May 29 Prime Minister Menderes presented an official party program focused on details of economic reform, agricultural policy, press freedom, and the upholding of secularism, with only a slight alteration of an existing CHP program for religious education.[82] Newspapers reporting on the party program commented on the DP administration's "cautious language," and rumors suggested a possible impending military coup.[83] When it became clear that İnönü would support the independence of the new administration and assume a role as opposition leader, the atmosphere became somewhat less tense, and on June 5 in an interview with the DP's official newspaper, *Zafer*, Menderes discussed the DP's decision to lift the ban on the Arabic *ezan*, which would take effect on the first night of Ramadan, June 16.[84] Despite the fact that the "*ezan* issue" occupied much of the press's attention after this point, Menderes discussed the issue relatively sparingly in other speeches, emphasizing instead an amnesty law for jailed journalists and the strong Turkish democracy. Menderes's *Zafer* interview on June 5, 1950, stands out as the most complete explanation of the party's philosophy behind the repeal of the ban on the Arabic *ezan*, and the interview clearly indicates the function of the figure of religion in political discourse at this time.[85]

At the beginning of the interview, Menderes offers an explanation of the history of the *ezan* law and past justifications of the ban on Arabic, which helps specify the function of religion in the political discourse of 1950, helps define the characteristics of legitimate religion, and clarifies the realm of legitimate state action toward religion. He categorically states that "all forms of fanaticism [*taassup*] give rise to harmful consequences for social life," and therefore social progress requires the "destruction of the mentality of fanaticism."[86] At the beginning of the interview, then, Menderes signals the ongoing legitimacy of certain state interventions against fanaticism wherever that fanaticism threatens the health of the social body. As Menderes continues the interview, he explains that it was this same truism of Turkish political thought that guided "Great Atatürk . . . to struggle against the mentality of fanaticism while beginning preparation of the preliminary reforms." With this in mind, Menderes argues, "the requirement to recite the *ezan* in Turkish should be considered as one such vitally necessary result" of the process at the time that "prepared the ground for today's free Turkey."[87] Offering a kind of historical analysis of the legitimacy of the ban on the Arabic *ezan*, Menderes describes this ban as a necessary and timely part of the reforms proposed by Atatürk, an example of the correct application of a general principle of good government. By marking the ban on the Arabic *ezan* as a past necessity appropriate to the historical situation, Menderes suggests that judgments concerning the legitimacy of a law must consider the historical context of that law and that good government must be appropriate to its contemporaneous moment.

By extending the logic of this historical analysis to the ban on the Arabic *ezan* as it exists in 1950, Menderes carefully attempts to position his repeal of this ban as a continued maintenance of the same principles that necessitated the ban in the first place. For instance, he expands the parameters of the category of fanaticism in his discussion of the ban on the Arabic *ezan*, arguing, "To insist on this measure [the ban] after all the intervening years and after it is no longer considered necessary constitutes fanaticism [*taassup*] against the freedom of conscience [*vicdan hürriyeti*]."[88] Describing a desire to defend the "freedom of conscience," Menderes seems to demonstrate a concern for the same principles that motivated Atatürk's reforms in the 1920s and 1930s. But although references to an opposition to "fanaticism" and a defense of "the freedom of conscience" considerably resemble the language used to justify the ban on Arabic in the first place, the significance of the phrase "freedom of conscience" in the discourse of 1950 in Turkey has shifted somewhat, influenced by developments in international human rights discourse after World War II.[89] That is, in Menderes's interview in *Zafer* the idea of "freedom of conscience" refers less to the appropriate physical location of religious belief (in one's own head) and more to the freedom from government or other intervention that would prevent individuals from publicly expressing their religious beliefs "either alone or in community with others."[90] In this formulation, zealous Kemalists who would insist on the maintenance of specific laws without considering the underlying principles of these laws are as guilty of fanaticism as those who insist on a return of the Caliphate. Early in the interview, then, Menderes articulates the way that his policies, specifically the repeal of the ban on the Arabic *ezan*, continue to maintain the foundational principles of the Turkish Republic.

The slight alteration of the significance of the idea of "freedom of conscience" in the political discourse of 1950 in Turkey corresponds to the alteration of a constellation of associated concepts in this discourse, and Menderes clearly explains the consequence of these various shifts in discourse. Transitioning to discussion of another of the Republic's foundational principles, he explains, "Like our other revolutionary reforms, the preservation of the foundation of secularism is possible today only because we remain connected to principles."[91] That is, Menderes suggests a connection between the foundation of the principle of secularism and the other significant principles of the Republic (perhaps the defense of the "freedom of conscience"). Keeping this connection in mind, then, Menderes goes on to argue that because recitation of the Arabic *ezan* "[demonstrates] no incongruity whatsoever with public order or general customs, the continuation of the ban regarding the *ezan* issue is damaging to the principle of secularism."[92] In Menderes's formulation, then, Kemalists' tenacious defense of specific regulations enacted by Atatürk, such as the *ezan* law, has begun to undermine the foundational principles of the secular Kemalist republic. For Menderes, the appropriate process of government legislation seems to consist of a continuous negotiation between foundational principles, common practice, and existing or new regulations. To the extent that the regulation regarding the Arabic *ezan* no longer appropriately negotiates these factors or to the extent that the ban on Arabic seems to have become (if it weren't before) a hindrance to the unencumbered "freedom of conscience" (with its altered meaning), this regulation must be removed before it significantly damages any of the Republic's foundational principles (secularism, defense of "freedom of conscience," etc.). Menderes's interview in *Zafer*, announcing the impending amendment to the law regulating the language of the *ezan*, then, corresponds to a significant shift in political discourse regarding "freedom of conscience" and the appropriate government negotiation of regulations and foundational principles in Turkey.

In the political speech of 1950 regarding the regulation of the *ezan* in Turkey, it is possible not only to recognize shifts in the significance of certain concepts in political discourse, such as "freedom of conscience," but also to recognize a shift in the way that the figure of religion emerged to organize knowledge of the operation of Turkish politics. The political discourse surrounding the ban on the Arabic *ezan* in 1932 marked a relatively straightforward confrontation between religion and government, one that emphasized the continuing project of the Turkish Revolution to wrest government from the hands of religion and to protect or purify religion in the process. By the election of 1950, however, the terms of this confrontation had shifted, and a figure of religion organized diverse events and policies (education reform, the funeral of a national hero, a protest in Parliament, and the *ezan* law amendment) by emphasizing fluctuations in and limits of the correct management of the population. As discussed earlier, Menderes's interview announcing the forthcoming repeal of the ban on the Arabic *ezan* emphasizes concepts such as "fanaticism," "freedom of conscience," and "secularism," but each of these concepts focuses primarily on the appropriate management of these concerns in the daily life of the population. After all, as Menderes states at the beginning of his interview, the danger of fanaticism is not that it endangers the ideals of the revolution but that it gives rise to "harmful consequences *for social life* [*cemiyet hayatı*]."[93] Menderes's later responses to his critics also emphasized proper management of competing extremes as he attempted to place himself between those who shouted that "religion is getting out of hand" and those who complained that "Atatürk's reforms are getting out of hand."[94] Most importantly, Menderes articulated the ongoing responsibility of a government to coordinate an appropriate relationship between foundational principles (secularism, freedom of conscience) and present legislative policy (the *ezan* law). At the beginning of the multiparty era in Turkey and by the time of the election in 1950, then, the figure of religion that circulated in the political discourse of Turkey seemed to emphasize the art of governmental rationality rather than the transcendental ideals of the Turkish Revolution, developing out of more than ten years of political debate that was limited to detailed accounts of electoral procedure, tax policy, and education reform.

Conclusion

This chapter outlines two moments in the political discourse of Turkey and the way that the figure of religion operates within each of these moments. On the one hand, the revolutionary moment in the discourse surrounding Turkey in 1932 constitutes an overlapping set of knowledges that emphasize the Central Asian origin of various phenomena, authorizing the activity of the state, the organization of institutions, and legitimate political action with reference to a transcendent logic of pure Turkish origins, the justness of the Turkish Revolution, and an image of the ideal future state. In this moment in political discourse, the figure of religion helps coordinate knowledge of a diverse array of events and legislation into a struggle between religious fundamentalists and the Kemalist state, a struggle that in turn marks out legitimate forms of worship and belief and that authorizes legislative activity and institutional operation according to the purity of the revolution. On the other hand, the discourse surrounding Turkey in 1950 marks the emergence of a moment of governmentality in which the legitimacy of state activity and political action is anchored by concerns about the propriety and efficiency of action in the present, including electoral procedure, economy, and other modes of population management. In this moment of governmentality, the figure of religion helps organize numerous events (the *ezan* law, a state funeral) and concepts (fanaticism, freedom of conscience) into a single category of governance and helps articulate a continuous process of properly balancing the foundational principles with the contemporary social landscape. By exploring the figure of religion in the political discourse of 1932 and 1950 in Turkey, this chapter offers an outline of a broader shift from a political discourse anchored by the purity of national origins and the ideal future nation to a political discourse that emphasizes the proper administration of the state through a balancing of ideals and present social life.

Although this chapter has focused on a single figure in the discourse of two different historical moments, the analysis is meant neither to trace the progression of this figure over time nor to offer an account of the changing significance of Islam in the politics of Turkey. Rather, this chapter attempts to demonstrate the ways in which a category or figure of religion emerges and operates within broader discourses at two separate intervals, focusing on the way that this category organizes knowledge and authorizes action differently at these two moments in history. As Talal Asad has argued, the analysis of religion cannot presume that religion is "a transhistorical and transcultural phenomenon" because this presumption overlooks the ways in which religion's "constituent elements and relationships are historically specific" and because it "invites us to separate [religion] conceptually from the domain of power."[95] That is, an analysis that traces the progression of religion over time would assume the existence of a transhistorical essence for that concept rather than offering an account of the concept's deployment and structure in history. An analysis that attempts to offer an account of the changing significance of religion in politics would position religion as a universal category acted upon by politics rather than accounting for the way that a concept of religion helps structure relationships of power in political discourse. This chapter has outlined the way that a figure of religion operates in 1932 and 1950, respectively, focusing on the way this figure helps to structure relationships of power at different times in Turkish history, authorizes legitimate forms of worship and expression in different ways, and coordinates its constituent concepts according to broader trends and regularities in the structure of political discourse. Even the analytic organization of this chapter has relied on related legislative actions regarding the language of the call to prayer in Turkey in order to avoid an unstated structuring presumption regarding the transhistorical nature of the figure of religion. In the end, this chapter removes the supposed unity of the figure of religion from the level of a presumption in analysis and places this supposed unity at the level of an object of analysis in the political discourse of 1932 and 1950 in Turkey.

3

Historical Revision and the Figure of the Military

On September 17, 1990, the Turkish government held a large state funeral ceremony and procession in Istanbul honoring former prime minister Adnan Menderes and two of his colleagues, former foreign affairs minister Fatin Rüştü Zorlu and former finance minister Hasan Polatkan. Twenty-nine years earlier all three men had been hanged and buried in unmarked graves at the military prison on İmralı Island in the Sea of Marmara following the military coup that deposed Prime Minister Menderes and President Celal Bayar and that had outlawed the Democrat Party.[1] The funeral ceremony in 1990 marked a final step in the official rehabilitation of Menderes and his colleagues, a process that had begun in 1987 with a law renaming a number of landmarks after the men and providing for their reburial and that continued in May 1990 with their official pardon by President Turgut Özal.[2] The events surrounding the funeral and procession spanned a number of days, including small ceremonies on İmralı Island on September 16 that accompanied the

A different analysis of the material in this chapter is given in Matthew deTar, "Absence of the Present: The Reburial of Adnan Menderes and the Condition of Possibility of Public Memory in Turkey," *Communication and Critical/Cultural Studies* 13, no. 1 (2016): 93–108, copyright © National Communication Association. Revision printed by permission of Informa UK Limited, trading as Taylor & Francis Group, www.tandfonline.com on behalf of National Communication Association.

exhuming of the "three martyrs" and a three-day television series on the Turkish state broadcasting network Türkiye Radyo Televizyon Kurumu entitled *1946 and After* (*46 ve sonrası*), which provided a retrospective on Menderes's party, the DP, interviews with family members and former DP politicians, and a seven-minute address by President Özal regarding the significance of the reburial.[3]

On the day of the ceremony, tens of thousands of people turned out to follow the procession of the coffins along a two-and-a-half kilometer route down the recently renamed Adnan Menderes Boulevard from Murat Paşa Mosque in Aksaray, Istanbul, to the newly built mausoleum in Edirnekapı, Istanbul.[4] Numerous government officials attended the ceremony at the mosque and walked in the procession to the mausoleum, including President Özal and his wife, the prime minister, the president of the Turkish Republic of Northern Cyprus, True Path Party (Doğru Yol Partisi) chairman Süleyman Demirel, and a number of former DP members. News coverage of the ceremony occupied the front pages of all newspapers in Turkey for weeks prior to the event, and Menderes's reburial provided an occasion for columnists on all sides of the political spectrum to debate the legacy of the coup on May 27, 1960, and the status of democracy in Turkey.[5]

Although Menderes's execution was widely unpopular when it occurred in 1961 and is generally regretted in Turkey,[6] his reburial in 1990 became a divisive issue among political parties and in public, and a number of strains of dissent emerged in the years leading up to the reburial that indicated a fractured public sentiment on the memorial. First and perhaps most unexpectedly, members of Menderes's, Zorlu's, and Polatkan's families argued that the planned memorial was either inadequate to the crime committed against their loved ones or not relevant to the memory of the men. For instance, in response to the law that renamed monuments in honor of the men, Hasan Polatkan's widow, Mutahhare, asked, "What does the Sarıyar Dam have to do with Hasan? Hasan was born and raised in Eskişehir. This does not restore his dignity."[7] Second, a significant and influential number of editorialists and politicians argued that the coup on May 27, 1960, and the Constitution of 1961 inaugurated an era of true liberalism in Turkey and that the reburial of Menderes denigrated the "Spirit of the May 27 Revolution."[8] Although supporters of the "Spirit of May 27" had largely been displaced to the outskirts of the Turkish political spectrum after the coup of September 12, 1980, by 1990 supporters of the 1960 coup had reemerged in mainstream newspapers and Parliament. Third, numerous prominent political opponents of President Turgut Özal argued that he was appropriating Menderes's memory for political purposes, attempting to associate Özal's Motherland Party (Anavatan Partisi) with the legacy of Menderes's Democrat Party in order to build support ahead of the general elections to be held in 1992.[9] A combination of the second and third criticisms of the reburial kept the leaders of two mainstream opposition parties, Erdal İnönü and Bülent Ecevit, from attending any of the ceremonies, and the third criticism led Süleyman Demirel to walk "with the people" in the funeral procession rather than with Özal and the members of Parliament.[10] Despite seemingly broad consensus that the execution of Menderes was one of the biggest regrets in Turkish history, Menderes's official rehabilitation quickly became a controversial event accompanied by discussions of the legacy of the military intervention on May 27, 1960.

Although the Turkish government's decision to rebury a former prime minister who was executed by a military junta might suggest an open environment for the reevaluation of the mistakes of the past, speech about the rehabilitation of Menderes in 1990 was circumscribed by the figure of the military as it related to the much more recent coup of September 12, 1980. That is, in 1987, when then Prime Minister Turgut Özal's civilian government announced its plans to rebury Menderes and his colleagues, this announcement occurred within a space of public discussion that was significantly constrained by official accounts of the 1980 coup and by the continuing statements of the leader of that coup, Kenan Evren, who served as Turkey's president from 1982 to 1989. Early in the period of military rule from 1980 to 1983, Evren and others articulated a figure of the military that both connected this figure to the timeless ideals of Atatürk and clearly separated the September 12 coup from the May 27 coup, emphasizing the failures of the junta in 1960 and the Constitution of 1961 that necessitated the intervention in 1980. In 1981, the governing body of the junta, the National Security Council (Milli Güvenlik Kurulu, MGK), even changed the register of official holidays to exclude May 27, which had been celebrated as a national holiday commemorating the military intervention of 1960.[11] The official distinction between the coup of May 27, 1960, and the coup of September 12, 1980, that developed in the years preceding Menderes's reburial indicates the complexity of the figure of the military that circulated in 1990, a figure that draws a clear distinction between two moments in the institutional history of the Turkish Armed Forces but also suggests a timelessness of purpose for the military throughout Turkish history. Discussion of the meaning of the reburial of Menderes in 1990 was significantly constrained by the intricate organization of elements within this figure in Turkish political discourse at the time, as the process of evaluating the mistakes of the past was negotiated largely within the logic of a present figure (in 1990) of the military.

The most significant feature of the relationship between the figure of the military and the rehabilitation of Menderes is the attendant coordination of a constellation of concepts that signify continuities between the events of 1960 and the ceremonies in 1990: government, nation, state, and army. The reburial and exoneration of Menderes required the identification of an entity that could be blamed for past actions and that could take responsibility for those actions in the present. Each of these four concepts (government, nation, state, and army) suggests the kind of unified, continuous entity that could reasonably assume responsibility for the actions of 1960 in the context of 1990, and each was mentioned by politicians, family members, and columnists between 1987 and 1990 in light of Menderes's imminent reburial. In a political environment where the legitimacy of the coup on September 12, 1980, and President Evren's authority were premised in part on important discontinuities with the coup on May 27, 1960, the struggle to assign responsibility in 1990 for Menderes's execution in 1961 was complicated by the circulation of the figure of the military in 1990. The figure of the military in 1990 limited the possible culprits for Menderes's execution, and, specifically, the army as an institution became unavailable as the kind of historically continuous entity that could be blamed for this past injustice.[12] The figure of the military conditioned the possibilities of public speech in such a way that the concept of the state (*devlet*) emerged as the most significant entity to be held accountable for past crimes, while the concepts of government, nation, and army receded somewhat in public debates regarding the Menderes reburial.

This chapter explores the relationship between the figure of the military and the concept of the state (*devlet*) in public discussions of the reburial of Menderes and his colleagues between 1987 and 1990. Over the past thirty years and certainly since 1996, the term *devlet*, "state," has developed an increasingly negative connotation in Turkish political speech, especially alongside the popular circulation of the associated idea of the *derin devlet*, "deep state." The term *deep state* refers to an ambiguous network of military leaders, politicians, judicial officials, members of the National Intelligence Organization (Milli İstihbarat Teşkilatı), civil society organizations, and elements of organized crime that employ covert and violent tactics to manipulate political processes in Turkey for varying interests.[13] The reburial of Menderes in 1990 occurred before the widespread circulation of the "deep state" concept in Turkey, and this chapter locates the idea of the "state" as it coalesced in the years before the widespread circulation of the term *deep state* (even though the former resembles the latter).[14] In order to trace the concept of the state and the figure of the military, this chapter begins with an account of the history of military interventions in Turkey before 1990, focusing particularly on the more recent September 12 coup as an event with significant influence on Turkish political discourse in 1990. As mentioned previously, the leaders of the September 12 coup developed a clear distinction between the coup of 1980 and the coup of 1960, and public memory of these two coups and of the intervention in 1971 contribute to the figure of the military as it circulated in 1990. Finally, this chapter provides an analysis of some of the debates in national newspapers regarding the plans to rebury Menderes and his colleagues, beginning in May 1987 with the announcement that Menderes would be reburied at an unspecified time and place in the future and continuing over the next few years until his eventual reburial on the twenty-ninth anniversary of his execution. Through this analysis, this chapter argues that the figure of the military in 1990 simultaneously produced and *was constituted by* public understanding of the "state," especially as this concept became necessary to refer to a continuous entity that could be blamed in 1990 for unjust actions in 1960.

A History of Military Interventions in Turkish Politics

1960–1961

Before Menderes's reburial in 1990, the Turkish Armed Forces had intervened to depose the civilian government three times, in 1960, 1971, and 1980, and each intervention profoundly shaped the concepts deployed in the debate about his reburial.[15] Prior to the coup on May 27, 1960, that resulted in Menderes's execution, the official institutional identity of the Turkish army committed it to maintenance of Atatürk's ideals but emphasized the distance between the military and politics. Officers legally had to resign from the military before they could participate in political activity.[16] Former officers had been prominently involved in all of Turkey's major political parties since the beginning of the multiparty era in 1946, including Menderes's Democrat Party. When Menderes became prime minister, he insisted on this separation between the military and the civilian government by replacing former officers in the government bureaucracy with civilians and forcing the retirement of numerous high-ranking military officers, including the chief of the General Staff and the commanders of all four branches of the armed forces.[17] Menderes's actions did not create significant tension between the military and the DP because Menderes had been instrumental in winning international praise for the Turkish Armed Forces through its involvement in the North Atlantic Treaty Organization and the Korean War.[18] Prior to the coup, the legitimacy or possibility of a military intervention was not really part of the Turkish political imagination because of the clear demarcation of the armed forces and politics.[19]

Despite the unprecedented nature of the 1960 coup, scholars have argued that the impending military coup was apparent to everyone but Menderes himself.[20] By late 1959, Menderes and İsmet İnönü, the leader of the CHP, were trading thinly veiled threats about the other's safety or liberty.[21] In early 1960, Menderes ordered the military to suppress protests against the DP and eventually declared emergency martial law in Istanbul and Ankara to prevent daily violence at rallies.[22] But Menderes's use of military units to suppress protests supporting the CHP or İnönü (a hero of the War of Independence and Atatürk's second in command) brought a new political character to the military's activities. Many members of the officer corps expressed their disapproval of Menderes's approach to the tension, and some even demonstrated publicly against him.[23] Although a small group of more junior officers had been developing plans to depose the DP since as early as 1955, the increased political tension, violence, and politicization of domestic military activities in 1959–60 provided this group with the means to convince or force senior-level commanders to support their plans for a forceful intervention.[24]

During the period of military rule, May 1960–October 1961, the junta's governing group, the National Unity Committee (Milli Birlik Komitesi, MBK), established two institutions that had significant influence on the figure of the military after 1960.[25] First, the new constitution established the National Security Council (MGK), an advisory council composed of the ministers of state, the president, the chief of the General Staff, and all four serving force commanders that would be in charge of security and defense policy in Turkey.[26] The MGK codified a permanent, formal role for the military in the Turkish political system. Second, in January 1961 the MBK established the Armed Forces Mutual Assistance Fund (Ordu Yardımlaşma Kurulu, OYAK), a pension system funded by officer salary deductions.[27] Since 1961, OYAK has grown to be the largest corporate conglomerate in Turkey, with an enormous role in all sectors of the Turkish domestic economy and a significant presence in international trade.[28] Although the MBK's involvement in government during 1960–61 and in the executions of Menderes, Zorlu, and Polatkan are generally remembered as the military's gravest mistake in national history, the new constitution deeply immersed the military in Turkish government and the economy.[29]

In the months following the coup, public support for military involvement in government quickly eroded. In early June 1960, the narrative justifying the coup as a temporary action necessary to defend democracy from a "single-party dictatorship" appealed to some politicians and parts of the public.[30] Whatever popular support the MBK had in May and June 1960 seemed lost by 1961, however. MBK chairman Cemal Gürsel's early assurances that no trials were planned gave way to arguments that Menderes had violated the Constitution and had committed treason and that therefore trials were necessary (to the coup's legitimacy).[31] Farcical corruption trials aimed at tarnishing reputations and treason trials with obvious logical flaws followed.[32] When the MBK held a vote in July 1961 to ratify the new constitution it had written, 38 percent of people voted against ratification in a gesture widely understood as a rebuke to the MBK's legitimacy.[33] As demonstrations supporting Menderes occurred in Ankara and elsewhere, hundreds of people were put on trial, and fifteen high level DP members were sentenced to death, including Bayar and Menderes (although twelve of these sentences were commuted).[34] Despite an attempted intervention by İnönü and pleas by foreign leaders (President John F. Kennedy, Queen Elizabeth, and Charles de Gaulle, among them), the executions of former foreign affairs minister Fatin Rüştü Zorlu and former finance minister Hasan Polatkan took place on September 16, 1961, followed by the execution of Adnan Menderes on September 17.[35]

The events of the summer and fall of 1961 indicate a limit to military authority in the public imagination. In the elections of October 1961 that restored civilian government, two political parties claiming to be the successors of the DP won a combined majority of seats in Parliament, returning to power many of the same political leaders who had been deposed in the coup the previous year.[36] In the early days after the coup, the military circulated as an institution committed to preserving Kemalist ideals, and the "Spirit of May 27" referenced forceful intervention into politics on behalf of these ideals. Electoral results and public demonstrations in the year after the coup suggest insistence on the previous separation between the military and civilian government. At this time, the military gained new valence as an institution that did not have the expertise or the authority to govern the country. The coup on May 27, 1960, both established institutions that tied the military to the legal and economic structure of Turkey and marked a popular limit to the military's authority to intervene in the affairs of civilian government.

1971

If the 1960 coup formalized the military's role in governing the nation, the 1971 intervention and subsequent political party disputes solidified an idea of the military as a thoroughly political body. Beginning in 1969, Prime Minister Süleyman Demirel began deploying riot police against leftist organizations and implying support for far-right militant groups who attacked these protestors, leading to a steady increase in politicized street violence on the left and right.[37] In response, the military broadcast an ultimatum over Turkish state radio on March 12, 1971 (the "Memorandum of 1971"): Prime Minister Demirel should step down or face a full military takeover.[38] Demirel stepped down and was replaced by Nihat Erim, a longtime associate of İsmet İnönü and a prominent member of the CHP since the 1940s.[39] Nihat Erim's government declared martial law in eleven provinces in April to quell continuing street violence, which resulted in the arrests of thousands of journalists for their political views and the closure of a number of leading newspapers.[40]

Following the establishment of a new government, the chief of the General Staff began to leak news that the Memorandum of 1971 had actually prevented more radical younger officers from staging a complete, armed military coup.[41] Rather than garnering public goodwill toward the generals' seeming restraint, these leaks confirmed public beliefs about political fragmentation within the military itself and marked the intervention as an act of military institutional politics rather than as a defense of foundational principles. By the time the MGK forced a number of constitutional amendments through Parliament in September 1971 (one of which strengthened the council's authority), the military's public legitimacy had seriously deteriorated, and Nihat Erim's government received a vote of no confidence in Parliament in December.[42] By the end of 1971, public criticism of the military intervention and of the military's commitment to democracy seriously eroded the general goodwill toward the military as a guardian of Kemalist principles and Turkish government.[43]

Public disapproval of the military intervention produced dramatic changes in the identity of the CHP and significantly altered the status of the military in Turkish national discourse. Although CHP chairman İsmet İnönü initially criticized the military intervention, he changed his mind a few days later, and the CHP's secretary-general, Bülent Ecevit, resigned in protest.[44] The tension between Ecevit and İnönü culminated in an intraparty vote in 1972 that led to Ecevit's assumption of leadership of the CHP.[45] Ecevit worked to rebrand the CHP as a social-democratic party, discarding the traditional emphasis on Kemalism and nationalism and thus leaving the founding state philosophy without an organized political representative in Turkey.[46] This transformation in the CHP helped cement a partisan identity for the Turkish Armed Forces as an institution committed to the "founding philosophy" just as internal political conflict within the armed forces also became visible.

1980–1983

The military intervention of 1980 was far more extensive than either of the actions in 1960 and 1971, and it more thoroughly incorporated the military apparatus into the day-to-day functioning of the state. At the time of this coup, deteriorating public security, a faltering economy, and the collapse of party politics threatened to plunge the country into civil war. In the summer of 1980, Turkey's murder rate averaged twenty every day, and professors, members of Parliament, journalists, and even former prime minister Nihat Erim had fallen victim to this violence.[47] Even the declaration of martial law in a number of provinces in 1979 did not decrease the violence.[48] Unemployment had skyrocketed, the Turkish lira was devalued 50 percent in January 1980, and the black market for basic commodities grew substantially.[49] Near-total political dysfunction between Justice Party (JP, Adalet Partisi) chairman Süleyman Demirel and CHP chairman Bülent Ecevit produced ten different governments between 1973 and 1980, with Ecevit and Demirel each holding the position of prime minister twice between 1977 and 1980.[50] When President Fahri Korutürk's term expired in April 1980, political deadlock left the Parliament unable to select a new president, and the seat was vacant through the September coup.[51]

In contrast to the institutional conflict within the military in 1960 and 1971, on September 12, 1980, Chief of the General Staff Kenan Evren led all of the force commanders and all other high-ranking generals in a massive operation that suspended Parliament and detained all political leaders in Turkey.[52] The MGK declared martial law throughout the country and gave field commanders extensive autonomy to restore order, resulting in more than 120,000 arrests in the following year, heavy restrictions on all forms of public speech, long-term curfews, and extensive reports of torture.[53] Political party leaders were detained at a military resort on the Aegean coast, keeping them out of the public but also preventing public perception of their poor treatment.[54] A month after the coup, Demirel and Ecevit were released, whereas Alparslan Türkeş, the leader of the Nationalist Action Party (Milliyetçi Hareket Partisi), and Necmettin Erbakan, the leader of the National Salvation Party (Millî Selâmet Partisi), were tried and imprisoned for inciting violence and participating in antisecular activity, respectively.[55] Although massive arrests and heavy restrictions on speech corresponded to a rapid decline in political violence, reports of extensive torture became increasingly common, and widespread fear of military rule developed.[56]

Despite public fear and dissatisfaction with martial law, the MGK established a Consultative Assembly in 1981 that embarked on a three-year period of vast institutional and political reform, including an entirely new constitution. In the months following the coup, the MGK appointed former admiral Bülend Ulusu as prime minister, and he formed a provisional government composed of military officers and some civilians, most notably Turgut Özal, an economist who had worked at the World Bank and served in Demirel's last cabinet. Some of the most significant legal reforms implemented by this provisional government were revisions to the National Security Council contained in Article 118 of the Turkish Constitution of 1982, which increased the size, authority, and scope of the MGK.[57] This article required the civilian Council of Ministers to give "priority consideration" to the MGK's recommendations.[58] An additional National Security Council Law of 1983 defined the scope of "national security" extremely broadly as "external and internal threat[s] to the constitutional order, national existence, [and] unity . . . in the political, social, cultural and economic spheres."[59] With this expansion of the MGK's authority, then, the highest-ranking generals in the armed forces became the most powerful unelected executive power in the country.[60]

The preparations for transition to civilian rule in 1982–83 further emphasized the public, political role that the military would have in the future. The first step was popular ratification of the new constitution, which included a provisional article making Kenan Evren president of the Republic for a seven-year term.[61] Although Evren campaigned throughout Turkey in 1982, no other candidates were allowed to run; no discussion of the Provisional Articles of the Constitution was allowed; no former politician could make statements "about the past or future political or legal system of Turkey"; and Prime Minister Ulusu explained that a "no" vote on constitutional ratification would leave the military in power.[62] After the Constitution was ratified by a large majority, the MGK organized two of its own political parties and allowed a third to run in the elections of November 1983.[63] Politicians active prior to 1980 were barred from politics for ten years, and the MGK closed proxy parties organized by Demirel and İsmet İnönü's son, Erdal.[64] Only Turgut Özal's Motherland Party appeared to have a semblance of autonomy from the MGK as the significant influence that the military would continue to wield over politics became clear.

Despite broad official and unofficial constraints on expression in the 1980s, political speech in the months and years after the elections in 1983 indicate antipathy to continued military control of politics.[65] Despite Turgut Özal's previous low profile, his Motherland Party won more than 45 percent of the popular vote in the elections, giving the party a comfortable majority of 211 seats in the newly reestablished 400-seat Parliament.[66] Restrictions on political parties unofficially relaxed after 1983, and two new parties had strong showings in local elections in 1984 and 1986: Erdal İnönü's Social Democracy Party (Sosyal Demokrasi Partisi, later Social Democratic Populist Party, Sosyaldemokrat Halkçı Partisi) and Demirel's proxy True Path Party. Demirel began to openly criticize Özal's party as not democratically legitimate, leading Özal to hold a popular referendum in 1987 to repeal the Provisional Article of the Constitution that barred Demirel and others from politics, a referendum that Özal then campaigned against.[67] When the referendum passed, Özal claimed the 49 percent of votes against it as his own supporters while also claiming restoration of the democratic legitimacy of his party.[68] Evren's authority to veto any changes to the Constitution during his presidential term meant that the figure of the military lingered over this entire political charade.[69] In the following months, Demirel continued to voice criticism of the nondemocratic nature of Özal's government and repeatedly argued that martial law commanders in 1979 had deliberately failed to restore stability in order to undermine public confidence in civilian government and to increase public support for a military intervention.[70] By the late 1980s, serious fissures appeared in the supposed broad public support of President Evren, support for the 1980 coup in general, and the democratic legitimacy of Özal's government.

The 1980 coup significantly restructured the figure of the military in a number of ways. As discussed earlier, Ecevit's leadership in the mid-1970s steered the CHP away from some elements of Kemalism, and by the time of the coup the military had staked an independent relationship to the "founding philosophy."[71] By 1980, the pension fund OYAK had become one of the largest corporate conglomerates in Turkey, and this independent economic interest committed the Turkish Armed Forces to maintaining a specific arrangement of political power.[72] Finally, consistent media campaigns throughout the 1980s and 1990s asserted a narrative relationship between the military and civilian government, wherein a "period of anarchy" or "chaotic days" had preceded the 1980 coup, and so the public had greeted military intervention with "relief."[73] Just after the coup, Evren used this historical frame to assert the reluctance of military commanders to intervene, explaining, "If we engage in politics today, it is because we felt it was our duty to save our country from a disastrous situation," but "whenever the army entered into politics . . . it was led into corruption."[74] The assertion of the military's reluctance to intervene, combined with its commitments to a founding philosophy and material economic and political interests, established a public image of the military as an institution committed to the defense of the fundamental principles of the Republic and to the maintenance of democracy in Turkey.

This public image of the figure of the military after 1980 influenced the relationship between the concepts "state" and "government" in a way that rewrote official history to produce the legitimacy of the figure itself. As Ümit Cizre Sakallioğlu argues, the 1980 coup "legitimized the military's historical mission and institutional political role as the guardian of the state."[75] The military became subtly delineated from the state, with the former serving as the institution of defense of the latter's principles. "The state" began to exist independently from the military and civilian government, with the military institutionalizing a role for itself as the supreme arbiter of the state's foundational principles against the volatility of civilian administrations. From this perspective as arbiter of foundational principles,

Evren built the official narrative of post-1980 Turkey to blame the Constitution of 1961 and the "illegitimate" coup of 1960 for the pre-1980 "anarchy."[76] Distinguishing between the 1960 coup and the 1980 "intervention" and asserting the earlier coup's illegitimacy reconstituted its official history in a way that produced the legitimacy of the later coup.[77] Evren's insistence that military intervention was a last resort further reinforced and reproduced this narrative.[78] By the time of Menderes's reburial, the concepts "state" and "government" emerged in coordination with the figure of the military to establish an official narrative that produced its own legitimacy as "official" by delegitimating the 1960 coup.

The Military, the State, and the Reburial of Menderes

In addition to official narratives that defined the state in relationship to the military, public debates about the reburial of Menderes immediately focused on the concept of the state. Although discussion of pardoning and reburying Menderes surfaced from time to time in the 1970s, debate about his official rehabilitation exploded in 1986 following the death of former president Celal Bayar at the age of 103.[79] Bayar had been tried and sentenced to death in 1961 along with Menderes, but Bayar's sentence had been commuted to life imprisonment because of his old age at the time (he was seventy-eight in 1961), and he was later exonerated in 1966 as part of a general amnesty.[80] Bayar wished to be buried alongside İsmet İnönü at Anıtkabir, Atatürk's mausoleum in Ankara, but intervening laws prohibited anyone else from being buried at the site, and Turgut Özal's government decided to hold a "state ceremony" for Bayar in Ankara.[81] In the months following Bayar's death, Menderes's rehabilitation again became a significant topic of debate in the press, and Menderes's son, Aydın Menderes, began to publicly lobby Özal for a state ceremony to restore his father's reputation.

When Aydın Menderes emerged in May 1987 as the primary spokesman of the families of the "three martyrs" Menderes, Zorlu, and Polatkan, the continued complex relationships between government, nation, and state became clear under the weight of the figure of the military. For instance, in a lengthy interview with the daily newspaper *Tercüman*, Aydın Menderes explains that, "as a family, our intention is not to blame anyone," but he continued on to pressure Özal: "Now I ask: Esteemed Prime Minister, will you secure the declaration of a state ceremony [*devlet töreni*] and the state's sorrow [*devletin üzüntüsü*] for the late Menderes and his friends?"[82] In response to this interview, however, Prime Minister Özal drew a careful distinction between the prime minister's authority as head of civilian government and the president's authority as head of state, saying that he had told Aydın Menderes that "we can hold a national ceremony [*millet töreni*], but we cannot hold a state ceremony [*devlet töreni*] . . . because a state ceremony is held by the President. . . . If the families do not want a national ceremony [*millet töreni*] . . . [then] unfortunately Adnan Menderes's body will stay at İmralı."[83] Because the Turkish president and head of state in 1987 was Kenan Evren, the former chief of the General Staff who had led the coup in 1980, Özal's statement marks the palpable, uncomfortable, and unstated influence of the figure of the military on the relationship between Adnan Menderes and the state. Nation, state, and civilian government all find their relationships governed by the figure of the military.

In a seeming effort to dissolve this tension with Aydın Menderes, Özal developed a proposal for rehabilitating Menderes, Zorlu, and Polatkan that remained vague on the details of the funeral ceremony, in effect delaying a confrontation between the concepts of the state, the army, and the legacy of Menderes. The law that passed Parliament on May 22, 1987, named a number of landmarks after the three men and stipulated that their bodies would "be transferred, in a funeral ceremony, from their graves on İmralı Island to a site deemed suitable by the Prime Minister and which would be constructed in their honor."[84] Almost all of the details of the form of the ceremony, its location, and its timing were left up to the discretion of the prime minister (Özal) by a Parliament dominated by his own Motherland Party, a fact that numerous opposition party leaders criticized at the time.[85] In response to the passage of this law, Aydın

Menderes suggested the need for the families' relief but also noted the lingering issue of the state's role in the ceremony, explaining that the families "have waited for 27 years, a state ceremony can also be waited for."[86] Following the passage of the law, Özal delivered a long apology to the families from his perspective "as a simple member of Parliament," further postponing the tension between the legacy of Menderes and the responsibility borne by the state.[87]

Discussion surrounding the original legislation regarding Menderes's reburial helps indicate the location of the concept of the state in relation to the figure of the military by marking the presumed unity of the state and the dissociation of the concepts of the state and the army. As Aydın Menderes and other advocates of a reburial ceremony focused their attention on the singular way in which a state ceremony (*devlet töreni*) would restore the reputations of Menderes, Zorlu, and Polatkan, the discussion of the state ceremony emphasized the way this event would show the state's responsibility for (one of) its past injustices. But the emphasis on the "state ceremony" presumed the existence of a transhistorical entity called "the state" that could apologize for its past actions. The unity and singularity of this idea of the state made it easily distinguishable from the institution of the Turkish Armed Forces, which also seemed like a plausible site of responsibility for the past injustice against Menderes and his colleagues. The armed forces' potential culpability was not mentioned in any news coverage of this legislation in 1987, however, not even by dailies highly sympathetic to the reburial efforts, such as *Tercüman*. This silence helped to reinforce a separation between the army and the reburial, singling out the state as the only potentially culpable entity that could be publicly named.[88] The post-1980 political environment included both mandated and de facto limitations on speech about the figure of the military, and a unified entity of "the state" that was distinct from the institution of the Turkish Armed Forces emerged from this network of explicit prohibitions and unarticulated taboos.

In 1987, the distinction between the state and the armed forces also implied a confrontation with Kenan Evren and leaders of the

1980 coup that was both dangerous and not entirely relevant to the project of rehabilitating victims of the 1960 coup. As mentioned previously, during the 1980s the MGK emphasized a marked difference between the military incursions of 1960 and 1980, especially with reference to the latter's leadership, goals, and relation to Turkish society.[89] The separation between these two coups conditioned Özal's argument that Aydın Menderes had addressed his complaint regarding the "state ceremony" to the wrong person because only Kenan Evren, the president and head of state, could declare a state ceremony. Requesting a state ceremony from the face of the 1980 coup would muddle the purpose of a *state* ceremony because it was not the army but the state that (for Aydın Menderes) had to be held accountable for past injustice. Because Evren was both head of state and a prominent former general, the distinction between the state and the armed forces in 1987 was blurred in the body of Evren, marking a limit in the reasonable pursuit of the rehabilitation of the three martyrs in 1987. In response to this limit, Özal's legislation that year effectively postponed the issue of a state ceremony and apology until a time "deemed suitable by the Prime Minister." This postponement also reinforced the separation of the army from the state, allowing for a state apology in the future when this apology would not also implicate the army. This complex negotiation of understandings about the armed forces, the state, and Menderes's reburial, then, helps to indicate the ways in which the figure of the military structured Turkish political discourse at the time.

This complex network of concepts resurfaced again in 1990 when plans for the reburial ceremony began in earnest. Upon the expiration of Kenan Evren's term in office on October 30, 1989, Parliament elected Turgut Özal as president of the Republic.[90] Özal and members of his Motherland Party immediately began to develop plans for a reburial ceremony to be held in 1990 on the twenty-ninth anniversary of Menderes's execution. On April 11, 1990, Parliament passed an amendment to the law it wrote in 1987 regarding the reburial, which officially reversed the convictions of Menderes, Zorlu, and Polatkan and inserted the word *state* into the description of the ceremony that would accompany their reburial. The three men's bodies would be "transferred in a state funeral ceremony [*devlet töreni*]" rather than simply "in a funeral ceremony [*tören*]."[91] Following this law, construction began on a $5.5 million mausoleum in Istanbul that would be known as Anıtmezar, and a date was set for the state ceremony, September 17, 1990, the twenty-ninth anniversary of Menderes's execution and the Monday after the tenth anniversary of the coup on September 12, 1980.[92]

Following these preparations for a state ceremony, Aydın Menderes again emerged as a spokesman for the families of the three martyrs to emphasize the significance of the state's action and to accept the state's "apology." In the days preceding the reburial ceremony, Aydın Menderes made a number of public statements declaring that "the state apologized" and clarifying the ceremony's purpose: "The point of the state ceremony [*devlet töreni*] is that a social consensus was reached. The point of it is that a wound has been bandaged that cannot reopen again."[93] For Aydın Menderes, the state ceremony articulates the state's sorrow for the execution of his father, helps to unify the public, and provides closure on the issue for society as a whole. Aydın Menderes's statements present an uncomplicated picture of the event, where there is no question of what the ceremony means about the army's past actions, and there is no recognition of the political tension surrounding the event. In fact, Aydın Menderes reemphasizes his earlier insistence that the ceremony is not intended to assign blame for the executions and "is not aimed at a settling of accounts of the past."[94] If the reburial of a prime minister executed by a military junta raised questions about the justness of the armed forces' past actions, then these questions are absent from Aydın Menderes's declaration that the state has apologized and that the wounds of the past can now heal.

Despite Aydın Menderes's seemingly uncomplicated description of the significance of the state ceremony, press coverage of the reburial in 1990 quickly focused on the Turkish Armed Forces' relationship to the planned ceremonies. For instance, when it became clear that neither Kenan Evren nor any high-ranking military official would be involved in the state ceremony, numerous reporters asked Evren why he wasn't participating. In response, Evren offered only oblique answers: "This is a state ceremony. I am merely a citizen," or "I am not now in the state, am I? The state ceremony is being held under that name."[95] Evren seemed to dismiss suggestions that his absence at the ceremony would have some kind of special meaning, implying both the autonomy of the state with Özal at its head as well as the 1980 coup leaders' neutrality toward the Menderes reburial. Given Evren's and the MGK's emphasis on the profound difference between the coups of 1960 and 1980, a state ceremony implicitly condemning the earlier coup could be understood to fit within the parameters of this narrative. Although Evren's absence at the ceremony raised doubt about the military leadership's support of the state ceremony, the large visible presence of Turkish soldiers in the ceremony had the seemingly opposite effect as newspapers lauded the procession of the three martyrs' coffins "nestled on the shoulders of soldiers."[96] If the relationship between the army, the state, and the Menderes reburial was unclear in 1987 when the ceremonies were first proposed, then this relationship remained similarly confusing to many reporters in 1990. Although the official rehabilitation of Menderes, Zorlu, and Polatkan emphasized the state's culpability for this past injustice, the Turkish Armed Forces' relationship to the Menderes reburial remained complex.

Emphasis on "the state" as the primary responsible entity in the Menderes reburial in 1990 was followed by public debate about Menderes's own historical relationship to "the state" in the 1950s. For the most part, discussion ranged between two interpretations of Menderes's historical relationship to something called the "state," with politicians such as Özal and Demirel emphasizing the populist reputation of Menderes's early years as a reformer of an authoritarian state apparatus, and politicians such as Erdal İnönü and Bülent Ecevit mentioning Menderes's dictatorial control over state mechanisms preceding the 1960 coup.[97] On one end of the political spectrum, coverage of the reburial in the newspaper *Tercüman* clearly displayed the former, more positive interpretation of the legacy of

Menderes with respect to the state, altering its front-page format on the day of the reburial so that the entire front page consisted of a drawing of Menderes looking down and away from the viewer, the Turkish flag in the background, and a quote from the day of Menderes's execution: "At this moment when I am about to bid farewell to life, I wish my state [*devlet*] and my nation [*millet*] eternal happiness" (see figure 2).[98] From *Tercüman*'s editorial position, then, Menderes represented "eternal" devotion to both the state and the nation, and therefore a state ceremony would restore the rightful relationship between Menderes and the state. Although all of *Tercüman*'s other coverage of the Menderes reburial also presented a similarly sympathetic picture of his legacy, the paper's dramatic portrayal of Menderes on the twenty-ninth anniversary of his execution and the day of his reburial emphasizes his patriotism toward the Turkish state.

At the other end of the political spectrum, the coverage presented by the newspaper *Cumhuriyet* leading up to the reburial offered a much less sympathetic view of Menderes's legacy with regard to the Turkish state. During the entire week of Menderes's reburial, *Cumhuriyet* ran a series of articles under the heading "Menderes's World," which offered a seemingly comprehensive retrospective on the ten years of DP control of Parliament (1950–60). The series began the day before the reburial with one article that questioned the effect of the Menderes era on Turkish society and another that reminded readers that Menderes had supposedly been Turkey's answer to fascism.[99] As the week continued, *Cumhuriyet* ran articles arguing that Menderes had used the idea of "populism" as a weapon against the CHP and that the DP represented a transition from a country run by "national" political parties to a country run by a single "state" party rather than the other way around, as most historiography usually describes the transition to multiparty democracy in 1950.[100] By the end of the week, *Cumhuriyet* made very clear its editorial position on the relationship between Menderes and the operation of the state, running articles titled "Menderes's Democracy" and "The DP and Parliamentarian Dictatorship," which emphasized Menderes's and the DP's increasingly authoritarian nature, especially after 1957.[101]

2. Drawing of Adnan Menderes by Erol Denli, *Tercüman*, September 17, 1990.

Cumhuriyet's coverage focused almost exclusively on Menderes's creeping control of the state apparatus and use of authoritarian tactics to marginalize the CHP.[102] Thus, *Cumhuriyet*'s coverage of the Menderes reburial presented a much different picture than *Tercüman* of Menderes's relationship to the state, emphasizing his abuse of the state to serve his own interests and his authoritarian appropriation of state mechanisms to limit democratic processes in Turkey.

Although news coverage of the reburial presented differing arguments about Menderes's relationship to the concept of the state, coverage surrounding the reburial also demonstrated ambivalence about the entity called "the state" in the first place. A few days before the state ceremony, on September 15, the mass-market, centrist paper *Günaydın* reported Aydın Menderes's declaration that "the state apologized" (as discussed earlier).[103] Directly above this article, *Günaydın* printed a captioned picture of a memorial ceremony for former president Cemal Gürsel, the leader of the coup on May 27, 1960, at the State Cemetery in Ankara on the twenty-fourth anniversary of his death.[104] The photo shows a number of generals and statesmen paying their respects to Gürsel by laying wreathes on his tomb. The placement of the Gürsel memorial photo's headline below the photo itself, the very small size of the photo's headline, and the alignment of the page in relation to the headline of the Aydın Menderes article suggest that the two stories share a headline that reads "The State Apologized." *Günaydın* reserved limited space for political news, and the accidental juxtaposition of elements on this page of the newspaper does not necessarily imply a deliberate editorial decision, but it does offer a glimpse of differing understandings of the nature of the state that circulated in Turkey at this time. On the one hand, according to Aydın Menderes, something called the state has apologized to his family for executing his father in 1961 and has begun the national healing process, but on the other hand the state honors the leader of the 1960 coup at a cemetery in Ankara. Insofar as the state is assumed to be a single entity involved in simultaneously apologizing for an unjust execution and honoring the leader of the junta that had performed the execution, the precise character of this entity, its guiding principles, its relationship to Turkish history and society, and its composition seem ambivalent and unstable in news coverage surrounding Menderes's reburial.

Ambivalence about the nature of the state even became the focus of editorials critical of the ceremony and its utility in Turkish political life. An editorialist for *Cumhuriyet*, Mehmed Kemal, interviewed people near the ceremony about what it meant for them, beginning with a *simit* vendor. When Kemal asks him who is being honored in the state ceremony, the *simit* seller responds that he doesn't know whose funeral is happening, only that "some important person died." Kemal then reports asking a woman nearby about the significance of the ceremony, who responds, "How many years had they forgotten him, now he comes to the front of their minds. They thought we would forget the cost." Kemal offers a number of interviews to build a case that the only impact of the Menderes reburial for ordinary people in Turkey is that the ceremony and mausoleum cost the country a lot of money. After this refutation of the practical utility of the reburial, Kemal goes on to argue that the ceremony doesn't serve even a symbolic function because "one state holds an execution, one state holds a ceremony. One state does the hanging that day, and another state does the pardoning 29 years later."[105] Arguing against the utility of the Menderes reburial, Kemal denies the presumed transhistorical unity of the state that would make it possible for the state to assume responsibility for past injustice. Emphasizing the ambivalent nature of the entity called the state through its lack of historical continuity, then, Kemal offers a glimpse of the way that transformations in the Turkish political, legal, and social structure since 1960 had made it difficult to assume unquestioningly a continuity between the entity that apologized in 1990 and the entity that had organized Menderes's execution in 1960.

Although accounts of the Menderes reburial in national newspapers suggested questions about the nature of the state as an entity, its historical continuity, or its relationship to the army, more radical opponents of the reburial ceremony suggested that the proper understanding of and respect for the state was contravened altogether in the "state ceremony" for Menderes. One such outspoken opponent of the reburial ceremony was Hüseyin Avni Güler, the chairman of the May 27th National Revolution Association (27 Mayıs Milli Devrim Derneği), a private group organized to maintain the "ideals" of the 1960 coup and preserve its reputation.[106] Güler's opposition to the state ceremony suggests a definition of the "state" very different from Aydın Menderes's "state," as Güler explains, "We are not against transferring the bodies to the families, we are against the illegal decision to hold a state ceremony." After declaring this opposition, Güler goes on to counter his implied understanding of the ceremony: "We are grateful to the Turkish Armed Forces for not being involved in the state ceremony."[107] For Güler, the reburial of Menderes implies criticism of the army's past acts, and Özal denigrates the state and implies criticism of the army in an "illegal" ceremony that resulted from Özal's abuse of power. From Güler's perspective, then, the army is inseparable from the idea of the state, and a ceremony billed as a state apology necessarily defames the institution of the army and its past acts. Güler's understanding of the concept of the state thus differs dramatically from Aydın Menderes's, and Güler's lack of separation between the state and army makes the "state ceremony" into almost a contradiction in terms, a state act disparaging the institution tasked with defending the foundational principles of the state.

It was precisely through a struggle over the meaning of "the state" and its relationship to the reburial ceremony in 1990 that the figure of the military visibly produced its own authority. In speech surrounding the reburial of Adnan Menderes and his colleagues in 1990, the concept "the state" was not truly available for reinterpretation but instead was simultaneously produced and relied on by a vast network of official narratives and institutional apparatuses. Güler's suggestion that the reburial defamed the Turkish Armed Forces was marginalized in a number of ways by the self-reinforcing relationship between "the state" and the figure of the military in 1990. First, official history separated the 1960 coup from the 1980 coup by emphasizing the intervening "period of anarchy" that resulted from deficiencies in the 1961 Constitution, and Güler's suggestion that the army in 1990 was being held responsible for the executions in 1960 contradicted the official relationship between these two historical moments. As explained earlier, this official history not only distinguishes between the armed forces at the earlier moment and the armed forces of the later moment but also distinguishes between the armed forces and the concept of the state in 1990. Güler's formulation was wholly out of sync with this set of past and present distinctions. Second, Güler's interpretation did not correspond to the clearly defined authority of armed forces leaders in the operation of the state as outlined in the law regulating the National Security Council. By implying that the MGK would have authorized a reburial that insulted the honor of the current Turkish Armed Forces, Güler's statement seemed to misunderstand the armed forces' broad authority to intervene in seemingly all aspects of Turkish political life through the MGK. Although Evren's silence was certainly confusing for journalists, it could also be understood as implicit support for a ceremony he didn't see as a threat. In the years surrounding the reburial of Adnan Menderes, the figure of the military and its array of histories and legal mechanisms constructed public knowledge and general assumptions about "the state" in a way that defined the mainstream of political speech and marginalized voices that relied on alternative conceptions of "the state." Contestation over the concept of the state made visible the influence of the figure of the military.

The network of conceptual relationships contained in the figure of the military also mitigated more mainstream and direct criticisms of the role of "the state" in the reburial by people such as Mehmed Kemal in *Cumhuriyet*. As quoted earlier, part of Mehmed Kemal's criticism of the reburial directly targeted the supposed transhistorical unity of the concept of the state. Within the constellation of concepts that could reasonably accept responsibility in the present for past actions, Kemal's altered conception of the state in turn complicates the relationship of a concept such as the army to the reburial. If the state that presents the reburial in 1990 cannot accept responsibility for past acts because it cannot claim a continuous historical unity (as Kemal asserts), then this alters the relationship between the reburial and concepts such as the army, government, and nation, suggesting that one of these other entities might reasonably be blamed for past injustice. The culpability of these other concepts was already fixed by the figure of the military in 1990, however, because the blameless nation would begin healing with the reburial, the army in 1990 was officially distinct from whatever institution existed in 1960, and, in a sense, it was the government itself that was executed along with its prime minister in 1960. The figure of the military fixes the meaning of "the state" by managing a broad network of concepts and knowledge, and Kemal's direct criticism of the role of "the state" in the reburial is mitigated in its inability to shift this vast definitional apparatus. "The state" remained the only entity that could apologize for the past in 1990 because its location was already determined in this definitional apparatus and authority of the military.

Finally, the figure of the military and its negotiation of relations of authority between concepts such as the army, the government, the nation, and the state helped manage understanding of even the most mainstream statements regarding the reburial, such as those made by Turgut Özal and Aydın Menderes. Despite the *Günaydın* headline on September 15, 1990, that read, "Adnan Menderes's Son Aydın Menderes: 'The State Apologized,'" Aydın Menderes's statement seems to produce rather than to describe the state's apology because Head of State Özal only ever implied such an apology by expressing either the state's sorrow or his personal apology. For instance, the day before the reburial, Özal reemphasized the official lack of direct blame associated with the reburial, explaining, "We want to heal old wounds and leave the final judgment to history."[108] That is, twenty-nine years after Menderes's execution, final judgments of culpability or even justice were to remain in the future in that both Özal and even Aydın Menderes emphasized national and family healing over the allocation of blame. According to the way that the figure of the military negotiated the relationships between the army, the state, and the reburial, however, the avoidance of a clear articulation of blame for the executions aligned with the complexity of the Turkish Armed Forces' relationship in 1990 to its own institutional history and also aligned with the still delicate nature of free political expression in Turkey following the 1980 coup. That is, if general knowledge about the form of Turkish political life recognized both the fragility of political expression as well as vast differences between the Turkey of 1990 and the Turkey of 1960, then it perhaps made more sense for a nation to come together in healing and for a state to express its sorrow for and support of the three martyrs than for the reburial ceremony to clearly mark culpability. The figure of the military that circulated in 1990 produced meaning for a constellation of concepts that defined the "mainstream" of political speech and circularly secured the authority of the figure itself.

Conclusion

After the coup in Turkey on September 12, 1980, relations of authority surrounding the Turkish Armed Forces and its role in politics helped refine public understanding of the concept "the state." The meaning of "the state" included elements of law, official history, and other social relationships, but it also resulted from a constellation of associated terms, including *nation*, *government*, and *army*. A set of concepts, institutions, and official histories produced a political environment in Turkey in the 1980s that limited possible articulations of "the state" in 1990. But disagreement over the timing and meaning of Menderes's reburial also indicated the complexly circular relationship between the military and this concept that secured the military's authority. In 1990, the concept of the state remained contested or ambiguous as newspaper columnists, Özal's political opponents, coincidences of newspaper layout, and even Mutahhare Polatkan (the widow of one of the "three martyrs") variously indicated hesitations about and resistance to the planned "state ceremony." The reburial ceremony therefore became a location where a singular definition for the concept of the state was *constituted* despite the fact that Özal and others presumed this concept already gave the ceremony its meaning. As the reburial helped produce the significance of "the state," it also helped secure the authority of the military as constituted by this network of concepts and knowledge in 1990.

The figure of the military not only generated and relied on the concept of the state to produce a specific arrangement of authority in Turkish political discourse in 1990 but would also influence the emergence of the idea of the "deep state" a few years later in the mid-1990s. As discussed earlier, the law regulating the National Security Council relied on an understanding of the state as a set of mechanisms of law, economy, national security, international relations, and so on, which embody a specific political philosophy (Kemalism). According to this law, civilian government is for the most part in charge of steering the state, but the MGK remains a kind of executive auditor over and "priority" adviser of civilian government. Official justifications of this authority for the MGK describe a need to circumvent government decisions that would steer the state in a direction that undermines its founding principles. The law and form of the MGK rely on a broad assumption that the leaders of civilian government may not always be capable of guiding the mechanisms of state in such a way that the state's own best interests and its independent foundational principles will be defended.[109] In an environment of political discourse where the state holds its own independent political philosophy and there is only limited legal confidence in civilian government, rumors that the whole state apparatus is controlled by an underground network of generals, judges, old-guard Kemalists, and criminals do not take much imaginative labor. When a fatal car crash near Susurluk, Turkey, in 1996 revealed that one car contained the deputy chief of the Istanbul Police, a deputy of Parliament, and an internationally wanted contract assassin and his falsified diplomatic passports, the immediate popularity of the concept of the deep state was the seemingly natural result.[110] The figure of the military that coordinated the concept of the state at the time of Menderes's reburial continued to influence the development of political discourse in Turkey, and the idea of the deep state has been only one of a number of effects of the figure of the military on common knowledge.

4

Article 301 and the Oscillations of the Figure of the Minority

On June 1, 2005, the now infamous Article 301 of the revised Turkish Penal Code took effect as part of preparations for the European Union (EU) accession process. The version of Article 301 of 2005 gave Turkish citizens the right to file a complaint to a prosecutor against another citizen for "insulting Turkishness, the Republic, or the Grand National Assembly of Turkey[,] . . . the Government of the Republic of Turkey, the judicial institutions of the State, the military or security structures."[1] Article 301 was a revised version of similar articles that had been part of the Turkish Penal Code since 1926, when the Turkish Parliament had based its new Penal Code on that of Mussolini's Italy.[2] In the years surrounding the formal introduction of Article 301, a group of ultranationalist lawyers used Article 301 and its predecessor to bring cases for "insulting Turkishness" against numerous prominent authors, journalists, publishers, and human rights advocates in an apparent attempt to disrupt EU negotiations. Nearly eighty prosecutions under Article 301 took place in 2005 and 2006 alone, and these prosecutions became a repeated point of contention between EU officials and Turkish diplomats.[3] Article 301's broad scope, vague language, and restrictive application by courts made it the subject of both international and domestic criticism.

Despite the apparent strategy to interfere with Turkey's EU bid, Article 301 prosecutions were not always transparently associated with EU accession, and these prosecutions produced a condensed domestic discussion of "Turkishness" and "the minority" that reflected these concepts' shifting and implicit limits. The boundary of "Turkishness" is in part constituted by the figure of the minority, a combination of legal definitions, citizenship rules, historical knowledge, and norms of public speech. Owing to the complexity of what makes up the "minority," its content fluctuated in media coverage of Article 301 trials, at times appearing as an ethnic or religious category, at times referencing law, at times presuming historical-political relationships, and at times even invoking narratives of modernity and development. Many of the most prominent trials under Article 301 also brought speech regarding specific minority populations into the courtroom, and references to the Armenian Genocide (1915–16) were a particularly frequent topic of prosecution. The fluctuating nature of "the minority" became apparent in the media coverage of these trials as politicians, columnists, and other public figures variously articulated norms of acceptable speech.

This chapter argues that the figure of the minority operates as a fluid, oscillating boundary mechanism for norms of public speech. The minority can reference ethnicity, republican citizenship, religion, a modernity narrative, and/or history. The figure of the minority can include one or several of these elements at different times, a rhetorical fluctuation that mobilizes authority, law, and public knowledge to produce the norms and boundaries in public speech. Scholars have recognized how the overlapping ethnic, religious, secular, and modern content of Turkish national identity produces narrow limits of the "ideal citizen" as well as how this ideal citizen has been challenged and transformed since 1980.[4] Rather than exploring "Turkishness" as a kind of "center" of an identity discourse, however, this chapter details the rhetorical production of the margin in the figure of the minority. The figure of the minority is not a narrow "ideal" but a shifting category. The "minority" is not a stable, overlapping intersection of criteria but a strategically malleable and unpredictably fluctuating figure in discourse. As this book argues, the "minority" is only one element of the vocabulary of Turkish nationalism, and thus the boundary it marks does not completely circumscribe the center.

This chapter focuses on the "minority" in three of the most prominent Article 301 cases spanning the years of this law's initial implementation: a case against journalist and activist Hrant Dink in 2004, the case targeting novelist Orhan Pamuk in 2005, and the prosecution of novelist Elif Şafak in 2006. Dink's prosecution began under the authority of Article 159 of the previous legal code, but his trial and sentencing occurred after Article 301 replaced the older law.[5] Pamuk was indicted retroactively after Article 301 took effect for remarks he made prior to the law's official implementation. Şafak's supposed offense and her trial occurred in 2006, after the law's official implementation and after media coverage of previous trials had more clearly connected Article 301 to the EU accession process. In each case, the figure of the minority appears to oscillate in its definitional content, producing a distributed, variable limit to acceptable public speech. Although critics of Article 301 have focused on the law's ambiguous phrase "insulting Turkishness" that produces limitations on public speech, the figure of the minority operates beyond law in coordination with a host of other kinds of knowledge to define the limits of speech and action.[6] Dink's, Pamuk's, and Şafak's prominent Article 301 cases became sites of the articulation of "the minority" in public discourse both about and beyond the law.

The chapter begins with an exploration of the legal apparatus associated with the figure of the minority and the concept of citizenship in Turkey, including Article 301 of the Penal Code, Articles of the Constitution of 1982, the National Security Council Law of 1983, and the specter of the Treaty of Sèvres of 1920 as compared to the continuing legal authority of the Treaty of Lausanne of 1923. The chapter then explores the relationship between the figure of the minority and specific minority groups in Turkey, such as Kurds, Alevis, and Armenians, in order to specify the role of civil society organizations representing these groups in the production of the figure of the minority. Finally, the chapter analyzes public discourse surrounding the trials of Hrant Dink, Orhan Pamuk, and Elif Şafak, focusing on the way "the minority" fluctuated in content during each trial. Although this chapter offers an account of the operation of the figure of the minority in Turkish political discourse, it does not really account for the experience of being a minority in Turkey. The figure of the minority is a nodal point in the hegemonic, semiofficial discourse regarding national identity and political life in Turkey. This discourse polices its borders by managing and defining some elements as external to itself—rhetorical operations that do not account for the experience of being on the periphery of this discourse so much as for the structure of its center. This chapter examines the figure of the minority as it continuously reasserts its role in the structure of Turkish political discourse, helping to reproduce knowledge and forms of authority that reinforce a hegemonic definition of national identity.

Citizenship, Security, Identity

Much of the legal apparatus that constitutes the figure of the minority in Turkey relies on an ambiguous combination of ethnicity and a republican theory of community membership to define the category "Turk." The Constitution of 1982 makes clear the more republican legal status of this category: "Everyone bound to the Turkish state through the bond of citizenship is a Turk."[7] Theoretically, then, the category "Turk" can describe numerous different ethnic groups and religious communities, assimilating them all under a citizenship category that binds them to the Turkish state.[8] Throughout the history of the Turkish Republic, however, "Turk" has almost uniformly been understood as a descriptor of ethnicity rather than of purely republican citizenship. As Ayşegül Aydıngün and İsmail Aydıngün have shown, parliamentary debates about the Constitution of 1924 focused explicitly on whether the category "Turk" was a republican category or an ethnicity, opting to define it ambiguously *as both* in Article 88 of the Constitution of 1924: "People of Turkey, regardless of religion and race, are Turks as regards Turkish citizenship."[9] The last words of Article 88, "as regards Turkish citizenship," were added to avoid the suggestion that non-Muslims, specifically Greeks and Armenians, were Turks in the same (ethnic) way that the Turkish nationalist elite were Turks.[10] This historical tension reappears in the wording of the Constitution of 1982 as well, where Article 66's phrasing can be heard to imply an additional Turkishness beyond the article's definition: "Everyone bound to the Turkish state *through the bond of citizenship* is a Turk."[11] Juxtaposed to the constitutional debates in 1924, the Constitution of 1982 implies other, perhaps ethnic kinds of bonds to the Turkish state, marking the category "Turk" as an overlapping ethnic and formally republican category.

These overlapping understandings of "Turk" allow descriptions of the rights-bearing individual to stand in for ethnicity even in strongly nationalist slogans. One of the most commonly reproduced nationalist phrases in Turkey comes from the last line of a short, commemorative speech given by Mustafa Kemal Atatürk on the tenth anniversary of the Turkish Republic: "How happy is he who calls himself a Turk! [Ne mutlu Türküm diyene!]."[12] This phrase or the entire speech is reproduced throughout the country on hillsides, state facilities, statues, museums, bumper stickers, and signs, and it frequently appears in political speech. The phrase can easily circulate to support a legal citizenship category rather than a description of ethnicity, as in former president Kenan Evren's interpretation: "'How happy is he who calls himself a Turk.' This philosophy includes every citizen who considers himself a Turk, regardless of creed, race or religion."[13] In both the legal documents and public speech that compose the hegemonic national discourse in Turkey, the category "Turk" circulates as a description of republican state citizenship despite the fact that it is almost universally understood to be an ethnic descriptor as well. The category "Turk" oscillates between a specific ethnicity and a bond with the state independent of a particular "creed, race or religion."

This official understanding of the category "Turk" as a simultaneous description of citizenship and implicit ethnicity has an important relationship to the articulation of national identity developed in legal instruments and official discourse in Turkey. For instance, after the preamble of the Constitution of 1982, the document describes the unity of Turkey with the brief sentence: "The Turkish state, with its territory and nation, is an indivisible entity" (Article 3).[14] This description of the indivisibility of the state distinguishes between the land area of the state and the nation. By marking the unity of the nation as inextricable from the indivisibility of the state, the Constitution suggests the existence of a single state culture or identity category that subsumes all others, and any discord with this identity category directly impinges on the existence of the state.[15] That is, Article 3 reinforces the understanding that Turkish national identity is a legal citizenship category rather than an ethnic or religious identity, and the bond between the nation of "Turks" and the state becomes a constitutive feature of the state itself. Insofar as "Turk" can also be understood as an ethnicity, one feature of this ethnicity might be loyalty to the state. In the legal documents that help constitute the official discourse of Turkish politics, then, descriptions of both citizenship and nation seem to preclude official recognition of ethnic, religious, or even political minority groups as members of the Turkish nation.

These ideas of citizenship and nation also influence general understanding of legal definitions of national security in Turkey and the form of threats to this security. Since the foundation of the Republic, political speech and legal documents have repeatedly employed a seemingly ambiguous formulation to describe threats to national security: "external and internal enemies." According to Mustafa Kemal's *Nutuk*, at the end of World War I the phrase *external enemies* described the victorious Entente Powers, who had drawn up the Treaty of Sèvres to parcel the land area of the Ottoman Empire to the victors, and *internal enemies* referred to any group of former Ottoman citizens perceived by the nationalists to be collaborating with the Entente in this endeavor, primarily Armenians and Greeks but also at times the sultan or his cabinet.[16] This vague idea of "external and internal enemies" appears in the National Security Council Law of 1983, which uses the phrase to make clear that the council will be involved in "the defense and protection of the state against every kind of external and internal threat to the constitutional order, national existence, [and] unity."[17] By maintaining this nearly century-old ambiguous description of "external and internal threats," contemporary legal documents on national security in Turkey provide flexible and dangerous descriptions of the parameters of the National Security Council, which can take action against "every kind of external and internal threat."[18]

The phrase "external and internal enemies" becomes somewhat more specific in its coordination with the legal and political understandings of citizenship and the nation in Turkey's hegemonic political discourse. As discussed earlier, the category "Turk" describes ethnicity, national identity, and legal citizenship, subsuming them into a formally indivisible concept. Similarly, when the National Security Council Law describes defending the state from threats to its "constitutional order, national existence, [and] unity," this description reinscribes the equivalence of state citizenship and national identity by presuming the indivisibility of the state and the nation. That is, the council must defend the state from a threat to its "national existence and unity" because the very definition of the state is premised on the equivalence of citizenship and national identity in the category "Turk."[19] The unity of a nation of "Turks" thus becomes as indispensable as territorial integrity to the life of the state.[20] Within this network of definitions of state, citizenship, ethnicity, and nation, any person who might resist the idea that the term *Turk* describes all citizens of Turkey poses a threat to national unity, and insofar as that person lives in Turkey, he or she becomes an "internal threat" to the state. The formal equivalence of state citizenship, ethnicity, and national identity helps constitute the figure of the minority by specifying the otherwise ambiguous idea of "external and internal enemies."

The coordination of ideas of citizenship, nation, and "external and internal enemies" that structure perception of national security in Turkey further mark the legal status of minority groups in the Republic by clearly establishing the relationship of different kinds of minorities to the state. As numerous scholars mention, the process of EU accession has produced a so-called Sèvres Syndrome, a belief that EU accession requires "national and territorial disintegration of the republican state" by attempting "to restore the conditions of the Treaty of Sèvres."[21] One frequently invoked measure for maintaining national integrity in the face of this "syndrome" is intermittent contemporary reference to the treaty that replaced Sèvres and Sèvres's attempts to wholly dismember the Ottoman Empire, the Treaty of Lausanne, which was signed after the Turkish nationalists had regained negotiating power by defeating the Greek army after World War I. The Turkish delegation at Lausanne replaced the standard international treaty language regarding rights secured by the League of Nations for religious, racial, and linguistic minorities with a statement differentiating between Muslims and non-Muslims and securing rights only for the latter group.[22] Turkish governments since the establishment of the Turkish Republic have been careful in international negotiations to preserve the definition of minorities established at Lausanne because this definition can be employed easily to maintain the unity of the category "Turk" by legally recognizing only minorities that foreign governments have historically been interested in protecting.[23] The contemporary circulation of a very limited legal definition of minority groups in Turkey operates in tandem with a general understanding of the indivisibility of citizenship and national identity, producing a sense in which the category "Muslim" is coterminous with the citizenship/identity category "Turk," whereas non-Muslims have only a tenuous relationship with the state and its national identity.

This coordination of citizenship, nation, security, and legal minority groups conditions understanding of Article 301 of the Turkish Penal Code. Although many scholars dismiss Article 301 as "antidemocratic" or "non-European," Turkish politicians and others have argued that the law approximates antidefamation laws regarding the symbols of the state (such as bans on flag desecration) in places such as Austria, Germany, France, and Switzerland.[24] The full text of the version of Article 301 written in 2005 states:

1. A person who publicly denigrates Turkishness, the Republic or the Grand National Assembly of Turkey, shall be sentenced a penalty of imprisonment for a term of six months to three years.

2. A person who publicly denigrates the Government of the Republic of Turkey, the judicial bodies of the State, the military or security organizations, shall be sentenced to a penalty of imprisonment for a term of six months to two years.
3. Where denigrating of Turkishness is committed by a Turkish citizen in another country, the penalty to be imposed shall be increased by one third.
4. Expressions of thought intended to criticize shall not constitute a crime.[25]

In the context of other legal and political apparatuses that constitute the figure of the minority, "insulting Turkishness" becomes a fluctuating activity that helps maintain the relations between the citizenship category "Turk," national identity, minority-group rights, and national security. Similar to the way the theoretically republican (and thus formally inclusive) category "Turk" describes a symbiosis of state and national identity, the idea of "Turkishness" (revised in 2008 to "the Turkish nation") describes a formal identity category that does not preclude membership due to "creed, race or religion."[26] According to this understanding of the idea of Turkishness, statements describing minority groups in conflict with the state or describing state mistreatment of its minority populations insult the category of Turkishness by suggesting that this category is not the inclusive, republican identity category it purports to be. Perhaps most importantly, the version of Article 301 articulated in 2005 increases penalties for insults made in a foreign country, suggesting a coordination of Article 301 with general knowledge about the national security idea of internal and external enemies because the article makes it a worse crime for an internal enemy to collaborate with an external enemy when insulting Turkishness. The limitations on speech produced by Article 301 therefore result not only from the text of the law but also from the broad operation of the figure of the minority in Turkish national discourse, which coordinates legal definitions and general understanding of citizenship, history, minority groups, and national security along with the articulation of Article 301.

Minority Populations and the Figure of the Minority in Turkey

Specific minority populations in Turkey are differently entangled in the fluctuating parameters of the figure of the minority, and these differences became more visible in the 1990s and 2000s. The Lausanne Treaty's delineation of only two population categories in Turkey, Muslim and non-Muslim, has produced overlapping effacement of Muslim minority groups in the Republic. For instance, Sunni Kurds face the rhetorical impasse of being required by official state discourse to articulate rights claims as religious rather than ethnic minorities even though Sunni Islam is already regulated by the state. But even when non-Sunni Muslim religious minorities, such as Alevis, attempt to articulate rights claims as religious minorities, these claims face a similar impasse in official discourse because the category "Muslim" in the Lausanne Treaty does not admit of any differentiation within Islam. Of course, none of these groups is internally homogeneous, and the effacement of Muslim religious minorities and Muslim ethnic minorities is especially significant in the case of Zaza Kurds, some of whom are Sunni and some of whom are Alevi.[27] The oscillating content of "the minority" as a figure produces unique constraints on Muslim ethnic and religious minority populations.

In the 1980s and 1990s, the Kurdistan Workers' Party (Partiya Karkarên Kurdistan, PKK) began to organize armed resistance to the Turkish state's policies of assimilation and oppression. These policies had prohibited public use of the Kurdish language, closed religious educational institutions serving as Kurdish cultural centers, and in the 1920s, 1930s, and 1990s instituted vast relocation efforts to forcibly disperse concentrations of Kurdish people in southeastern provinces.[28] Prior to the 1990s, policies to "assimilate" Kurds grew out of a narrative of the new Turkish Republic's civilizing mission and the inclusiveness of its modern republican state identity category "Turk." This narrative constituted Kurds as "future Turks" currently plagued by economic underdevelopment, cultural backwardness, and a reactionary politics associated with religion.[29] This narrative was reinforced in the early Republic by colloquial understandings of Kurds as "mountain Turks" and by characterizations of Kurdish separatist movements (most notably the Şeyh Said Rebellion of 1925) as religious revolts.[30] By the end of the 1990s, however, increasing violence and international attention to the Kurdish population (in both northern Iraq and Turkey) altered Turkish official discourse on the Kurds, leading to intermittent official recognition of Kurds as an ethnic minority.[31] As official discourse relating to Kurds increasingly marks the distinct ethnicity of this population, the limits of the ability of the figure of the minority to negotiate the state's relation to its population become increasingly evident, especially with regard to understandings of the category "Turk" and threats to national security from "internal enemies."

Alevi civil society organizations also made visible the complicated fictions of "the minority" in lawsuits brought in Turkish and international courts to secure equality of state financing of religious facilities and guarantees on rights to religious practice. Turkish nationalist discourse typically characterizes Alevis as already assimilated supporters of the secular state establishment, and Turkish courts struggle with categorizing Alevis as either an ethnic group or a religious group.[32] In 2002, a Turkish court described Alevism as a "cultural variant" within Turkish society rather than as a religious subgroup of Islam or the religion of an ethnic group within the Republic.[33] In 2005, a Turkish court described Alevism as a "serious, coherent religious belief" in dicta.[34] The interaction between European and Turkish courts further complicates these definitions, with German Alevi groups securing a legal status for Alevism as a religion independent from Islam because this status provides financial privileges within the German state.[35] Insofar as Alevis continue to be understood as the "assimilated minorities" in Turkey, then, the terms of this assimilation remain tenuous, and Alevi groups' activity in Turkish courts challenges the discursive function of the figure of the minority.

Despite Kurdish and Alevi resistance to the operation of the figure of the minority, the term *minority* can still circulate with a generally negative connotation, even among those groups. The separation of non-Muslims and Muslims in the Lausanne Treaty combines with the formally indivisible concept "Turk" and the discourse of "internal enemies" to mark non-Muslims as suspect members of the Republic with questionable allegiance to the state. The early republican characterization of non-Muslims as unreliable citizens appears in descriptions of non-Muslim minorities as "foreign citizens" (*yabancı vatandaş*), producing the sense that *minority* is a derogatory term.[36] Turkish Alevi groups' opposition to European Alevis' legal definition of Alevism as a minority religion recirculates the presumed negative status of the minority, and Turkish Alevis reject "minority" status because it indicates lack of "belonging to the nation and even being in contradictory terms with it."[37] Similarly, many Kurds reject a minority status because it seems to efface the historical significance of Kurdish soldiers' role in fighting for the Turkish nationalists in the Independence War and in helping to establish the Turkish Republic.[38] This is true even of Kurdish separatist groups in Turkey, such as the PKK, which reject a status as minorities in favor of a designation as a "people" with a history of strong resistance to foreign oppression (both Turkish and Western).[39] That is, a negative connotation of the term *minority* as either a description of people with questionable allegiance to the state or a description of generally untrustworthy people continues to structure Alevi and Kurdish groups articulation of their location with respect to the Turkish state, and rights claims by these groups frequently avoid official categorization of Alevis or Kurds as minorities because of the complex stigma associated with this category.

Historical Knowledge of "the Minority"

State-sponsored production of historical knowledge about the Armenian Genocide and the conflict with the PKK in the 1980s and 1990s constricted knowledge of Turkey's minority populations in such a way that "the minority" became an uncomfortable and unknown topic of conversation. The Constitution of 1982 established the Atatürk High Institution of Culture, Language, and History (Atatürk Kültür, Dil ve Tarih Yüksek Kurumu), an organization attached to the Office of the Prime Minister, which operates "under the moral aegis of Atatürk" and administers a number of other well-known institutions such as the Turkish Historical Society.[40] These organizations have sponsored research that consistently contradicts international academic consensus on the historical treatment of minority populations in the late Ottoman Empire and in the Turkish Republic. When, for instance, Orhan Pamuk stated in 2005 that "30 thousand Kurds and 1 million Armenians have been killed here,"[41] this statement challenged the state-sponsored histories of these minority populations written in the recent and distant past. The Ministry of Education's classroom textbooks reinforce official history by avoiding reference to massacres of Armenians in World War I and instead describing massacres of Anatolian Muslims by Armenians during this period.[42] Similarly, classroom discussion of Kurds does not acknowledge Kurdish ethnicity, instead explaining that communist and Marxist radicals have fomented divisions between "spotlessly clean and completely Turkish" Muslims, inciting the "so-called 'Kurdish' citizens" against the Turkish state.[43] The Ministry of Education curriculum creates a general assumption of "innocence" in Turkey, and international accounts of the Armenian Genocide or abuses of human rights perpetrated against Kurds by the Turkish Armed Forces in the 1990s sound like serious, unjustified accusations made by foreigners.[44] State institutions' regulation and alteration of knowledge of problematic events in the histories of Armenians and Kurds limit public discussion of these histories simply by producing an atmosphere of indifference or lack of information.[45]

Although Turkish state historians acknowledge that numerous Armenians died in eastern Anatolia in 1915, they disagree with most other academics regarding the manner, scope, and significance of these deaths and especially regarding the use of the term *genocide*.[46] Following a decade of international conferences, including an extremely high-profile conference in Istanbul held just before Hrant Dink's trial in 2005, Ronald Grigor Suny, Fatma Müge Göçek, Norman M. Naimark, and others developed academic consensus among

Turks, Armenians, and other historians on the Armenian Genocide in the edited collection *A Question of Genocide*.[47] According to this consensus history, after Russia declared war on the Ottoman Empire in November 1914, the Ottoman government began to perceive the large Christian Armenian population of eastern Anatolia as a threat to national security, given their close proximity and religious similarities to Russia.[48] Following this perception, "sometime in March 1915 a decision was made to deport [Armenians] systematically and, by issuing oral orders and sending out secret emissaries, to massacre them in the process."[49] Over the course of the next year, at least one million Armenians were killed either by starvation or by systematic execution following a policy of ethnic cleansing and ethnic homogenization intended to remove all non-Turkish peoples (Armenians, Assyrians, and Greeks) from eastern Anatolia.[50] Although the majority of Armenian deaths occurred in 1915, massacres of Armenians and other minorities in eastern Anatolia by Turkish soldiers continued as late as 1920.[51] These events were the result of deliberate action on the part of the Ottoman government, in particular members of the Committee of Union and Progress (CUP, İttihad ve Terakki Cemiyeti) which controlled the Ottoman Parliament and most mechanisms of the Ottoman state. Many of the people directly involved in the organization and planning of the genocide had prominent roles in the Turkish nationalist movement and in the government of the post-Ottoman republic. Suny and Göçek argue that despite long-standing anti-Armenian sentiment among many Ottoman elites since at least the turn of the twentieth century, plans for genocide only began to be developed in 1915.[52]

Political motivations for silence about or denial of the genocide began to develop almost immediately after the end of World War I. In the wake of the war, British authorities and Ottoman officials organized war crimes trials in Istanbul to prosecute members of the Ottoman government who had helped organize massacres or been complicit in the killing of Armenians. These trials resulted in execution sentences for numerous former Ottoman officials for their role in planning or ordering massacres.[53] Although the war crimes trials produced extensive evidence of the former Ottoman officials' culpability in the mass killings of Armenians, these trials were disbanded in 1922.[54] Taner Akçam argues that when British authorities began to link the trials with partition of Ottoman territories, the Turkish nationalist elite began resisting the trials as a whole.[55] For Erik Zürcher, in contrast, Turkish nationalist leaders' motivation for disbanding the trials and denying the genocide resulted from the fact that the mass killing of Armenians and the forcible removal of Armenians from their property directly contributed to the development of an Anatolian Muslim "middle class," which the Turkish nationalists saw as their constituents.[56] The genocide had been organized in such a way that members of the local Muslim population were directly involved in killing Armenians but not in a way that prevented retribution by the Armenian population against Muslims, and so tens of thousands of Muslims were also killed in Anatolia during this time.[57] For Zürcher, CUP officials mobilized vast ethnic violence between Muslims and non-Muslims, and if CUP successor political parties had acknowledged the genocide or supported the war crimes trials, they would have appeared as hypocrites and lost support of the Muslim population of Anatolia, the only remaining population there after the massacres.[58] The politicization of the Armenian Genocide thus began immediately following the end of World War I and has only intensified in the ensuing century.[59]

Turkish state policy of silence about the genocide was largely successful in avoiding any international discussion about the events of 1915–20 until Holocaust remembrance activities became common in the 1960s.[60] Beginning in the 1970s, Turkish state institutions became more openly active in the denial of the genocide, and after the 1980 coup this denial became more academic and sophisticated, taking the form of documentary histories.[61] Scholars have speculated on the reasons for continuing the Turkish state policy of silence on the Armenian Genocide, but the persistence of this policy is probably related to the extensive implication of early nationalist leaders in the massacres.[62] Although many of the CUP members with the most direct ties to the genocide were either executed by Armenian assassins in the years following World War I or exiled, jailed, or executed by the Turkish nationalists in the Independence Tribunals of 1925–26, the Turkish state's acknowledgment of the nationalist leaders' implication in the genocide and its aftermath would require an extensive revision of state discourse on national identity and history.[63] Thus, Turkish state institutions instead employ a logic of denial that takes the following forms: (*a*) there was no state-sponsored genocide, and Armenian deaths were accidental or the result of war; (*b*) what happened wasn't as bad as people say because only three hundred to six hundred thousand Armenians died rather than the one to two million that some sources claim; (*c*) the victims brought it on themselves through a "civil war" in the East, where Armenian massacres of Muslims had to be stopped; and, anyway, (*d*) others have done worse.[64] State-sponsored historical and cultural societies in Turkey continue to produce research that effaces the fact, scope, and systematic nature of the massacres and contradicts broad international consensus on the Armenian Genocide.

In distinction to official histories of the "Armenian Question," the production of public knowledge about the Kurdish population in Turkey operates according to a much less formal process. Basic facts regarding state suppression of Kurds are sometimes contested, but for the most part political interpretations of recent history are a critical site of contestation. Tension between Turkish state institutions and the Kurdish population in southeastern Turkey increased dramatically after 1984, when Marxist militant Kurdish groups such as the PKK emerged as a significant threat to security in the region.[65] As Kemal Kirişci and Gareth Winrow argue, the PKK's understanding of this conflict as an ethnic separatist movement shifted Kurdish popular perception of Kurds' relationship to the Turkish state, significantly increasing Kurdish public perception of a Kurdish ethnic identity distinct from Turkishness.[66] Increased armed hostility led Turkish military and government officials to consistently characterize the "Kurdish Question" as a terrorism issue, reinforcing tension between Turks and Kurds at a time of dramatically increased identification with Kurdish ethnicity and drastically overstating Kurdish public support for the PKK's violence.[67] Most official understanding of the conflict with Kurdish militants has developed in this less formal manner through shifting public perception of identity.

Turkish military policy regarding the conflict with Kurdish militants has also had a profound impact on public understanding of the conflict itself. Given the Turkish Armed Forces' difficulties in accessing remote, mountainous villages in southeastern Turkey, the Village Guard (Köy Korucuları, officially Türkiye Güvenlik Köy Korucuları) system was established in 1985, a state-funded system of paramilitary groups justified as a way to employ and arm local villagers for their own defense against PKK raids.[68] This system escalated hostilities as the PKK began attacking villages that joined the Guard system, and numerous Village Guards have been implicated in human rights violations, corruption, drug smuggling, extortion, and intra- and intervillage hostilities. Nevertheless, the Turkish government steadily increased funding for the system, and by 1998 seventy thousand Village Guards were paid $210 million dollars in total annually.[69] In coordination with the Guard system, the Turkish military has forcibly evacuated thousands of villages in remote parts of the Southeast (primarily along the Iranian and Iraqi borders), burning the villages after evacuation to prevent their use by PKK militants but blaming the fires on the PKK.[70] These evacuations displaced approximately three hundred thousand people by 1995, and scholars estimate that the entire conflict has led to an internal migration of between one and four million people, either from rural to urban centers in the Southeast or from the Southeast to Istanbul and the Marmara region.[71] By 1996, the majority of Turkish Kurds lived outside of southeastern Turkey.[72] High rates of migration and intracommunal violence have led both to the increased public visibility of Kurdish people and to increased association of Kurds with violent conflict in Turkey.

The most significant site of contestation about the Kurdish conflict in the 1980s and 1990s is the general attribution of blame for fatalities. By 2005, when Pamuk stated that "30 thousand Kurds were killed" in the conflict, this number was not a contentious estimate, and official accounts of the total number of civilian and military deaths during the 1980s and 1990s usually stood around thirty-seven thousand.[73] As the conflict escalated after 1993, much of the narrative justifying continued military activity centered on capturing or executing the leader of the PKK, Abdullah Öcalan, in order to restore peace. Political statements that vilified Öcalan frequently mentioned the PKK tactic (beginning in 1987–90) of burning or attacking Kurdish villages in order to ensure their cooperation with the PKK, a tactic that dissolved the majority of Kurdish public support for the PKK.[74] Following Öcalan's capture, public trial, and life imprisonment in 1999, Turkish media outlets began referring to Öcalan as "the Murderer of 35,000 People."[75] This popular designation indicates a general understanding of culpability for fatalities in southeastern Turkey from 1984 to 1999, all of which are considered the fault of an illegitimate group of militants and their leader. Justifications for Turkish military action in the Southeast that emphasize Öcalan's personal culpability and Turkish military policies that increased intra-Kurdish violence have helped develop a public understanding of the Kurdish conflict that recognizes only the PKK's role in killing Kurds and Turks alike.

Foreign Citizen: The Trial of Hrant Dink

The vast background of legal definitions, citizenship rules, and popular historical knowledge described in the previous section circulated in the figure of the minority in Article 301 trials in the mid-2000s, enabling "the minority" to fluctuate in each case. In the weeks prior to Hrant Dink's indictment, media attention on Dink dramatically intensified following the publication of his article on famed Turkish aviator Sabiha Gökçen (1913–2001), the world's first female combat pilot and Atatürk's adopted daughter, in February 2004.[76] Dink's article, entitled "The Secret of Sabiha-Hatun," reported that Gökçen was actually an Armenian orphaned by the genocide of 1915, a story based on interviews with a Turkish woman of Armenian descent claiming to be Gökçen's niece.[77] Two weeks after the article's original publication in Dink's bilingual Armenian–Turkish weekly *Agos* on February 6, the wider-circulation daily newspaper *Hürriyet* picked up the story in sensationalist fashion, reporting "Sabiha Gökçen's 80-Year-Old Secret" in massive front-page lettering.[78] The next day the Office of the Chief of the General Staff issued a press release to all Turkish newspapers warning against "dangerous and unhealthy ideas" recently circulated about the "precious [national] symbol" Gökçen and stating that "the nation" expects the Turkish media to show "more sensitivity to Atatürk's moral being, system of thought, [and] the Turkish Republic's fundamental principles and values."[79] Despite the statement's seemingly clear implication that allegations about Gökçen's Armenian ancestry disparage her (and by extension Atatürk and the Turkish nation), the statement went on to remind its readers that Atatürk's nationalism "is not based on ethnic or religious foundations" and then quoted from Article 66 of the Constitution to emphasize that "everyone bound to the Turkish State through the bond of citizenship is a Turk."[80] At the beginning of the media firestorm surrounding Dink's Gökçen article, the figure of the minority already ambiguously alternated between an ethnic (Armenian) subject and a legal (noncitizen) subject.

Simultaneous with the publication of the Gökçen article, Dink was also publishing a series of articles in *Agos* called "On Armenian Identity," targeted at Armenians and especially diaspora Armenians in Europe and the United States. A primary argument of this series was that Armenian fixation on "the Turk" as a constitutive "Other" to Armenian identity was unproductive in the same way that Turkish "paranoia" about Armenians undermined healthy democracy in Turkey.[81] Dink developed a detailed idea of how diaspora Armenians had produced a fictional concept of "the Turk" and argued that they should emancipate themselves from enmity toward this concept of "the Turk" to build a healthy Armenian state. Continuing this argument, the eighth installment of this series began, "The clean blood that will replace the poisonous blood of 'the Turk' [concept] is present in the noble vein that the Armenian will establish with Armenia."[82] Although Dink had been publishing this series since November 2003, this decontextualized excerpt from one installment in February 2004 circulated to a new audience of hostile media pundits following *Hürriyet*'s publication of the article on Sabiha Gökçen.

As editorialists seized on this excerpt, they either republished it without quotation marks around "the Turk" to imply a kind of eugenics, or they transformed it into a simpler, clear attack on Turks: "Turkish blood is poisonous." Simple omission of the quotation marks in the original excerpt became the basis for *Cumhuriyet* columnist Deniz Som to argue that Dink proposed an "intravenous blood purification operation" more abhorrent than something conceived by Hitler, making Dink's article an extremely crude example of what Som called "minority racism."[83] For Emin Çölaşan, a *Hürriyet* columnist, the EU accession process was being used to undermine Turkey as people published nonsensical and offensive statements. Çölaşan argued sarcastically, "We are rapidly progressing toward the EU! Everything is allowed, everything is free! From Imam marriage to Arabic writing to the poisonous blood of the Turk."[84] In addition to editorialists' attacks on Dink, in the week following *Hürriyet*'s Gökçen article he was threatened by the Istanbul governor and the secret police in the governor's office and by groups of protestors outside the offices of *Agos*.[85] Interviewers even misquoted Dink to his face, asking him why he had said "Turkish blood is poisonous," and Dink became concerned he would be remembered as "the guy who said the Turks have poisoned blood."[86] After the Gökçen article, Dink's call to Armenians to resist the trap of enmity toward Turks was widely misread as an attack on Turks and a statement of ethnic division.[87]

In the court case brought against Dink, the misreading of Dink as promoting ethnic division became a complex mechanism of producing both Dink's foreignness and his similarity/proximity to Turks. About a month after *Hürriyet* published the article on Gökçen in 2004, Kemal Kerinçsiz, a lawyer and founder of the ultranationalist Great Union of Jurists (Büyük Hukukçular Birliği), filed a complaint to open a formal investigation, and charges were then brought against Dink for "insulting Turkishness" in three of his "On Armenian

Identity" essays, focusing especially on the "poisonous blood" quote in the eighth essay.[88] When Judge Metin Aydın convicted Dink of "insulting Turkishness" on October 7, 2005, he explained that any court judgment is based on the nation's morals and values because "every country has its own values. . . . In many countries, when you say blood, the ancestors' blood in every inch of the land comes to mind. . . . [Dink's essay] is disrespectful to the Turkish ancestors, martyrs, and the values that make up the nation, and of course it is degrading and hurtful."[89] The framing of Judge Aydın's justification of his reasoning for the conviction in terms relevant to any national culture and explanation of what things are specifically "degrading and hurtful" to Turks suggests an audience of foreigners, and to the extent that there was international media attention on the case, the judge's explanation could target that audience. But insofar as the court opinion was also addressed primarily to the defendant, Dink, the language implies a limit to what Dink is presumed to know about Turks, marking Dink himself as a foreigner.[90] The court thus subtly (re)produces an ethnic division between Dink and Turks in its finding that Dink's "article is not a statement of thought made for the purpose of criticism but is of a degrading and hurtful nature."[91]

Although the tone of the opinion implies Dink's difference from Turks, it also makes clear that his writing is especially insulting because it is so well versed in Turkish cultural references. The judge expansively reinterpreted Dink's essay to include an insult to Atatürk and all Turks by arguing that Dink's "poisonous blood" quote is a "distortion" of Atatürk's "Address to the Youth."[92] This address includes one of the most famous Atatürk quotations that is still memorized in Turkish schools and is etched in thirty-foot-tall gold lettering on the outside wall of Atatürk's mausoleum: "The strength you will need for [preserving Turkey's independence] is in the noble blood which flows in your veins."[93] For Judge Aydın, the words of the "Address to the Youth" "were subtly and skillfully distorted by Dink," and the opinion explains, "Since Atatürk knew very well that this motherland was saved by [our ancestors'] blood, he said that the power the youth needed in every difficult situation was in this blood.

However, the accused stated that this blood was poisonous."[94] Judge Aydın's decision not only characterizes the "poisonous blood" quote as insulting to Turkishness on its own but also marks Dink's words as even more offensive because they so "skillfully" distort one of Atatürk's most famous quotations. Whether this "distortion" was intentional on Dink's part, the opinion positions Dink as especially insulting to Turkishness because of his perceived cultural proximity, similar to the threat of an "internal enemy" of Turkey.

The oscillating characterizations of Dink as both foreign and Turkish continued through Dink's assassination outside the *Agos* offices on January 19, 2007. Dink had appealed his conviction in domestic courts until he had exhausted his options in May 2006, and he was preparing an appeal to the European Court of Human Rights at the time of his assassination.[95] After Dink lost his final domestic appeal in 2006, *Milliyet* journalist Derya Sazak published an interview with the nationalist historian Mehmet Perinçek, who claimed that new evidence from Russian archives demonstrated there had been no genocide against Armenians in 1915, but rather that Armenian forces had waged a desperate "suicide mission" in eastern Anatolia. The interview was explicitly framed as a response to Dink, arguing that Dink had taken the side of the West on the "Armenian Issue" when, according to Perinçek, "Armenians killed just as many Turks," and "Turkey should be able to say, 'We defended our homeland.'"[96] At the moment when Dink's appeals were exhausted in Turkey, he remained an outsider, and his Armenian heritage made it easy to imply analogies between Dink and Armenian forces in 1915 who collaborated with foreigners to attack Turkey.

When Dink was assassinated on the streets of Istanbul the following year, however, his foreignness was reduced on one side of the political spectrum to an unassimilable constitutive trace within Turkishness as a whole as thousands of marchers at his funeral held signs reading, "We Are All Hrant, We Are All Armenians." Daniella Kuzmanovic argues that after Dink's assassination, Turkish mainstream media appropriated Dink as "ours" in a way that both expressed and relieved feelings of collective guilt for his murder.[97]

According to Gülay Türkmen-Dervişoğlu, the expressions of public guilt following Dink's murder mourned the death of an official narrative of Turkish benevolence toward Armenians perhaps more than Dink himself.[98] At the other end of the political spectrum, nationalists reacted with alternative signs reading "We Are All Turks, We Are All Mustafa Kemal [Atatürk]," or they suggested that the murder was a plot to discredit ultranationalists.[99] These more nationalist slogans responded to demonstrations of collective guilt with a globally familiar defensiveness, interpreting mourning for Dink as a threat to the stability of Turkishness. On both sides of the political spectrum, there was a kind of broad consensus that Dink's death was a rupture in Turkishness itself, a crisis in the figure of the minority in its constitutive relationship with "the Turk." As mainstream media swung toward an inclusionary attitude to Dink after his murder, the unassimilable nature of Dink's Armenianness became visible as the ethnic Other/noncitizen figure of the minority that constitutes Turkishness.

Reactionary Criminal: The Trial of Orhan Pamuk

On August 31, 2005, about a month prior to Dink's trial, one of Turkey's most famous and best-selling novelists, Orhan Pamuk, was also indicted for "insulting Turkishness" under Article 301. In February 2005, Pamuk had given an interview with a German arts and culture magazine, *Das Magazin*, in which he discussed his novel *Snow* (*Kar*, 2002) and its reception in Turkey.[100] Although the interview focused primarily on the challenges of Turkey's accession to the EU and the political symbolism in the book, the interview circulated in Turkish newspapers as a single brief statement: "Thirty thousand Kurds were killed here. And a million Armenians. And almost no one dares mention it. So I do."[101] Reactions to Pamuk's statement were almost uniformly hostile as professors at Turkish universities denounced it as "a great falsehood"; the mayor of a city in southwestern Turkey, Isparta, collected and burned Pamuk's books; and Pamuk himself had to delay his return to Turkey owing to concerns about his own safety.[102] Pamuk had been a central target of anti-intellectual and anti-European sentiment in the past in Turkey, but the backlash to his interview was particularly severe. As in Dink's case, the oscillating limitations surrounding the figure of the minority reappeared in Pamuk's case in slightly different form.

Within the intense criticism of Pamuk for his statement that "30 thousand Kurds and 1 million Armenians have been killed here," three themes emerged to combine definitions of legal citizenship with popular knowledge of national identity in the figure of the minority.[103] First, critics insinuated that Pamuk himself must be some kind of minority or at least that his opinions made him a traitor to his country. Second, because Pamuk did not seem to support the official discourse of the Turkish Republic, he was labeled "backward" or "nonmodern," and his statement was accordingly dismissed as not befitting the discourse of the modern republic. Finally, descriptions of Pamuk's interview developed a subtle distinction between the craft of a fiction writer and the knowledge of actual historians, and Pamuk's comments, especially regarding the Armenian Genocide, were labeled a species of fiction. In Pamuk's case, the figure of the minority combined a concept of modernity with the idea of an "internal enemy" to reinforce the Turkish state's official history of the Armenian Genocide.

Although Pamuk's statement drew an intense reaction precisely because Pamuk himself fit well within the parameters of the category "Turk," numerous critics also insinuated that Pamuk had a secret minority past or was in some way collaborating with minorities or foreigners. For instance, two weeks after Pamuk's interview appeared in translation in Turkey, an Armenian writer living in England, Nouritza Matossian, published praise for Pamuk's statement in the British newspaper the *Observer.* Reports of Matossian's article quickly circulated in Turkey as mainstream newspapers announced that Armenians had declared Orhan Pamuk their hero but that this declaration was tied to someone who had an outstanding criminal complaint against him in Turkey.[104] Pamuk's status as the criminal hero to minorities worked in tandem with related criticisms at the time that Pamuk had made the statement regarding Armenian and

Kurdish deaths in order to sell more books in Europe by disparaging his country.[105] Although criticisms of Pamuk that emphasized his close ties to minorities and his treasonous behavior for economic gain seem like exaggerated slander, these criticisms circulated common aspects of the figure of the minority regarding the inferiority of minorities and the threats to national security posed by the collaboration of internal and external enemies. Common responses to Pamuk's statement that labeled him a secret minority and an immoral sellout therefore operated within the logic of the figure of the minority, locating Pamuk within official understandings of national security and formal definitions of minorities and citizenship.

Turkish citizenship also circulates as a "modern" republican category that can include anyone with a bond to the state, and this understanding of citizenship transformed Pamuk's statement into the expression of a premodern, backward, or reactionary individual. As mentioned previously, official discourse in Turkey recognized Kurds in the early republic as an assimilable but backward group known as "mountain Turks." This appellation has a close affinity with the more contemporary epithet "black Turk" (*kara Türk*), which describes undereducated, socially conservative, religious, and poorer citizens of Turkey, sometimes referring to Kurds as an ethnic group but frequently suggesting an individual who is out of step with modern Turkey because of a lack of education or overly fervent religious devotion.[106] Within a few days of the translation of Pamuk's interview into Turkish, an editorialist coined the term *black writer* (*kara yazar*) to describe Pamuk's moral character, arguing that Pamuk had "put his interior blackness [*karalık*] in the title of a book," referring to Pamuk's novel *The Black Book* (*Kara kitap*, 1990).[107] This editorial also mistranslated the iconic statement from Pamuk's interview to erase any nuance in the statement's original wording, quoting Pamuk as saying, "Turks murdered one million Armenians and thirty thousand Kurds."[108] The altered translation makes Pamuk's statement sound more inflammatory by explicitly blaming Turks for the genocide of 1915, helping to reinforce the idea of Pamuk as a "black writer" and uncivilized reactionary. Criticism of Pamuk's statement transformed him into a nonmodern and perhaps irrational agitator, someone who could be dismissed as out of touch with modern Turkey and its republican, inclusive citizenship category "Turk."

Criticism of Pamuk was not always polemical in its rejection of his statement, and many critics relied on the argument that Pamuk was not qualified to make statements about the "Armenian Question." For instance, the day Pamuk's interview was translated and printed in newspapers in Turkey, the centrist, wide-circulation daily *Vatan* printed a forum article with statements by five professors at Turkish universities or policy centers entitled "Did We Slaughter 1 Million Armenians and 30 Thousand Kurds?" Among the professors interviewed for the article, Hikmet Özdemir, the chair of the Turkish Historical Society's Armenian Division, said that the statement "'we slaughtered one million Armenians' is a great falsehood" and explained, "As a scientist, I do not make claims without absolute certainty." Özdemir not only dismissed the veracity of Pamuk's statement but also questioned Pamuk's authority to make this kind of controversial statement, suggesting that Pamuk's careless accusation was not the product of "science." Halil İnalcık, professor of history at Boğaziçi University, echoed concern about Pamuk's qualifications, explaining that "literature is different from the study of history. We take pride in Pamuk as a writer renowned not only in Turkey but all over the world. But historical comments are not fantasy, dreams, or preconceptions but are put forward based on documentation."[109] These statements outlined an important but subtle argument about Pamuk's lack of knowledge of historical matters, reappropriating his status as a fiction writer to delegitimize his statements about the Armenian Genocide as fictional. These kinds of academic dismissals of Pamuk's statement as inflammatory and uninformed suggest a correspondence between the figure of the minority in official discourse and a range of academic disciplines and institutions producing social-scientific research with the state's financial support.

Criticisms of Pamuk coalesced around themes that operate in harmony with the way that the figure of the minority organizes knowledge about Turkish citizenship, national security, and the legal status of minorities. Editorialists who dismissed Pamuk as collaborating with minorities or foreigners activated ideas about the continuing threat from internal and external enemies in the Republic and displayed general disdain for minority status in relation to the principles of the state. Similarly, attacks on Pamuk that labeled him a "black writer" suggested his inability to participate in modern, rational discussion and pointed to his divergence from the ideal characteristics of the republican citizenship and identity category "Turk." Most importantly, academics who suggested that Pamuk was not properly informed about history or was unqualified to make statements about the past reinforced the entire discourse in which the figure of the minority operated, marking a limit to the legitimate production of knowledge regarding events that might challenge the official operation of the figure of the minority. The statements by academics who dismissed Pamuk's "interpretation" of events as "fantasy" or "dreams" rather than "science" reinforced the way that the figure of the minority circulates through the entire authorized production of knowledge in the Turkish state and the network of techniques and disciplines that maintain this state discourse. Public speech criticizing Pamuk's statement regarding historical deaths of Armenians and Kurds mobilized a range of informal knowledge regarding national identity that defined the figure of the minority.

The Sometimes-Ethnic Citizen: The Trial of Elif Şafak

By the time of Elif Şafak's trial in September 2006, the tenor of media coverage of Kerinçsiz's campaign against journalists, authors, and public intellectuals had shifted somewhat. Certainly, ultranationalists sent Şafak death threats and called her a "pawn of the enemies of Turkey," and lawyers affiliated with Kerinçsiz subjected Şafak to the kind of vitriol used against Pamuk and Dink.[110] But in Şafak's case many of the newspapers and columnists who had attacked Dink and Pamuk so fiercely were now more focused on Article 301 itself and the possibility of amending it.[111] This shifted response is perhaps owing to the manifestly implausible nature of the case against Şafak: she had supposedly "insulted Turkishness" by having an Armenian American character in her novel *The Bastard of Istanbul* (2006, written and published in English and then translated into Turkish as *Baba ve Piç* the same year) say (among other things), "I am the grandchild of genocide survivors who lost all their relatives to the hands of Turkish butchers in 1915, but I myself have been brainwashed to deny the genocide because I was raised by some Turk named Mustapha!"[112] The frequently repeated question "How can a fictional character be judged in court?" helped position Şafak as a kind of bystander to the trial rather than its subject.[113] The absurdity of bringing the law into the fictional world of a novel helped make the law itself the subject of debate.

Şafak's case was a shorter saga than Dink's or Pamuk's, and the concomitant debate about amending Article 301 was inextricable from discussions of the EU accession negotiations that began in October 2005. Charges were brought against Şafak in July 2006; her trial took about an hour on September 21, 2006, and shortly after she was acquitted, Şafak explained, "I don't think I was the main target there. I think the main target is Turkey's EU process, and they [Kerinçsiz and others] want to block that process."[114] Indeed, on the day of the trial, Kerinçsiz's group of lawyers staged protests and made comments at the courthouse almost wholly focused on the EU. This group altered an EU flag to include a swastika inside the circle of stars and the phrase "EU fascism," and Kerinçsiz argued that the judges in Şafak's trial could not make an objective decision because EU officials had attended the trial "like *ağa* fathers."[115] Kerinçsiz formalized this sentiment in the official appeal of Şafak's case, which alleged that EU officials' presence at the trial "as if they were armistice commissioners ready to inspect the court all runs counter to the independence of the court and prevents the court from making an objective and unbiased ruling. . . . The judge should have prevented foreigners from coming undauntedly to the hearing and trying secretly to inspect and influence [the trial]."[116] Moving away from the facts of the case and in a familiar criticism of European exploitation of Turkey, Kerinçsiz positioned Turkey's sovereignty as under siege. In Şafak's case, refiguring Turkey as marginalized and oppressed by Europe almost completely elided *The Bastard of Istanbul* as the subject of the case, (re)obscuring Armenian minority experience of memory and forgetting the genocide that is the subject of the book.

Because commentary about Şafak's case tied Article 301 directly to discussion of EU accession negotiations, reference to amendment or repeal of Article 301 became politically dangerous ahead of the elections in 2007. Both Justice and Development Party (Adalet ve Kalkınma Partisi, AKP) and CHP officials implied that they favored changing Article 301 or preventing its abuse, which had led to cases like Şafak's, but neither party would risk the political fallout presumed to accompany amendment or repeal.[117] As the AKP justice minister Cemil Çiçek explained, "There are proposals to take out 'Turkishness' from the law. But wouldn't some people then ask us if we are ashamed of being Turks?"[118] Elected from outside the dominant Kemalist/nationalist paradigm, the AKP of 2006 still had to carefully manage its status as an outsider party in complete control of Parliament in an atmosphere where the military sent out public memoranda warning about the limits of propriety (as after Dink's Gökçen article).[119] From Şafak's own perspective, even if "there is division within the [AKP]," Çiçek himself was especially clear in his defense of the Kemalist/nationalist paradigm as "he clearly labeled us 'traitor.'"[120] The risk to the AKP of appearing as an "internal enemy," a "pawn of the enemies of Turkey," a "yes-man for Europe," or otherwise not Turkish led officials such as Çiçek to recirculate some of the ultranationalist characterizations of Şafak during her trial.

The political impossibility of addressing Article 301 also demonstrated the looming influence of the minority as both an ethnic descriptor and a citizenship category that shaped speech surrounding Şafak's case. For members of both the AKP and the CHP, condemnations of Şafak's trial always came with important caveats. The CHP's secretary-general, Onur Öymen, explained, "Even if we don't like [Şafak's] thoughts, we respect the freedom of opinion. . . . But on one condition: we do not accept endangering the state's security by taking refuge in this freedom of thought. Just as EU countries make special laws to protect their own security, if they have that right, we should have that right too."[121] For Öymen, dismissing Şafak's case is correct, but he clarifies both that he doesn't agree with Şafak and that the security of the state should limit certain freedoms. In reference to Article 301, Öymen's framing makes defense of "Turkishness" into a matter of state security, indicating the way a legal, republican citizenship category, "Turk," blends with the affect of a threatened ethnicity. Öymen situates "freedom of thought" as an unjustified refuge for those wishing to attack either Turkishness or the state or both.

In a similar evasion of the specifics of Şafak's trial, Prime Minister Recep Tayyip Erdoğan (head of the AKP) also emphasized the justness of limiting speech freedom, even if he supported the result of Şafak's trial. After explaining to reporters that he had called Şafak to congratulate her on the court's decision to drop the charges against her, Erdoğan also clarified: "I always say, you don't exercise freedom by infringing on another's freedom. I'm not saying this about Ms. [Şafak's] novel. Let me emphasize that. But I have heard some commentators [say,] '[Article 301] is a limitation on freedoms.' I disagree with that. Entering another's area of freedom is not freedom. This does not give rise to the right to insult the Turkish Republic. It does not give rise to the right to insult the government of the Turkish Republic."[122] For Erdoğan, individual rights to free speech must be balanced with a kind of cultural right against defamation of all Turks, which occurs when individuals insult the Turkish Republic. *Hürriyet* columnist Cüneyt Ülsever mirrored Erdoğan's sentiment in a way that emphasized this cultural right of Turks: "It is not possible to allow some people to humiliate or insult others either at the individual or social level. . . . In order to prevent those who abuse the right to sue others, we must not turn the idea that 'freedoms have no boundaries' (such as removing Article 301 totally) into our understanding of freedom."[123] In both Erdoğan's and Ülsever's statements about Şafak's trial, the figure of the minority equates republican citizenship with an ethnicity, making criticisms of the Republic's relationship to minorities appear as unprotected hate speech against an ethnic group of "Turks" and helping to justify the enforcement of Article 301.

Conclusion

The trials of Dink, Pamuk, Şafak, and numerous other prominent intellectuals in Turkey mark "the minority" as a fluctuating figure that variously appears as ethnicity, republican citizenship category, historical geopolitical relationship, and modernity narrative. "The minority" situates Dink as both ethnic "Other" and uniquely proximate to Turkishness, blurs the boundaries between ethnicity and legal citizenship category, and eventually, after Dink's assassination, folds Dink's perceived foreignness into Turkishness as a constitutive supplement. In Pamuk's case, the figure of the minority echoes historical characterizations of state security against the "internal enemy," positions Pamuk as irrational or reactionary (descriptors typically reserved for "bad" expressions of Islam, as in chapter 2), and reserves for official state discourse the authority of scientific rigor and academic institutions. By the time of Şafak's trial, Article 301 seemed to embody Turkishness itself, becoming politically untouchable in its equation of republican citizenship with ethnicity. This equation positions Turkish sovereignty and state security as under siege when both domestic and EU critics of Article 301 suggest the law's amendment. "The minority" is an oscillating boundary concept that marks the norms of acceptable speech in coordination with a range of academic disciplines, state institutions, and popular knowledge.

The oscillations of the minority characterize both its figural form and its function as an element of discourse. Discourses are not uniform narratives, logical arguments, or coherent thoughts. As Thomas Nakayama and Robert Krizek have said about the discourse of whiteness in the United States, concepts in a discourse contradict themselves or each other as a means of spreading their authority to more discursive terrain. Just as whiteness is not a content but instead a strategy for securing a certain kind of hegemony, Turkishness might be better defined by its border concepts than by an inherent essence.[124] "The minority" in Turkey is one of these border concepts, a mechanism for securing the hegemony of nationalist discourse rather than a locatable content. It operates to exclude via ethnicity in Dink's case and to mark imagined threats to Turkish sovereignty in Pamuk's and Şafak's cases. It defines the premodern, noncosmopolitan reactionary in Pamuk's case, while combining modern, republican citizenship with ethnicity in Şafak's case. The contradictions shift and disperse as "the minority" figures relationships of authority across cases. The figure of the minority arranges ethnicity, history, law, and narratives of modernity into oscillating relationships that differently (and sometimes divergently) articulate the limits of appropriate public speech.

5

Reflections of Liminality in the Figure of Europe

On September 12, 1963, Turkish government leaders and European officials gathered in Ankara for a large treaty-signing ceremony to commemorate Turkey's becoming a candidate member of the European Economic Community (EEC). At the time of Turkey's application, the EEC was a fledgling organization, one of two competing organizations for economic cooperation in Europe, and EEC member states had not determined what process to follow in admitting countries that required economic transformation in order to compete in the EEC (such as Greece and Turkey). Despite the fact that the treaty envisioned a phased process of Turkish integration into the EEC lasting at least seventeen and not more than twenty-two years, Turkish mainstream politicians and media almost universally hailed the ceremony as marking Turkey's formal entry into Europe. According to the newspaper *Hürriyet* on September 13, 1963, the Ankara Agreement marked "the most permanent and productive step in Turkey's efforts of the last 150 years to westernize and become an equal member of the Western world."[1] The EEC's acceptance of Turkey's application circulated domestically as a symbol of Turkey's status as a political equal among a select group of European states, positioning EEC membership within a long history of Ottoman and then Turkish efforts to implement reforms that would "modernize" the country and secure its political influence in Europe. The signing ceremony suggested a significant moment in the march of Turkish history toward the goal of "joining Europe."

More than forty years later, on October 3, 2005, Turkey began formal accession negotiations with the EU, which had subsumed the EEC in 1991. By the time EU negotiations began, though, the process had already been defined by delay: amendments and deferrals of Turkey's EEC application had necessitated a new (re)application to the EU, and delays throughout the late 1990s and early 2000s had continued a pattern of amendment, renegotiation, and shifting criteria that had prevented Turkey's EEC membership and slowed its application to the EU. By 2005, more than thirty thousand legally binding criteria had been split into thirty-five "chapters" covering legal, political, economic, and social reforms with which Turkey had to comply in order to join the EU.[2] Although numerous Turkish media outlets and politicians again hailed the beginning of EU accession talks as a historic moment for Turkey's progress toward Europe, domestic opposition parties directly challenged the presumption that EU accession would represent a step forward in Turkey's political equality with Europe. Whereas foreign minister and AKP founding member Abdullah Gül lauded accession talks as signaling a "new era" and an "immense and positive development" in Turkey's march toward Europe, Deniz Baykal, leader of the opposition CHP, argued that the EU was making "unreasonable demands" that would lead to a "second-class status" for Turkey.[3] In 2005, a clear political divide regarding Turkey's EU accession centered on differing interpretations of the political relationship between Europe and Turkey implied by the vastness of the accession process.

The divergent responses to these moments of European diplomatic relations align with the narrative and theoretical understandings of modernization and westernization that are unique to Turkey. As Perin Gürel explains, "westernization" has long been figured in Turkey as a double-edged sword, simultaneously "desirable and damaging . . . necessary and potentially corrupting."[4] Turkish and Ottoman state officials and intelligentsia have thus debated the proper scope of "selective westernization," attempting to take the "good things" from "the West" while avoiding unwanted social and cultural effects.[5] For Andrew Davison, a cautious and hybrid approach to westernization characterized the social theory of Ziya Gökalp, the late Ottoman intellectual whose philosophy of a uniquely Turkish modernity became foundational for the leaders of the new Republic.[6] Begüm Adalet argues that even when American academics produced "universal" modernization theories that used Turkey as both template and test case in the 1950s and 1960s, Turkish academics actively challenged and adapted these theories in heterogeneous ways.[7] The EEC treaty of 1963 was interpreted to imply imminent political equality between Turkey and Europe, whereas EU accession in 2005 outlined vast political, legal, social, and economic reforms stipulated by the EU. Differing responses to the negotiations of 1963 and 2005 could easily be understood as reflecting historically consistent Turkish skepticism toward European colonial impulses.

The moments when "modernization" appears as a topic of Turkish public speech are not simply examples of Turkey's long-standing strategic and selective attitude toward westernization, however. These moments make visible the way "Europe" is constituted as a consistent figure in public speech. The figure of Europe that circulated in domestic political speech in 1963 and 2005 consistently positioned Turkey in a liminal space "in between" Europe and Asia or on the margin of Europe or as a "bridge" between East and West. The valuation of this metaphorical positioning could differ from moment to moment because the bridge metaphor can imply equality in difference, whereas marginality implies power imbalance. But in Turkish public discourse, both broad support for EEC integration in 1963 and debate about EU accession in 2005 constructed a figure of Europe as an always-more-"modern" ideal and reflected an image of Turkey as always in the process of catching up. The figure of Europe implies Turkey's "movement" corresponding to transhistorical narratives of development and modernization, but the figure of Europe circulates in Turkey to make the status of movement static. In 1963 and 2005, "Europe" emerged as a construct of Turkish political discourse that produced Turkish liminality as a permanent transition, helping to secure the discursive terrain for narratives of strategic or selective modernization.

This chapter addresses "Europe" as a figure constituted in Turkish public speech, a *specific* definition for a concept that assumes a universal status. Scholars have noted how the name "Europe" can simultaneously reference a geographical place, a political philosophy, and a cultural identity, thus embodying a confrontation between unity and difference, universality and particularity.[8] "Europe" structures knowledge production in the social sciences, democratization, and development, and "Europe's" universality can take a multiplicity of forms, constituting universality differently from different perspectives.[9] Rather than being one of many "alternative modernities," this chapter treats "Europe" as the overlapping name in common (not the proper name) of alternative universalities.[10] "Europe" circulates in domestic Turkish political speech as a means of rhetorically constituting a universality that references permanent liminality, even though this name, "Europe," means different things to different groups simultaneously. Part of the rhetorical power of "Europe" is that this figure presumes a universal character in Turkey *as well as* in its other appearances around the globe (including "in" Europe). "Europe" appears universal while indexing specific, local histories and experiences.

To speak of the figure of Europe in Turkey is to tread dangerously near a homogenization of something like "Turkish national identity," "Turkish consciousness," or even "Turkey" as an anthropomorphized international actor. This chapter focuses on a single definition and set of functions for the figure of Europe, analyzing this figure as it constitutes a static liminality for Turkey. Although this definition is historically familiar and at times hegemonic, it is far from universal *in Turkey*. The figure of Europe can be an important inventional resource for minority communities in Turkey to resist state policy and official narratives. Alevi groups have leveraged Turkish political parties' commitment to EU institutions to force legislative change at the European Court of Human Rights, sometimes in ways that even create splits between different Turkish Alevi groups.[11] Kurdish groups in Turkey, including the PKK, have recognized the AKP's oscillating commitments to the EU and "democratization" as opportunities to secure domestic political reform and basic freedoms for Turkish Kurds.[12] An analysis of Europe as a figure in political speech does not provide an image of something like dominant "Turkish national identity" because this book's argument is that nationalism is an interaction *between* figures. This chapter outlines a historically consistent figure as it is constituted in elite discourse but does not universalize elite discourse as constitutive of a supposedly homogeneous Turkey.

This chapter argues that the figure of Europe circulates in domestic Turkish political speech to structure elements of Turkish political life as "transitional." The content of Europe as a figure constituted in its circulation in Turkey reflects popular awareness in Turkey of the Orientalist representations of Turks that circulate in Europe. Europe gains content as the imagined target of attempted reversals of Orientalist tropes in Turkey, a process that Meltem Ahıska refers to as "Occidentalism."[13] That is, the Orientalist representations of Turkey that circulate in Europe—the "terrible Turk," the exotic harem woman—are also familiar within Turkey as European misconceptions of Turks. Representations of Europe in Turkey are, in turn, produced from a perspective that recognizes the misperception and marginalization of Turkey through these tropes. The figure of Europe therefore implies both the recognizably Orientalized subject position of "Turk" and the reconstitution of the imagined perspective of the orientalizing European. Understandings of the "transitional" status of Turkey produced by the figure of Europe are intricately bound up in this network of reflected fictions.

In contrast with the vast literature on policy, politics, and Turkey–EU relations, this chapter is not a history of the impact of international relations on Turkish national identity.[14] Although the chapter begins its analysis with a brief history of Ottoman and Turkish resistance to Orientalist representations of Turkey, it does not attempt to casually survey centuries of treaties, policies, and international relations in order to demonstrate how each development produced some sort of homogenous "Turkish national identity." Rather, insofar as struggles over representation continue to be spoken about *casually* in popular histories and public memory, they are integral to the background of unthought presumptions in 1963 and 2005 when the figure of Europe was constituted in public speech. Following this brief history, the chapter focuses on the way the figure of Europe enabled a near-universal celebration of the Ankara Agreement in 1963, an event that disappeared from public attention almost as soon as it emerged in newspaper headlines and political speech. In 2005, the content of the figure of Europe produced a very different political debate surrounding EU accession, and the chapter moves on to consider the altered implications of this figure forty years after the Ankara Agreement. This rhetorical approach to Europe takes the figure as a linguistic and affective construct in Turkey rather than as an external political entity, a construct that produces its own authority as a universal concept.

A Brief History of the Figure of Europe

Although Turkish official history has long emphasized a radical break separating the Turkish nation from the Ottoman Empire, a number of watershed events in Ottoman history circulate as common knowledge in contemporary Turkey to serve as the background to the figure of Europe. Perhaps the oldest concept from Ottoman diplomatic relations that continues to circulate in contemporary Turkey comprises treaties known as the "Capitulations," a type of treaty between the Ottoman Empire and a number of different European states and Russia that made foreign residents within the Ottoman Empire subject only to the laws of their home European states. These treaties were typically not reciprocal and granted foreign residents vast economic benefits and preferential treatment, and they were originally intended to encourage European merchants to operate within the empire at a time when Ottoman military strength was a threat to foreign traders.[15] The Capitulations ranged over a span of four hundred years of the Ottoman Empire, and by the nineteenth century these treaties had already long run their mercantilist course, instead becoming a means by which the Ottoman Empire was forced into "dependent integration" into the world economy and European countries took political and economic advantage of the Ottomans.[16] The Capitulations officially ended with the birth of the Turkish Republic (a fact that helps legitimate the nationalist movement), and when international economic and political ties between Turkey and Europe became topics of public speech in 1963 and 2005, the discussion echoed against this common knowledge of the earlier exchange imbalance.

Around the same time that the Capitulations began to become tools for taking advantage of the Ottomans, the empire also began to be known colloquially as the "Sick Man of Europe."[17] In the late nineteenth century and especially after massive territorial losses in the war with the Russian Empire in 1878, European confidence in the solvency of Ottoman financial and political institutions began to erode.[18] By the beginning of World War I, the Ottomans had ceded territory to successful nationalist independence movements in the Balkans, Greece, Romania, and Bulgaria, and the empire's war debts necessitated foreign (European) credit. With the circulation of the "Sick Man" designation for the empire, European countries also became interested in protecting their own financial interests within the empire, and the empire's relative "health" became less important to foreign countries than proper positioning for potential economic and territorial gains if the Ottoman Empire were to run into serious problems in the future. The Capitulations and the "Sick Man" designation circulate in contemporary Turkey to consolidate the history of European self-interest exercised against the Ottoman Empire, helping to constitute the imagined perspective from which a figure of "Europe" views political relations with an orientalized Turkey.[19]

This history of understanding Europe's colonialist designs on the Ottoman Empire combines with the legitimacy of the Turkish nationalist movement in contemporary understanding of the Treaty of Sèvres and the Treaty of Lausanne. After the Ottoman defeat in World War I, the Treaty of Sèvres of 1920 defined protectorates and territorial cessions that gave all remaining Ottoman territory in Europe to Greece; made a British-administered "international zone" around Istanbul and the Dardanelles; transferred the entire Ottoman Mediterranean and Aegean coasts to France, Italy, and Greece; established an independent Armenia twice the size of contemporary Armenia; envisioned a Kurdistan administered by the French and British; and left the Ottomans with just central and northern Anatolia.[20] The necessity and legitimacy of the Turkish nationalist movement were constituted on the basis of this near-complete partition of the Ottoman Empire, and when the nationalist war from 1919 to 1922 resulted in the Treaty of Lausanne in 1923, the success of the war and the treaty were measured against the partition planned at Sèvres.[21] As mentioned in chapter 4, the Treaty of Sèvres reappears in contemporary Turkey as the "Sèvres Syndrome," a fear that EU accession will result in the disintegration of Turkey through a combination of economic concessions, political compromises that cede Turkish authority to supranational institutions, and the extension of civil rights to Kurds, Armenians, Greeks, Alevis, and other minority groups.[22] The official history of the Turkish Republic therefore constitutes the territorial sovereignty of the nation as the embodiment of successful resistance to a long history of European designs on the Ottoman Empire, and the representation of the figure of Europe in 1963 and 2005 presumed familiarity with this history as the condition of Turkey's existence.

Beyond the Turkish nationalist military resistance to Europe's planned partition and marginalization of the empire, Ottoman and Turkish officials also have a long history of resisting Orientalist representations by Europe. Prior to the circulation of the "Sick Man" designation, in 1839 the Ottoman sultan Mahmud II initiated a vast series of reforms known as the Tanzimat, which continued through 1871 under his son Abdülmecid I and aimed to centralize Ottoman government and "modernize" a number of its institutions.[23] Among myriad reforms, the Tanzimat established an Ottoman central bank, stock market, proto-Parliament, and new civil and penal codes, and it reorganized the Ottoman military—all in order to continue to exert power among the system of European states.[24] Beyond the kind of governmental reform meant to compete in international politics and to counter the image of the "Sick Man," Ottoman sultans directly refuted the Orientalist representations of the Ottoman Empire that circulated in media such as fiction and photography. For instance, in 1893 Sultan Abdülhamid II produced a set of fifty-one photograph albums with images of the Ottoman court, cityscapes, and daily life in the empire and sent them to the British Museum Library and the US Library of Congress.[25] Nearly with the invention of photography, concern about this medium's ability to circulate negative stereotypes of the empire that implied political subservience motivated restrictions on photography studios in the empire.[26] The figure of Europe reflects imagined misrepresentations of Turkey in contemporary political discourse and historical resistance to these misrepresentations.[27]

In this history of political reform, contested representation, and armed resistance, Europe becomes visible as a figure that reprojects a transitional, marginal, or liminal status for Turkey. For Ahıska, this folded reprojection creates a caricature of the West as an orientalizing agent that is structured by the power dynamics of Orientalism and reflects a sense of having-been-orientalized. The Capitulations were an Ottoman attempt to "catch up" in the new interstate economy that had become the means by which the empire remained dependent on Europe. The "Sick Man" designation conveyed concern for the empire's forward progress, simultaneously implying that a "healthy" Europe might need to intervene to restore the empire's well-being. Tanzimat reforms can be situated as belated attempts to "modernize" in order to compete, and the late Ottoman concern for pictorial representations of the empire already discerned a power imbalance that might have political implications. Finally, references to a "Sèvres Syndrome" mark concern about the relative stability of the ground on which Turkish modernity rests, suggesting that it might recede or be undermined by European design. The figure of Europe reflects nearly two centuries of political history in a way that consistently marks Turkey as "in between," a bridge, or developing, and the consistency of this liminal status was apparent in both 1963 and 2005.

Economic Development, Political Equality, and the EEC in 1963

Shortly after Turkey's application for membership in the EEC in 1959, EEC ministers expressed concerns about Turkey's economic and political preparedness to join, especially given Turkey's limitations on press freedom, labor union rights, and civil society organizations.[28] In 1961, the EEC formally postponed negotiations with Turkey, a year and a half after the military coup in Turkey in 1960 and about a week after coup leaders executed the civilian leaders of the displaced government.[29] Following the restoration of civilian government in October 1961, negotiations with the EEC resumed in March 1962, but discussion of these negotiations emerged only sporadically in the Turkish press until May 1963, when details of the EEC Association Agreement began to be finalized and it seemed as if the negotiations would be successful. As these negotiations became a more common topic of news media coverage between May and September 1963 (when the Ankara Agreement was signed), this coverage emphasized a number of layers of Turkey's status as "transitional" in relation to Europe.[30] First, although there was intermittent skepticism about the extended length of the negotiation process between Turkey and the EEC, numerous politicians, editorialists, and journalists emphasized the myriad ways in which Turkey would profit from its status as a country in transition, one that was becoming European. Second, at the same time the EEC Association Agreement became a means by which Turkey could profit from its location on the margin of the EEC, the whole EEC itself began to be characterized as a stepping stone for Turkey to enter a political union with Europe. Indeed, numerous media accounts of the Ankara Agreement signing ceremony on September 12, 1963, declared this idea of transition to have been confirmed, with the ceremony marking the "turning point" from which "Turkey is to be considered European."[31] As the impending Association Agreement with the EEC became a common topic in the Turkish press, this coverage highlighted the way that Turkey was imagined on the margin, in transition, or liminal in relation to a figure of Europe.

Although Turkey's status as transitional in relation to Europe was not universally celebrated in news media, the infrequent critiques of the negotiation process primarily targeted the length of the transition period rather than the utility of EEC membership.[32] For instance, a few weeks after details of the Association Agreement began to emerge in the press in 1963, the mainstream conservative intellectual paper *Cumhuriyet* printed an editorial cartoon showing the president of Turkey riding a snail labeled "Turkey–Common Market." A caption clarified that the image represented the "snail-paced income to Turkey that results predominantly from exports."[33] Although much of the media coverage of the EEC negotiations (including in *Cumhuriyet*) had celebrated the benefits of EEC membership to the Turkish economy, this cartoon suggested that these benefits were exaggerated. Similarly, the day after the Ankara Agreement signing ceremony, when Turkish newspaper headlines declared that Turkey had officially entered Europe, the newspaper *Milliyet* published an editorial cartoon showing a personified Turkey sitting in the waiting room of the "Common Market" building, with the internal door leading from the waiting room to the rest of the building closed.[34] This cartoon appeared at the bottom of the front page on a day when the headlines above the fold declared, "Turkey Has Officially Become a Part of Europe," and so the cartoon's implied criticism was perhaps mitigated by the exuberance of the lead story.[35] In both cases, the moderate implied cynicism toward the EEC Association Agreement confirmed a broad perception of Turkey's liminal position with respect to the figure of Europe, marking an uncommon frustration with this position.

The more common interpretation of Turkey's status in transition toward Europe emphasized the unique way in which Turkey could benefit or had benefited from being located on the periphery but moving toward Europe. One of the most celebrated early details of the Association Agreement was the total amount of the aid package that Turkey would receive during the first phase of the agreement. In order to encourage agricultural and industrial growth in the domestic Turkish economy so that it could effectively compete in the European Common Market, the six EEC member states agreed to grant a set of preferential import quotas for Turkish products and agricultural goods that would last for five years. Turkish newspapers hailed the preferential quotas in headlines declaring the fact that "we will get 175 million dollars in aid" from the Common Market.[36] Although these headlines overemphasized the contribution to the Turkish economy by focusing on the total dollar amount of the aid package, the stories under these headlines also consistently emphasized that delayed negotiations over Turkey's application to the EEC had significantly benefited Turkey. When Turkey applied to be a member of the EEC seven weeks after Greece applied in 1959, there was broad agreement in the EEC that these two applications would be negotiated parallel to one another.[37] When, however, negotiations with Turkey were delayed after the 1960 coup, the Greek Association Agreement became the model for the Turkish agreement. When the amount of the Turkish aid package, $175 million, was reported in May 1963, Turkish papers wasted no time in making clear that "this amount shows an increase over the amount of aid previously envisioned. Indeed, the previous aid package to Turkey was supposed to be 125 million dollars like it was for Greece."[38] Although the process of Turkey's negotiations with the EEC had left Turkey in limbo for an extended amount of time, newspapers emphasized the benefits of this delay.

The seemingly strategic nature of Turkey's position on the margin of and in transition toward Europe surfaced again in July 1963 as the final details of the Ankara Agreement were announced. Simultaneous to the EEC negotiations, the Turkish State Planning Organization (Devlet Planlama Teşkilatı), an agency established by the junta of 1960 to direct Turkey's version of state-run import substitution industrialization, released a five-year plan that covered the same period as the first phase of the Ankara Agreement. As numerous scholars have noted, however, the five-year plans issued by the Turkish State Planning Organization in the 1960s contained no noticeable policy initiatives aimed at transforming the Turkish statist economic model so that it would meet the European Common Market's liberal economic demands.[39] Although economic historians have criticized this lack of coordination between state agencies as the reason why Turkish integration into the EEC was never achieved, Turkish domestic newspapers again interpreted a strategic benefit to a Turkish economy situated somewhere between a state-planned model and a liberal model. For instance, one editorial cartoonist regarded the position of Turkey's economic model as something like "having one's cake and eating it too," with an image of the Turkish prime minister seated to eat at a table labeled "Planned Economy" while reaching his fork over to a table labeled "Common Market" in order to eat off that plate as well (see figure 3).[40] As the final details of the Association Agreement between Turkey and the EEC were announced, then, this agreement began to be characterized as an attempt to profit from being positioned on the margin of Europe.[41] If the figure of Europe that circulated in Turkey at this time made clear Turkey's transitional position "in between" Europe and the East, this position did not always imply a lesser status for Turkey and could be imagined instead as strategically beneficial to Turkey's interests.

Although Turkey's liminal status with regard to the EEC was therefore frequently characterized as advantageous for Turkey, this understanding of Turkey's liminal status was layered within a broad consensus that EEC membership was itself an interim goal on Turkey's road to becoming European. Early in Turkish press coverage of the EEC negotiations, the EEC itself was constituted as a transitional organization presumed eventually to include all of Europe. For instance, in a column titled "Should We Join the Common Market?," Osman Okyar argued that the decision to support EEC membership was easy because "the issue facing Turkey is whether to enter a union that is destined to one day cover the whole of Europe. To not enter means to be left alone and to struggle on your own."[42] EEC membership therefore seemed like an unquestioned good, and Okyar presumed that Turkey should get in on the ground floor of this good investment. This presumption also resonated with the practical

3. *Cumhuriyet*, July 6, 1963. Reprinted with permission.

competition between the EEC and the European Free Trade Association, a rival European economic community that in 1963 included seven members, most notably the United Kingdom (which would exit in 1973 to join the EEC). According to one guest columnist in *Milliyet*, economics professor Hulusi Sidal, Turkish membership in the EEC would "spoil the equilibrium" between these two economic communities, shifting power toward the EEC, and would "raise concerns for England especially" about the future of the European Free Trade Association.[43] In editorials assessing the value of Common Market membership for Turkey, then, this value was determined not by the economic viability of membership for Turkey but by the importance of exerting political influence and adopting the Common Market model early (especially earlier than England).

In addition to characterizing the EEC itself as a transitional organization that would eventually cover all economic activity in Europe, celebration of the Ankara Agreement distinctively positioned the EEC as a first step in a European political union that would secure Turkey's status as European and its political equality within Europe. In the days leading up to the Ankara Agreement signing ceremony, almost every major newspaper ran a story asserting the impending political equality between Europe and Turkey. For Kayhan Sağlamer in *Cumhuriyet*, the simple fact of "our being accepted into the Common Market countries, before all else demonstrates their consent to Turkey's being 'European.'"[44] For a columnist in *Milliyet*, this new identity eclipsed the stated purpose of the *economic* union: "The most important part of the initial plan, rather than the economic benefits ensured, is having registered ourselves as being European to the European community . . . and that we have undoubtedly assured ourselves a place in the [future] European Political Union."[45] For both of these columnists, the significance of establishing Turkey's "Europeanness" was that—"*before all else*"—this Europeanness was established by Europe itself. Entry into the EEC did not just enable Turkish newspapers and columnists to declare Turkey's European status but also allowed this status to be framed as something conferred on Turkey by the figure of Europe. The figure of Europe circulated in Turkey as the locus of a judgment about Turkey, and in 1963 this figure reflected a self-understanding of Turkey as a politically equal player in a future European political union.

As the figure of Europe reflected this desired favorable judgment of Turkey, European officials' clichés of congratulations at the Ankara ceremony served to reinforce this reflection. Joseph Luns, Dutch foreign minister and president of the Council of Ministers of the Common Market, repeated a well-worn theme in diplomatic speech, declaring that Turkey had "continued on the same road established by Atatürk" in joining the Common Market. Walter Hallstein, president of the EEC Commission, echoed this sentiment: "Turkey, in becoming a part of Europe, has extended the strong character of Atatürk in every forward step."[46] Reinforcing the idea that representatives of "Europe" had declared Turkey European, these congratulatory remarks also allowed Turkish newspapers to celebrate a connection between Atatürk's vision and the EEC, where this connection might otherwise have remained implied. The reflected self-image of Turkey contained in the figure of Europe thus legitimated the Turkish nationalist project by situating the declaration of Turkey's Europeanness within early Turkish nationalism's modernization narratives. The somewhat predictable remarks by European officials at the Ankara Agreement signing ceremony helped reinforce the unique way that Turkish political discourse desired the approving gaze of the figure of Europe.

It was, however, precisely this combination of a reflected desire and an approving gaze that structured the permanence of Turkey's status as transitional within the figure of Europe. The day after the Ankara Agreement was signed, newspapers could not have been more emphatic about the significance of this achievement: "For Turkish economic and political history, Thursday, September 12, 1963, was a turning point. From this point on, Turkey is to be counted as European."[47] Yet registering this "turning point" in shifted Turkish discourse about Europe was seemingly impossible because the figure of Europe continued to circulate as a reflecting apparatus for Turkey's desire to be "more modern." In January 1964, when the Ankara Agreement was finally ratified by the Turkish Parliament, Turhan Feyzioğlu, former deputy prime minister, one of the chief proponents of the EEC Association Agreement, and a key negotiator with the EEC in 1962 and 1963, stated only that "this agreement brings Turkey closer to the West."[48] Against the celebratory atmosphere of September 1963, Feyzioğlu's statement seemed almost pessimistic.[49] If the figure of Europe reflected a particular desire for a gaze of approval, this approval could be achieved only sporadically, and the continued circulation of the figure eventually reasserted this desire, locating Europe as the always-more-modern aspiration of Turkish political identity. As the moment of Turkey's "entry" into Europe receded, then, the figure of Europe began to reappear in a way that positioned Turkey as permanently in transition toward Europe.

In the broad enthusiasm for EEC membership that emerged in 1963, the figure of Europe consistently positioned Turkey as liminal, even when Turkey was declared to be European. This liminal status emphasized the economic transformation Turkey would need to make, however, implying a certain amount of political equality between Turkey and other *European* EEC member states. From the initial enthusiasm over the $175 million aid package to the effect of Turkey's membership on competing European economic communities to the declaration that Europe had recognized Turkey as European, each moment of the discussion of EEC membership in 1963 implied the political influence of Turkey on Europe and an equality of diplomatic relations between Turkey and European countries. Even the moderate skepticism about EEC membership in 1963 focused on the pace of economic reform and the extent of economic benefits rather than marking any negative effect the Association Agreement might have on Turkey's global political status.[50] Although the figure of Europe located Turkey as in transition in 1963, the character of this transition was economic rather than political. The near-universal celebration of the Ankara Agreement focused on a presumed achievement of political equality, acknowledging the need for economic "development" but positioning this development as taking place after the recognition of Turkey's Europeanness.

Political Transition and EU Accession in 2005

When accession negotiations officially opened between Turkey and the European Union in October 2005, the conditions of membership in this political union were incomparably more complex than they had been when Turkey applied for membership in the EEC in 1963. Membership in the EEC had two formal requirements: applicant states needed to have capitalist market economies, and they needed to be geographically located in Europe. By 2005, however, EU accession had become a detailed, years-long series of negotiations, requiring broad harmonization of any accession candidate country with the laws and legal precedent of EU courts in areas as diverse as intellectual-property law, human rights and minority rights, food safety, and judicial independence as well as requiring that the candidate meet the economic standards of the common currency and Common Market.[51] The breadth of the harmonization process left little doubt about the political nature of any accession candidate's transformation, and the complexity of the harmonization process created a multifaceted debate in Turkish domestic political discourse about whether EU accession was desirable or not.

Although a spectrum of political positions developed with regard to Turkey's EU accession in 2005, a figure of Europe that served as the marker of Turkey's transitionality consistently circulated through all of these positions. In domestic political debate about Turkey's EU candidacy, three general positions emerged that negotiated the figure of Europe in different ways. First, the leaders of the AKP, who controlled Parliament and had negotiated the final stages of the accession framework, declared their strong support for the accession negotiations as well as the broad global-historical significance of the negotiations, while simultaneously emphasizing the year 2005 as a moment of change for Europe as a whole in accepting Turkey. Second, the leaders of the CHP, the largest opposition party and formerly a proponent of EU accession, criticized the terms of accession that the AKP had reached with EU officials, arguing that the AKP's accession framework would not lead to full EU membership but eventually only to a "privileged partnership" between Turkey and the EU.[52] Both the CHP and the AKP perceived a privileged partnership to be a kind of second-class status in Turkey's relationship to Europe.[53] Finally, the Nationalist Action Party (Milliyetçi Hareket Partisi, MHP) and a number of smaller ultranationalist parties proclaimed outright opposition to EU accession because it would require a political transition that they interpreted either as dangerous for Turkey or as implying Turkey's political inferiority in relation to Europe.[54] Although Turkish political parties offered numerous interpretations of the official beginning of EU accession negotiations, all of these interpretations indicated the circulating figure of Europe that positioned Turkey in a liminal relationship to Europe.

Prior to the beginning of official accession negotiations in 2005, EU officials had delayed a decision about Turkey's eligibility for EU candidacy and only officially announced in December 2004 the conditions Turkey would need to meet to become eligible.[55] In the months preceding this announcement, prime minister and AKP leader Recep Tayyip Erdoğan began to frame the global-historical significance of Turkey's bid for EU membership as important for both Turkey *and* Europe. At a meeting of the Boğazici University Alumni Foundation in October 2004, Erdoğan argued that the only way the EU could prevent a "clash of civilizations" was to admit Turkey into the EU. For Erdoğan, if Turkey were not admitted, the EU "should be ready for a clash of civilizations in this world. We have to choose the unity of civilizations. Otherwise, there will be a high cost to humanity and neither [we] nor the following generations can pay this price."[56] Signaling Turkey's strategic significance after the terrorist attacks on the United States on September 11, 2001, through a seeming threat, Erdoğan positioned Turkey as a necessary ally that Europe needed to court for the protection of global "civilization." Beyond the strategic significance of Turkey's geographical position, however, Erdoğan's emphasis on a "unity of civilizations" helped frame Turkey as the lynchpin of global harmony between Islam and the West. Erdoğan's statement described a unique strength of political identity for Turkey as the necessary bridge between Europe and the Middle East.[57]

AKP officials maintained this general narrative concerning Turkey's relationship with Europe through the formal opening of accession negotiations in 2005, emphasizing Turkey's strength of political character in public discussion of an accession process that implied vast political transition. Foreign affairs minister and former prime minister Abdullah Gül, one of the chief negotiators of the final stages of the EU Accession Agreement and founding member of the AKP, voiced his own strong support for Turkey's EU membership during the official opening of accession negotiations in Luxembourg. For Gül, "what we are doing here today is powerful and significant enough to change the course of history. Turkey's membership in the EU will prove, once and for all, that Europe is defined by common values. The true divide lies not between civilizations but between civilized people and the few who use violence and terror to try to destroy the common values which bind us all. It will also signify that the EU has a strategic vision and is able to see the broader picture in the best interest of the international community."[58] Gül's statement encapsulated the AKP's nuanced position as he attempted to mark the opening of EU accession negotiations as transformational for Turkey while simultaneously "saving face" for Turkey by asserting an unchanging Turkish political identity with respect to Europe.[59] Although the accession negotiations could "change the course of history," Gül also made clear that Turkey and the EU already shared a common set of values, implying that this historic change would not affect Turkish political identity. In fact, Turkish membership in the EU would be a chance for Europe to live up to the promise of its (secular) values, to "prove, once and for all, that Europe is defined by common values" rather than solely by the Christianity common to current member states. Echoing Erdoğan's "clash of civilizations" theme, Gül marked the beginning of accession negotiations as momentous for Turkey and transformative of Europe.

Just as Erdoğan's remarks in 2004 about a clash of civilizations contained the twinge of a threat toward the EU, Gül's statement did not end without including a kind of warning to current EU member states. Reviewing the unique history of Turkey's close association with the EU, Gül explained, "Turkey's economic performance since the completion of the Customs Union a decade ago [in 1995], the only candidate to do so before membership, has demonstrated that we are a fully functioning market economy. We are confident that the European Union will overcome the current skepticism toward enlargement . . . [and] extend to Turkey the equal treatment which it accorded other candidates in the past."[60] For Gül and many of his domestic critics, the opening of accession negotiations produced doubt when the Austrian delegation attempted to prevent the accession on the day before negotiations began, and a palpable lack of unanimity within the EU regarding Turkey's candidacy made it difficult to believe the process was being negotiated in good faith. In asserting Turkey's wariness as a warning, and in attempting to frame it as continuing support for the accession process, however, Gül had to emphasize the ways Turkey had already been an exception to the process of accession. In demonstrating Turkey's willingness to bend Europe's own rules to suit Europe, Gül's assertion of an unwavering Turkish political identity got lost in a desire for approval from Europe. Despite the "clash of civilizations" theme and careful attempts to assert strength of character for Turkey, the figure of

Europe continued to circulate in a way that subtly marginalized its creator.

For the AKP's domestic political opposition, criticisms of the EU accession framework contained much less subtlety regarding a European negotiating partner because they were aimed almost solely at a domestic audience and the AKP. In this more straightforward criticism of the EU accession negotiations and the AKP, anxiety about Turkey's relationship to the figure of Europe became even more apparent. For Deniz Baykal, longtime leader of the CHP and past proponent of Turkey's EU accession, the main problem with the AKP-negotiated accession framework was that it did not explicitly rule out a "privileged partnership" and therefore "open[ed] the door for second-class status for Turkey instead of full membership."[61] In an attempt to discredit his domestic political rival, Baykal emphasized the Turkish concern that EU negotiations might lead to an officially marginal position for Turkey in the EU rather than to political equality. Defending this position, Baykal argued, "Shall we sing the same songs? Shall we join the choir of deceivers? Our duty is to tell the truth. . . . It is evident that the outcome of negotiations will not be full membership. The king has no clothes."[62] For Baykal, then, the concern was not only that EU accession talks *might* lead to something other than membership but also that the AKP had been deliberately misled by the EU and was now trying to convince the Turkish people that accession was inevitable despite the invisibility of such assurances from the EU.[63] Baykal's insistent criticism of his domestic political rivals betrayed a newly "Occidentalist" concern for being duped by a Europe intent on taking advantage of Turkey.[64]

Baykal's criticism of the AKP was relatively moderate compared to the criticisms pronounced by ultranationalist politicians, and these smaller-party leaders' more radical statements significantly elaborated on the operation of the figure of Europe in Turkish political discourse in 2005. For MHP leader Devlet Bahçeli, the EU accession talks were a process of "appeasing the EU" that asked Turkey to make sacrifices that "put every advance Turkey has made since 1923 in jeopardy." Bahçeli argued that the accession talks endangered

Turkey by requiring a recognition of "the so-called Armenian genocide" and encouraged the "ethnic separatism" of the Kurdish minority.[65] Felicity Party (Saadet Partisi) deputy Recai Kutan emphasized the danger to Turkey posed by EU accession, arguing that giving Kurds and Alevis minority status was "traitorous."[66] Former MHP member Yaşar Okuyan vastly expanded this argument, declaring that the EU accession "documents include statements about the so-called Armenian genocide, the Greek Cypriot administration and minorities—issues that nobody pays attention to. The Dec. 17 [2004] document is the second Sèvres Treaty, while the negotiating framework [of October 2005] is the roadmap for it."[67] For ultranationalist politicians such as Okuyan, the EU accession documents would allow Europe to partition Turkey in the same way that European countries planned to partition the Ottoman Empire after World War I. These far-right politicians' criticisms of EU accession made visible the continuing circulation of a figure of Europe imagined as a threat to Turkish sovereignty and political identity, locating Turkey in a vulnerable, marginal position with respect to this figure.

Traversing the spectrum of Turkish political party discourse regarding EU accession in 2005 suggests a broad agreement on the function of the figure of Europe despite the fact that parties represented a number of conflicting policy positions regarding the EU. Even though the AKP strongly supported the political reforms necessitated by EU accession, it was still concerned about the possible political marginalization of Turkey by Europe, as evidenced in Gül's wariness about European member states' intent for negotiations.[68] Similarly, both Gül's and Erdoğan's modest threats to the EU indicated a continued sensitivity to the way that Europe positioned Turkey as liminal. At times, AKP leaders tried to capitalize on Turkey's status as the bridge between "civilizations," and at times they tried to underscore common values with Europe, but they consistently recognized the political nature of EU-mandated reforms. On the ultranationalist right, this same concern for the marginal status of Turkey vis-à-vis Europe combined with historical anxieties about territorial sovereignty that characterized early nationalist discourse, leading to assertions of the danger of political transformation and insistence on Turkish political strength that had to reject EU membership. Although the policies advocated by these parties differed substantially (including the CHP's seeming middle ground), they all were conditioned by and reproduced a figure of Europe in Turkish political discourse that reflected a liminal, marginal status for Turkey as a bridge between Europe and the East. In public discussion of EU accession negotiations in 2005, the figure of Europe provided a consistent reflection of a Turkish self-understanding that positioned Turkey as politically transitional and simultaneously imagined this transitionality from a caricatured orientalizing perspective of "Europe."

Conclusion

At two moments in the history of Turkey, the figure of Europe circulated with remarkably consistent form and effect despite very different debates surrounding its content. In 1963 and 2005, this figure outlined a structure of movement, naming "Europe" or "European" as an idealized end and positioning Turkey as in transition toward this end. At both moments, the pace of transition or the length of the process became topics of debate, satire, and critique, and yet this criticism was consistent in making pace and length the responsibility of the imagined addressee/agent "Europe." In constituting Europe as both addressee and orientalizing agent, and in positioning Turkey as permanently transitional, the figure of Europe marks a shifting teleology that cannot be traversed. When two different supranational institutions entered into the orbit of this figure in 1963 and 2005, these institutions momentarily gave content to the figure. In 1963, the European Economic Community emphasized the economic development Turkey needed to make and allowed public discourse to infer Turkey's already established political equality in the coming European political union. In 2005, however, reforms required by EU accession left much less space for an implied political equality, and the anxiety over the figure of Europe emerged in direct criticism of accession. The economic emphasis of 1963 aligned with the "bridge" metaphor of liminality, whereas the political character of transition in 2005 corresponded more to a development model of liminality. In both cases, the figure of Europe defined Turkey's location as liminal.

At a time when commentary on Turkey focuses on growing authoritarianism and decreased speech freedoms, it may seem odd to return to historical debates about European institutions that are all but functionally over in Turkey. As the cracks in the AKP Coalition become clearer after the local elections of 2019, however, it is important to return to the continuing significance of "Europe" as a concept around which authority is mobilized. As election campaigns for local Turkish municipalities ramped up at the beginning of 2019, the country was reeling from a currency crisis and skyrocketing food-price inflation that left President Erdoğan's AKP candidates more vulnerable to challengers than they had been in decades.[69] Much of President Erdoğan's campaign in support of mayoral candidates across Turkey in 2019 centered around a clash between East and West and the West's antipathy to Turkey and Islam, and so "Europe" became an interpretive structure through which he reasserted the AKP's (and his own) legitimacy.[70] In Erdoğan's framing, food scarcity and price inflation resulted from "food terrorism,"[71] especially the deliberate "games launched against Turkey" by "Hans and George" (a Turkish idiom for average Western foreigners).[72] To the extent that opposition-party candidates continued to talk about rising food prices, they became (for Erdoğan and his supporters) knowing conspirators who encouraged foreign interference. Erdoğan described his election coalition bloc, the People's Alliance (Cumhur İttifakı), as, in contrast to this meddling, rooted in the values of the nationalist struggle against occupiers following World War I.[73] Erdoğan described a Turkey on the cusp of prosperity that was threatened yet again by foreign interference, thus recirculating both the form and the specific historical content of the figure of Europe. Erdoğan's reframing of a severe economic crisis as deliberately imposed by the West and its Turkish co-conspirators becomes plausible (and in some places effective) precisely because of the historical circulation of the figure of Europe, which helps to shore up AKP legitimacy in a fraught electoral situation.[74]

Although the American and European press have rightly criticized growing authoritarianism in Turkey, especially the lack of free speech and an independent judiciary since 2016, these criticisms circulate in juxtaposition with the figure of Europe in Turkish political discourse to naturalize that figure's constitutive role in this discourse.[75] To the extent that foreign-media coverage of Turkey continues to reproduce clichéd framing questions about whether Turkey is "turning away" from the West, democracy, the North Atlantic Treaty Organization, or Europe, these media presume that "Europe" is an ideal philosophical project, a valued geography, or perhaps a "neutral" supranational political institution (the EU).[76] These clichés about Turkey's position vis-à-vis Europe naturalize the figure of Europe while mistaking its function in Turkish politics, where it remains both an Orientalist threat as well as an ideal of development rather than simply a universal good. This figure of Europe operates alongside more than a century of intermittent consideration of selective and strategic westernization. In this environment, circulating media clichés about Turkey "turning away" from Europe make the whole of Western media (i.e., the "anti-Erdoğan media") appear complicit in Europe's Orientalist designs on Turkey, a theme that commonly circulates in pro-AKP Turkish newspapers such as *Sabah*.[77] As the name "Europe" circulates to designate differing specific entities (philosophy, geography, institution), the specificity of these "Europes" must be emphasized to destabilize the presumed universality of Europe.

Epilogue

Figures, Rhetoric, Political Discourse

Overlapping Figures in the Sledgehammer Coup Plot

On January 20, 2010, the progressive Turkish daily *Taraf* broke news of a plan developed by high-ranking military officers to overthrow the ruling AKP. The Sledgehammer Security Operation Plan (Balyoz Güvenlik Harekat Planı) was alleged to have been developed at a meeting in March 2003, shortly after the moderate-conservative AKP won a landslide victory in the Turkish general elections of November 2002.[1] According to the evidence presented by *Taraf*, the Sledgehammer report included plans to foment violence and public chaos in Turkey that would undermine public confidence in the AKP, lead to the declaration of martial law in some areas of the country, and create the conditions for a military overthrow of elected government.[2] The report included plans for security forces to bomb some of the most popular historic mosques in Istanbul (Beyazit and Fatih) immediately after the Friday prayers and to blame these attacks on the PKK and al-Qaeda.[3] These attacks would be accompanied by a military skirmish with the Greek air force, which would be instigated by a Turkish fighter pilot entering Greek airspace and would result either in the downing of the Turkish jet by the Greeks or the deliberate crashing of the Turkish jet by the pilot, which would be blamed on the Greeks.[4] The Sledgehammer Plan went on to identify 137 journalists who, following these attacks, would be relied on to accuse the AKP of failing to guarantee public security, which would presumably lead to massive public protests and general civil unrest.[5] After *Taraf* reported the Sledgehammer plot, the newspaper released its own massive collection of documents to state prosecutors, and 196 retired and active-duty officers were on trial in Turkey by December 2010 for their role in planning to overthrow the government, including the former head of the First Army, the former air forces commander, and the former naval forces commander.[6]

The Sledgehammer coup plot was developed at a time in Turkey when Kemalist elites had begun to express intense anxiety about the future of the country, especially given the recent election in 2002 of a political party (the AKP) with leaders who openly acknowledged their own faith. In the face of the perceived threat posed by the AKP to the secular government of Turkey, the military officers who developed the Sledgehammer Security Operation Plan supposedly intended to "return Turkey to its dynamism of 1923," restoring "all the gains of the Republic, which have been eroded until now." Among the ways in which the coup leaders would "turn the clock back to 1923," the documents stated, "the [call to prayer] will be recited in Turkish and the damage to Turkish culture caused by Arabs and Kurds will be repaired."[7] That is, the documents released by *Taraf* constructed a desire to repeal legislative measures more than seventy years old and return the state apparatus of contemporary Turkey to a legal form resembling the state as it existed before Atatürk died in 1938. In the wake of the electoral victory of a party (the AKP) without strong ties to the class of politicians, judges, and other officials who had exercised near total control over the bureaucracy of the Turkish state until 2002, coverage of the Sledgehammer Plan suggested that military leaders developed the plan to reassert and defend this group's traditional hegemony over Turkish politics. The documents reported by *Taraf* evidenced a broad concern for the relationship between the military and Atatürk's ideals in the face of a supposed threat to those ideals by religious "reactionaries" and minority groups such as "Arabs and Kurds."

Following the disclosure and subsequent investigation of the Sledgehammer Plan in 2010, one of the most common themes circulating in the international and domestic press emphasized this episode as a "milestone" for Turkish democracy.[8] According to this account, the avoidance of a military coup and the subsequent investigation and criminal trial of the coup planners demonstrated a triumph of the rule of law over totalitarianism and of civilian government over military dictatorship.[9] That is, evaluation of the Sledgehammer scandal emphasized the positive progress of Turkey in its steady historical march toward democracy, liberalism, and Europe. Even the most outspoken critics of the AKP formulated their accusations within the logic of the progress of Turkish democracy. For Kemalist critics of the AKP such as Pınar Doğan and Dani Rodrik, the daughter and son-in-law of Çetin Doğan, former head of the First Army and lead suspect in the Sledgehammer trials, the investigations and prosecutions of suspects in the Sledgehammer plot demonstrated the authoritarian tendencies of the AKP and a vast conspiracy to manipulate mechanisms of the otherwise democratic Turkish state.[10] Both support for the Sledgehammer trials and criticism of the AKP's prosecution of its opponents focused on the relative democratic merit of a particular course of action, and political or legal responses to the Sledgehammer plot were justified in relation to Turkey's perceived democratization. In the responses to the Sledgehammer accusations, then, it is possible to recognize the continuing influence of an idea of Europe and the "progress of Turkish democracy" on interpretations of the meaning of this episode.

When more than three hundred suspects were sentenced to long prison terms for their involvement in developing the Sledgehammer Plan in 2012, reactions both for and against these verdicts continued to assert the implications to Turkish democracy, the relationship of a religious party to the military, and the significance of the event to the historic ideals of Turkey.[11] In March 2015, however, after some defendants had been in jail for more than five years, the High Criminal Court in Istanbul canceled the convictions of all of the defendants because of the new submission of expert analysis showing that much of the electronic evidence presented in trial (such as PowerPoint slides and other computer files) was forged or fabricated.[12] In the aftermath of this decision, numerous former military officers won civil suit cases against the Turkish state for wrongful imprisonment.[13] Although the acquittals occasioned celebration for some political figures and presented an opportunity to criticize the AKP's "authoritarian" tendency, some editorialists also marked their disappointment in AKP officials for overstating the case and undermining what might have been a historic victory for justice over a military establishment that continues to intervene in politics.[14] Lale Kemal went so far as to argue that the acquittals were the result of "a de facto alliance" between the AKP and "its once-adversary, the historic bastion of the secular republic, the TSK [Turkish Armed Forces]" as the AKP increasingly "opted for a drift towards authoritarianism departing from democratic reforms."[15] Even in the face of overturned convictions, falsified evidence, and a far-fetched action plan, there remains a sense of plausibility to the accusations and a palpable disappointment surrounding a kind of "missed opportunity" for the Turkish court system to assert power over the military.

The account of figures developed in this book makes possible a reflection on this disappointment and the remainder of plausibility that continues to circulate in Turkish public discourse regarding the (potentially fictional) Sledgehammer coup plot. The documents revealed in the Sledgehammer scandal and the subsequent discussion of this plot evidence the continued operation of each of the figures of Turkish political discourse analyzed in this book: Atatürk, the military, religion, the minority, and Europe. One form of the operation of these figures in the Sledgehammer scandal can be summarized as a narrative: in response to the threat of religious fundamentalism in the form of the AKP and in response to the degradation of national identity by minorities such as "the Arabs and Kurds," the military perceived a duty to shore up the institutions of the Republic by any means necessary and to protect Atatürk's vision of Turkey as a modern, European nation. This specific narrative expression of the operation of the figures of religion, the minority, the military, Atatürk, and Europe in the Sledgehammer scandal represents one particular constellation of these figures, one particular ordering of political relationships and forms of power in Turkey. The trials of prominent military officials that emerged in response to the Sledgehammer scandal momentarily represented a slight reordering of these figures, however, suggesting a challenge to the military's hegemony over the legacy of Atatürk and a more nuanced account of the relationship between religion and political parties in Turkey. The account of each of these figures developed in this book makes it possible to recognize the way this narrative contains a semblance of historical accuracy in its ordering of relations of authority that continue to circulate in Turkey. The plausibility of Sledgehammer's form exceeds the far-fetchedness of its content.

The surface-level plausibility of the form of this plot has less to do with the supposed fact of planned military intervention than it does with the historical relationships between the figures signaled in the plot. A form of nationalism, a historical consciousness, a familiar mode of perception is palpable if not contained, recirculated if not explicit in the coup plot narrative. The way that religion is politicized, the military becomes savior, the minority poses a threat, and Atatürk remains a motivating impulse toward "Europeanness"—all attest to historical relations of authority that inform a particular nationalist consciousness. The coup plot is plausible not because of the fact that the AKP seems to pose a threat to the authority of the military in the present. In fact, with the possible fabrication of the entire plot exposed, it becomes very difficult to locate in which "present" the AKP poses a threat to the military: 2003, when the supposed coup plot was hatched, or 2010, when its details were exposed in the media?[16] Rather, the coup plot is plausible because of the peculiarity of its far-fetchedness. The details are not just any details; rather, they map a constellation of power relations that is the Kemalist-nationalist imagination. The circulating power relationships between the figures that structure this plot are the familiar terrain that constitutes Turkish nationalist discourse, and this ordering of authority is therefore an accurate account of the nationalist imaginary if not of the events of 2003.

Although the location of plausibility therefore shifts from the details of content to the form of relations of power, this plausibility goes to the heart of rhetorical analysis. The conditions of plausibility are the touchstone for Aristotle. Plausibility as grounded in social norms marks the history of rhetorical theory. But in the coup plot narrative, the conditions of plausibility are resituated, defined not by a moment or an exigence or an intent but by the circulation of figures. The narrative that describes the plot is simultaneously new and ludicrously familiar because the relations of authority that emerge between figures in the plot are themselves things that constitute the nationalist imagination. Do relations of authority have content as they circulate? Perhaps not, and yet their aesthetics are familiar and recognizable here.

How should both the study of nationalism and the study of rhetoric proceed in the face of this kind of familiarity? Christa J. Olson suggests that the tradition of rhetorical theory related to invention and topoi must be retheorized to address contemporary nationalist imaginings.[17] In a parallel vein, I argue here that rhetorical figures need a new theorization to describe familiar recirculations of power because the complexity of Turkish nationalism necessitates this retheorization. Power is not reducible to content in the Sledgehammer case: the intentional downing of a Turkish jet in an imagined skirmish with the Greek military is perhaps something out of the mid-1970s, but it is so confusingly related to a false-flag "terrorist" bombing of mosques in Istanbul as to be not interpretable except through the lens of circulating power relations signaled in specific figures of speech.[18] Power exists in relations between figures of discourse in this case—between religion and Europe or between the minority and the military—in whatever formulation these figures appear and in a way that exceeds the content of the events that make up a moment in the figure. It is the familiarity of the connections between these figures that makes the Sledgehammer plot legible, plausible, recognizable. It is the layering of representational processes, social norms, and forms of circulation that constitutes the authority between and within "figures" of speech and that makes a collection of these figures familiar and recognizable as a nationalist discourse.

Destabilization through Repetition

This book began by articulating a series of questions about representation, meaning, circulation, and social norm, the set of which requires a theory of discursive form and figural circulation to address the way authority establishes the conditions of possibility of public speech. Each chapter of this book demonstrates the operation and significance of a figure or figures at a given historical moment, and as a whole the chapters provide a glimpse of the coordination of knowledge and modes of authority that constitute Turkish national identity. As stated in the introduction, one of the arguments of this book is that national identity cannot be analogized to the evolving description of an individual, but, rather, national identity is constituted by a range of implicit understandings regarding the operation of figures that structure political discourse. This book develops an analysis of these implicit understandings as they circulate in official, semiofficial, and elite speech about politics in Turkey, and, to this extent, the focus is official nationalist discourse rather than national identity as a whole. Recognition of the analytic perspective becomes especially important in chapter 4, when analysis of the figure of the minority establishes the parameters of the concept "Turk," marking "the minority" as a conceptual position in a nationalist, republican historical ideology rather than using it to investigate experience of being a minority in Turkey. It is imperative to mark the limits of the analytic perspective in order to avoid reinscribing official nationalist discourse as the only articulation of political identity available in contemporary Turkey.

Focusing on official nationalist discourse enables a destabilization of this discourse's presumed authority as well as of the concepts that maintain that authority, such as the concept of the state. Both chapter 1 and chapter 3 concentrate on moments of discourse in which something like "the state" could become the object of analysis, but these chapters preserve the singularity of these moments. The first chapter offers an account of nascent institutions of the new Turkish Republic and nationalist leaders' histories of the Republic, but it offers very little description of the idea of "the state" in Turkey in 1927. In fact, the chapter explores a number of concepts, including the military and Atatürk, that unify disparate events recounted in Atatürk's *Nutuk*, but "the nation" rather than "the state" stands out as the primary unifying entity of Turkish political discourse in 1927. To translate this analysis into the language of the later Republic would be to naturalize the rhetorical processes that produce the authority of a concept such as "the state" later in the Republic's history. By 1990 and the reburial of Menderes covered in chapter 3, for instance, various ideas of "the state" emerged to organize knowledge of a public relation to history, the significance of the reburial, and the operation of institutions such as the army. But the appearance of the concept of the state in 1990 and the relations of authority named by it were directly connected to the whole constellation of concepts that constituted the figure of the military at this time. A juxtaposition of the official nationalist discourse of Turkey in 1927 and the nationalist discourse of Turkey in 1990 as analyzed in chapter 1 and chapter 3 accounts for the emergence, dispersal, and later reconfiguration of "the state" as a category constituted by relations in discourse rather than as an entity with a transhistorical ontological essence.[19] Through the development of vignettes of figures in a discourse of official Turkish nationalism, singular moments in the emergence and dispersal of authority also become the comparative means of destabilizing the presumed transhistorical authority of concepts such as the state at any given moment in history.

Analogous to Yael Navaro-Yashin's argument that "'Turkish Culture,' as such, does not exist,"[20] the figures of Turkish nationalism analyzed here do not name static, transhistorical essences or stable ideational content. Figures are fluid affective locations of the mobilization of historical knowledge, political authority, and social norms. Figures circulate to articulate national identity at discreet moments, but "national identity" always exceeds this momentary articulation, like an abstract norm present only in performance but not circumscribed by its performance.[21] Most importantly, figures are rhetorical functions, they *act on and in* speech rather than neutrally describing institutions, individuals, groups, or phenomena. Presuming that the military, Europe, minorities, religion, and Atatürk are singular entities moving through time mistakes rhetorical function for reality: we become *persuaded* that religion is a transhistorical essence, a concrete thing, rather than recognizing how we have been persuaded by this figure. In order to analyze Turkish nationalism, indeed any nationalism, we must attend to the rhetorical arrangement and production of authority and treat national identity as a discourse with shifting, expanding figures and tensions rather than simplifying national identity into the narrative coherence of reductive historiography.[22]

This approach to nationalism quickly makes it impossible really to answer seemingly basic questions about a text such as Atatürk's *Nutuk*: What are the uses of this speech? To what does this speech respond? Who produces this speech? Although it is possible to come up with a range of responses to these questions, in the case of *Nutuk* these responses not only are partial but also create misleading accounts of the speech. One of the most important historians of the late Ottoman Empire and the early Turkish Republic, Erik J. Zürcher, has offered a number of unprecedented and deeply insightful accounts of *Nutuk* and the historical period it covers, demonstrating the way the text powerfully and completely discredits Atatürk's former political opponents.[23] To read *Nutuk* as a strategic project to discredit political opponents, however, a critic must privilege Atatürk as the origin point of the speech and read the historical documents collected in the speech in the way that Atatürk intended them to be read rather than for the truly unique way in which the documents, *on their surface*, challenge the account Atatürk attempts to give of them. To read *Nutuk* as a strategic attempt to discredit opponents is already to begin to naturalize the rhetorical force of *Nutuk* and thus to overlook the way the text acts on the documents it collects. Beginning with Atatürk's famous six-day speech, then, a fidelity to the rhetorical force of each moment of discourse has required a critical method that can juxtapose the contingency of authority to its rhetorically constructed permanence.

In developing a rhetorical analytic from the complex operation of Turkish nationalism, *Figures That Speak* departs, in some respects, from numerous trends in Turkish studies, including some contemporary common sense. To write about Turkey during the period from the 1950s to the 1980s was to reproduce the official modernization narrative of the Turkish state in scholarly form.[24] To write about Turkey in the 1990s was to consider the fate of Kemalism and the role of the military in democracy.[25] To write about Turkey in the 2000s was to write about the "Turkish model" of democracy and optimistically imagine EU integration and Muslim democracy.[26] To write about Turkey since 2013 is to write about growing authoritarianism, populism, and declining democratic freedoms.[27] Even where scholars disagree about aspects of contemporary Turkish politics, there seems to be implicit consensus that Turkey has undergone profound change since the AKP gained a parliamentary majority in 2002.[28] For Jenny White, the AKP is rewriting national identity in Turkey; for Maureen Freely, ultranationalist violence is a response to the AKP's perceived threats to the Kemalist nationalist order.[29] This book departs from and challenges many of these trends in scholarship about Turkey, locating the organizational concepts of these trends as rhetorical figures that compose Turkish nationalism.[30] If the surface of Turkish politics has changed dramatically over the decades, the vocabulary for sorting and performing these changes remains constant: Europe, the military, religion, the minority, Atatürk.

Public and political speech provides a fertile site for the analysis of figures of nationalist discourse because the ideological structuring of norms, knowledge, and authority are performed on the surface of speech. Political authority and legitimacy are constituted and sustained discursively at the most general level of political speech, in what must be taken for granted in order for speech to "make sense." The Sledgehammer coup plot makes sense only in relation to a network of historical power relations contained in numerous different figures of speech mobilized in the moment. A rhetorical approach to

Turkish nationalism can account for the mechanism by which the far-fetched might seem familiar because this familiarity is the basis of persuasion. But this analysis requires a mode of interpretation of speeches that does not necessarily privilege the intent of the speaker or the effects of speech on an audience but instead privileges the unique way political speech distills and articulates a range of beliefs and assumptions. In the analysis of public and political speech, one can locate the naturalization and reinscription of contingent knowledge and arrangements of authority as well as the way this knowledge and authority emerge and disperse according to contingent logics at a given moment.

By tracing the emergence and dispersal of the discourse of Turkish nationalism at moments in history, each chapter of *Figures That Speak* shows the relationships of authority within and between key figures in this discourse. In each chapter, these figures become momentarily legible through an accumulation of political speech and action, law and history, knowledge and assumption. Each chapter outlines the contingent emergence of this momentary legibility rather than identifying its true origin, and each chapter indicates the dispersal of authority rather than marking its trajectory toward antecedent events. This analysis avoids naturalizing the moments of texts' origin because assumed origins rhetorically structure texts themselves. This analysis avoids linking the chapters together in a clear conceptual progression because the idea of progression (toward/away from modernity, Europe, democracy, etc.) rhetorically structures public understanding of Turkish politics. If the goal of political, historical, and cultural analysis is to offer critical accounts of political, historical, and cultural processes, then analysis can succeed only when it avoids reinscribing these processes in scholarly analysis by attending to their rhetorical, figural structure. *Figures That Speak* maps shifting, momentary, circulating arrangements of authority and legitimacy, offers an account of a specific form of political discourse, and indicates the unique position of rhetorical analysis in the exploration of contemporary political discourse.

Notes

Bibliography

Index

Notes

Introduction

1. Erik J. Zürcher, "The Politician as Historian, Historians in Politics: On the *Nutuk* (Speech) of Mustafa Kemal Pasha," in *The Young Turk Legacy and Nation Building: From the Ottoman Empire to Atatürk's Turkey* (London: I. B. Taurus, 2010), 10–11.

2. M. Şükrü Hanioğlu, *Atatürk: An Intellectual Biography* (Princeton, NJ: Princeton Univ. Press, 2011), 144.

3. Zeynep Kezer, *Building Modern Turkey: State, Space, and Ideology in the Early Republic* (Pittsburgh: Univ. of Pittsburgh Press, 2015), 1, 200. See also Sam Kaplan, *The Pedagogical State: Education and the Politics of National Culture in Post-1980 Turkey* (Stanford, CA: Stanford Univ. Press, 2006); Hale Yılmaz, *Becoming Turkish: Nationalist Reforms and Cultural Negotiations in Early Republican Turkey, 1923–1945* (Syracuse, NY: Syracuse Univ. Press, 2013), 181–82.

4. See, for instance, Zürcher, "Politician as Historian"; Hülya Adak, "National Myths and Self-Na(rra)tions: Mustafa Kemal's *Nutuk* and Halide Edib's *Memoirs* and *The Turkish Ordeal*," *South Atlantic Quarterly* 102, nos. 2–3 (Spring–Summer 2003): 509–27.

5. In *Constitutive Visions: Indigeneity and Commonplaces of National Identity in Republican Ecuador* (University Park: Pennsylvania State Univ. Press, 2014), Christa J. Olson offers a rich reformulation of topos in the context of Ecuadorian nationalism.

6. Jeanne Fahnestock, *Rhetorical Figures in Science* (New York: Oxford Univ. Press, 1999), x.

7. Fahnestock, *Rhetorical Figures in Science*, 8, analyzing the anonymous early Roman text (circa 80 BCE) *Rhetorica ad Herennium*, trans. Harry Caplan (Cambridge, MA: Harvard Univ. Press, 1954), attributed to Cicero. Figures of speech were commonly defined by linguistic markers (substitutions, repetitions, tropes such as metaphor, etc.), and figures of thought were defined by effect (frank speech or *parrhesia*, personification or *prosopopoeia*, understatement or *litotes*,

etc.). Fahnestock argues elsewhere that the seeds of a tripartite division of figures of speech, tropes, and figures of thought can be located in Aristotle's *Rhetoric*. See Jeanne Fahnestock, "Aristotle and Theories of Figuration," in *Rereading Aristotle's* Rhetoric, ed. Alan G. Gross and Arthur E. Walzer (Carbondale: Southern Illinois Univ. Press, 2000), 167. George A. Kennedy suggests that the division between figures of speech and figures of thought circulated prior to the *Ad Herennium* in ancient Greece in the work of Aristotle's student Theophrastus or in Demetrius's treatise *On Style* or in Stoic grammatical theory. See George A. Kennedy, *A New History of Classical Rhetoric* (Princeton, NJ: Princeton Univ. Press, 1994), 6, 89, 92.

8. Fahnestock, *Rhetorical Figures in Science*, 11.

9. Aristotle, *Aristotle on Rhetoric: A Theory of Civic Discourse*, 2nd ed., trans. George A. Kennedy (New York: Oxford Univ. Press, 2007), 222, 308; Fahnestock, "Aristotle and Theories of Figuration," 166–67. See also John T. Kirby, "Aristotle on Metaphor," *American Journal of Philology* 118, no. 4 (1997): 517–54; Richard Moran, "Artifice and Persuasion: The Work of Metaphor in the *Rhetoric*," in *Essays on Aristotle's* Rhetoric, ed. Amélie Oksenberg Rorty (Berkeley: Univ. of California Press, 1996), 385–98.

10. Paul de Man, "Semiology and Rhetoric," in *Allegories of Reading: Figural Language in Rousseau, Nietzsche, Rilke, and Proust* (New Haven, CT: Yale Univ. Press, 1979), 3–19. See also Patricia Parker, "Metaphor and Catachresis," in *The Ends of Rhetoric: History, Theory, Practice*, ed. John Bender and David E. Wellbery (Stanford, CA: Stanford Univ. Press, 1990), 60–73; Jacques Derrida, "White Mythology: Metaphor in the Text of Philosophy," in *Margins of Philosophy*, trans. Alan Bass (Chicago: Univ. of Chicago Press, 1982), 207–71.

11. Robert Hariman, *Political Style: The Artistry of Power* (Chicago: Univ. of Chicago Press, 1995), 180–81. See also Robert Hariman, "Prudence/Performance," *Rhetoric Society Quarterly* 21, no. 2 (1991): 28.

12. Judith Butler, *Undoing Gender* (New York: Routledge, 2004), 48.

13. To some extent, contemporary rhetorical theorists' interpretation of Aristotle's *Rhetoric* as a theory of practical wisdom, or *phronesis*, compliments Butler's theory of performance and social norm. See Thomas B. Farrell, *Norms of Rhetorical Culture* (New Haven, CT: Yale Univ. Press, 1993); Eugene Garver, *Aristotle's* Rhetoric: *An Art of Character* (Chicago: Univ. of Chicago Press, 1994); Janet M. Atwill, *Rhetoric Reclaimed: Aristotle and the Liberal Arts Tradition* (Ithaca, NY: Cornell Univ. Press, 1998).

14. Carolyn Miller, Barbara Warnick, and Christa J. Olson have developed analyses of Aristotle's treatment of topos that is analogous to my argument here about figure. Miller argues that topos "must occupy the border between the known and the unknown" in order both to serve as a site of novelty and to make novelty

appropriate and recognizable ("The Aristotelian *Topos*: Hunting for Novelty," in *Rereading Aristotle's* Rhetoric, ed. Gross and Walzer, 141). For Warnick, "the *Rhetoric*'s common topics emerge from structures in the discourse and life experience of a culture and reflect its ways of thinking and being," both circulating recognizable content and acting as the site of invention ("Two Systems of Invention: The Topics in the *Rhetoric* and *The New Rhetoric*," in *Rereading Aristotle's* Rhetoric, ed. Gross and Walzer, 120). For Olson, topoi "provide a stable tether point, allowing rhetors and publics to negotiate shifting terrain," repurposing the past from the perspective of the present rather than mimetically reproducing the past (*Constitutive Visions*, 7).

15. See Fahnestock, *Rhetorical Figures in Science*, 37, 40. In "The Conceptual Unity of Aristotle's *Rhetoric*," *Philosophy and Rhetoric* 34, no. 4 (2001): 275–91, Alan Gross and Marcelo Dascal explain trope in Aristotle as a kind of argumentative inference in a vein similar to Fahnestock. Brian Vickers performs a similar anxiety about contingency as a ground for linguistic meaning in his polemic against Paul de Man (*In Defense of Rhetoric* [New York: Oxford Univ. Press, 1988], 453–67).

16. Butler, *Undoing Gender*, 48.

17. Butler, *Undoing Gender*, 48.

18. In "Being, Time, and Definition: Toward a Semiotics of Figural Rhetoric," *Philosophy and Rhetoric* 33, no. 2 (2000): 116–36, Carol Poster advocates for situated historical analysis of individual figures and the category of figure that would also avoid a static universal definition of figure(s) because this definition has demonstrably changed with rhetoric itself and because figure as a concept answers different questions in the history of rhetoric.

19. De Man, "Semiology and Rhetoric," 10.

20. "The proper," in this sense, borrows directly from Butler's approach to norms (*Undoing Gender*, 40–56).

21. By rebuilding the classical concept "figure" in a way that emphasizes the contingency of propriety, figure can be constituted by local difference globally rather than appearing as a unified transhistorical, transnational analytic tool for making sense of diverse instances of speech. In this way, this book responds to the projects of comparative rhetoric, Américan rhetoric, and regional rhetoric by globalizing rhetorical studies in a way that transforms analytic methods rather than simply proliferating cases. For such projects, see LuMing Mao, "Beyond Bias, Binary, and Border: Mapping Out the Future of Comparative Rhetoric," *Rhetoric Society Quarterly* 43, no. 3 (2013): 209–25; Christa J. Olson and René Augustín De los Santos, "Expanding the Idea of América," *Rhetoric Society Quarterly* 45, no. 3 (2015): 193–98; Jenny Rice, "From Architectonic to Tectonics: Introducing Regional Rhetorics," *Rhetoric Society Quarterly* 42, no. 3 (2012): 201–13.

22. Sara Ahmed, "Affective Economies," *Social Text* 22, no. 2 (2004): 119, 120.

23. Sara Ahmed, *The Cultural Politics of Emotion* (Edinburgh: Edinburgh Univ. Press, 2004), 8.

24. Sara Ahmed, "Atmospheric Walls," feministkilljoys, Sept. 15, 2014, at https://feministkilljoys.com/2014/09/15/atmospheric-walls/. For more on atmospheres of affect, see Theresa Brennan, *The Transmission of Affect* (Ithaca, NY: Cornell Univ. Press, 2004); Angharad Closs Stephens, "The Affective Atmospheres of Nationalism," *Cultural Geographies* 23, no. 2 (2016): 181–98.

25. Parts of this section have been published in an expanded consideration of the relationship between Foucault's work and nationalism in Matthew deTar, "Nationalism, Rhetoric, and Discursive Form," *Journal of Contemporary Thought* 44 (2016): 15–26.

26. Michel Foucault, *The Archaeology of Knowledge and The Discourse on Language*, trans. A. M. Sheridan Smith (New York: Harper Colophon Books, 1976), 35.

27. Foucault, *Archaeology of Knowledge*, 44.

28. Foucault, *Archaeology of Knowledge*, 87.

29. Foucault, *Archaeology of Knowledge*, 99.

30. Foucault, *Archaeology of Knowledge*, 85.

31. Foucault, *Archaeology of Knowledge*, 169. See also Michel Foucault, "Nietzsche, Genealogy, History," in *The Foucault Reader*, ed. Paul Rabinow (1984; reprint, New York: Vintage Books, 2010), 76–100.

32. Foucault, *Archaeology of Knowledge*, 117.

33. Foucault, *Archaeology of Knowledge*, 109.

34. Debra Hawhee and Christa Olson advocate a combination of synchronic and diachronic approaches to history that appears to slip back into a linear model of tracing change. See Debra Hawhee and Christa J. Olson, "Pan-historiography: The Challenges of Writing History across Time and Space," in *Theorizing Histories of Rhetoric*, ed. Michelle Ballif (Carbondale: Southern Illinois Univ. Press, 2013), 93, 96.

35. The problems of agency and exigence as categories in rhetorical analysis are long-standing concerns. See, for instance, Barbara A. Biesecker, "Rethinking the Rhetorical Situation from within the Thematic of 'Différance,'" *Philosophy and Rhetoric* 22, no. 2 (1989): 110–30; Dilip Parameshwar Gaonkar, "The Idea of Rhetoric in the Rhetoric of Science," in *Rhetorical Hermeneutics: Invention and Interpretation in the Age of Science*, ed. Alan G. Gross and William M. Keith (Albany: State Univ. of New York Press, 1997), 25–85. Gaonkar also outlines the methodological pitfalls avoided by an archaeological approach to discourse

in "Foucault on Discourse: Methods and Temptations," *Journal of the American Forensic Association* 18, no. 4 (1982): 246–57.

36. Foucault, *Archaeology of Knowledge*, 169.

37. Dave Tell, "Rhetoric and Power: An Inquiry into Foucault's Critique of Confession," *Philosophy and Rhetoric* 43, no. 2 (2010): 99, 113.

38. Benedict Anderson, *Imagined Communities: Reflections on the Origins and Spread of Nationalism*, rev. ed. (New York: Verso, 1991). Similar approaches are taken in Ernest Gellner, *Nations and Nationalism* (Ithaca, NY: Cornell Univ. Press, 1983); Eugen Weber, *Peasants into Frenchmen: The Modernization of Rural France, 1870–1914* (Stanford, CA: Stanford Univ. Press, 1976); E. J. Hobsbawm, *Nations and Nationalism since 1780: Programme, Myth, Reality*, 2nd ed. (New York: Cambridge Univ. Press, 1993).

39. Anderson, *Imagined Communities*, 81.

40. Craig Calhoun, *Nationalism* (Minneapolis: Univ. of Minnesota Press, 1997), 4–5. See also Pheng Cheah and Jonathan Culler, eds., *Grounds of Comparison: Around the Work of Benedict Anderson* (New York: Routledge, 2003).

41. Rogers Brubaker, *Nationalism Reframed: Nationhood and the National Question in the New Europe* (New York: Cambridge Univ. Press, 1996), 15, original emphasis. See also Rogers Brubaker, "Categories of Analysis and Categories of Practice: A Note on the Study of Muslims in European Countries of Immigration," *Ethnic and Racial Studies* 36, no. 1 (2013): 1–8.

42. Numerous scholars have studied the naturalization of specific features of the nation—such as economy, territory, borders, and community—that produce the authority and consistency of the nation. See, for example, Manu Goswami, *Producing India: From Colonial Economy to National Space* (Chicago: Univ. of Chicago Press, 2004); Nadia Abu El-Haj, *Facts on the Ground: Archaeological Practice and Territorial Self-Fashioning in Israeli Society* (Chicago: Univ. of Chicago Press, 2001); Peter Sahlins, *Boundaries: The Making of France and Spain in the Pyrenees* (Berkeley: Univ. of California Press, 1989); Lisa Wedeen, *Peripheral Visions: Publics, Power, and Performance in Yemen* (Chicago: Univ. of Chicago Press, 2008).

43. Rhetorical studies scholarship on nationalism tends to begin with narratives, ideologies, and myths, or it treats national identity as a kind of evolving conversation (rather than as a discursive form), thus naturalizing some of the rhetorical processes that produce the authority in nationalism. See, for example, Vanessa B. Beasley, *You, the People: American National Identity in Presidential Rhetoric* (College Station: Texas A&M Univ. Press, 2004); Trevor Parry-Giles and Shawn J. Parry-Giles, *The Prime-Time Presidency:* The West Wing *and U.S. Nationalism* (Chicago: Univ. of Illinois Press, 2006); M. Lane Bruner, *Strategies of Remembrance: The Rhetorical Dimensions of National Identity Construction*

(Columbia: Univ. of South Carolina Press, 2002); Gregory Clark, *Rhetorical Landscapes in America: Variations on a Theme from Kenneth Burke* (Columbia: Univ. of South Carolina Press, 2004); Jolanta A. Drzewiecka, "Reinventing and Contesting Identities in Constitutive Discourses: Between Diaspora and Its Others," *Communication Quarterly* 50, no. 1 (2002): 1–23; Don Paul Abbott, "The Genius of the Nation: Rhetoric and Nationalism in Eighteenth-Century Britain," *Rhetoric Society Quarterly* 40, no. 2 (2010): 105–27.

44. Talal Asad, *Formations of the Secular: Christianity, Islam, Modernity* (Stanford, CA: Stanford Univ. Press, 2003), 17.

45. The idea of a "constellation of terms" resembles J. G. A. Pocock's approach in *The Machiavellian Moment: Florentine Political Thought and the Atlantic Republican Tradition*, 2nd ed. (Princeton, NJ: Princeton Univ. Press, 2003). The "constellation" metaphor is an apt description of concepts in a discourse, but the linear approach to historical progression in Pocock's work is one I wish to avoid.

46. Asad, *Formations of the Secular*, 13, original emphasis.

47. Lisa Wedeen develops a critique of Anderson that emphasizes overlapping and simultaneous experiences of temporality that constitute national imaginings rather than Anderson's singular idea of "homogeneous, empty time" (*Peripheral Visions*, 5–14).

48. See Foucault, "Nietzsche, Genealogy, History"; Tell, "Rhetoric and Power," 100.

49. See, for instance, Jean-François Lyotard, *The Différend: Phrases in Dispute*, trans. Georges Van Den Abbeele (Minneapolis: Univ. of Minnesota Press, 1988); various essays in Derrida, *Margins of Philosophy*, including "White Mythology," 207–71, and "Signature Event Context," 307–30; Judith Butler, Ernesto Laclau, and Slavoj Žižek, *Contingency, Hegemony, Universality: Contemporary Dialogues on the Left* (New York: Verso, 2000); Hanna Fenichel Pitkin, *The Concept of Representation* (Berkeley: Univ. of California Press, 1967).

50. Gayatri Chakravorty Spivak, "Can the Subaltern Speak?," in *Marxism and the Interpretation of Culture*, ed. Cary Nelson and Lawrence Grossberg (Urbana: Univ. of Illinois Press, 1988), 271–313. See also Linda Alcoff, "The Problem of Speaking for Others," *Cultural Critique* 20 (1991–92): 5–32.

51. Hayden White makes a similar argument about problems of representation that are characteristic of historiography generally (also singling out Foucault in a footnote). See Hayden White, *Metahistory: The Historical Imagination in Nineteenth-Century Europe* (Baltimore: Johns Hopkins Univ. Press, 1973), 2.

52. See the essays in Rosalind C. Morris, ed., *Can the Subaltern Speak? Reflections on the History of an Idea* (New York: Columbia Univ. Press, 2010), especially Abdul JanMohamed, "Between Speaking and Dying: Some Imperatives in the Emergence of the Subaltern in the Context of US Slavery," 139–55.

53. For expanded arguments about how to engage Foucault's work after Spivak's critique, see Robert J. C. Young, *White Mythologies: Writing History and the West*, 2nd ed. (New York: Routledge, 2004), 49–50; Matthew deTar, "Decolonizing Rhetorical History," in *Reframing Rhetorical History: Cases, Theories, and Methodologies*, ed. Jason Edward Black and Kathleen J. Turner (Tuscaloosa: Univ. of Alabama Press, forthcoming).

54. Aristotle, *Rhetoric*. See also Farrell, *Norms of Rhetorical Culture*.

55. Judith Butler, *Frames of War: When Is Life Grievable?* (New York: Verso, 2010), 3–4.

56. Brian T. Edwards, "*Tahrir*: Ends of Circulation," *Public Culture* 23, no. 3 (2011): 493–504. Edwards forges a middle ground in debates about circulation theory waged in the journal *Public Culture*. See, for instance, Benjamin Lee and Edward LiPuma, "Cultures of Circulation: The Imaginations of Modernity," *Public Culture* 14, no. 1 (2002): 191–213, and Dilip Parameshwar Gaonkar and Elizabeth A. Povinelli, "Technologies of Public Forms: Circulation, Transfiguration, Recognition," *Public Culture* 15, no. 3 (2003): 385–97.

57. Catherine Chaput, "Rhetorical Circulation in Late Capitalism: Neoliberalism and the Overdetermination of Affective Energy," *Philosophy and Rhetoric* 43, no. 1 (2010): 1–25. Chaput draws on Jenny Edbauer, "Unframing Models of Public Distribution: From Rhetorical Situation to Rhetorical Ecologies," *Rhetoric Society Quarterly* 35, no. 4 (2005): 5–24. The interpretation of Marx that informs Chaput's essay shares affinities with Slavoj Žižek's interpretation of Marx in *The Sublime Object of Ideology* (New York: Verso, 1989).

58. Approaching figures as organic products of their context provides a corrective to and extension of René Augustín De los Santos, "'The Future of Our History': Rhetorics of Transformation and Power in Plutarco Elías Calles' 1928 *Informe*," *Rhetoric Society Quarterly* 45, no. 3 (2015): 199–211. Although De los Santos argues for new kinds of analytic concepts because the Western canon of analytic concepts reflects their use only in the United States, he proceeds to employ a concept of "definition" still rooted in that tradition.

59. This approach to rhetorical history does not strictly correspond to any of David Zarefsky's "four senses of rhetorical history" because each of those senses presumes or implies either the centrality of the speaking agent or the legibility of history as a complete object. See David Zarefsky, "Four Senses of Rhetorical History," in *Doing Rhetorical History: Concepts and Cases*, ed. Kathleen J. Turner (Tuscaloosa: Univ. of Alabama Press, 1998), 19–32; see also Cara A. Finnegan, "Doing Rhetorical History of the Visual: The Photograph and the Archive," in *Defining Visual Rhetorics*, ed. Charles A. Hill and Marguerite Helmers (Mahwah, NJ: Lawrence Erlbaum, 2004), 195–214. My approach maintains skepticism of history as a form of knowledge in order to avoid naturalizing the authority of history.

60. Foucault, *Archaeology of Knowledge*, 109.

61. Robert Hariman, "Theory without Modernity," in *Prudence: Classical Virtue, Postmodern Practice*, ed. Robert Hariman (University Park: Pennsylvania State Univ. Press, 2003), 1–32; Warnick, "Two Systems of Invention"; Miller, "The Aristotelian *Topos*."

62. Butler, *Undoing Gender*, 41.

63. Butler, *Undoing Gender*, 52.

64. Abbott, "The Genius of the Nation."

65. Paul de Man, *The Rhetoric of Romanticism* (New York: Columbia Univ. Press, 1984).

66. Yael Navaro-Yashin, *Faces of the State: Secularism and Public Life in Turkey* (Princeton, NJ: Princeton Univ. Press, 2002), 10.

67. Navaro-Yashin, *Faces of the State*, 10.

68. Mehmet Döşemeci, *Debating Turkish Modernity: Civilization, Nationalism, and the EEC* (New York: Cambridge Univ. Press, 2013), 223–26. See also Nergis Ertürk, *Grammatology and Literary Modernity in Turkey* (New York: Oxford Univ. Press, 2011).

69. Döşemeci, *Debating Turkish Modernity*, 225. See also Dipesh Chakrabarty, *Provincializing Europe: Postcolonial Thought and Historical Difference* (Princeton, NJ: Princeton Univ. Press, 2000); Partha Chatterjee, *The Nation and Its Fragments* (Princeton, NJ: Princeton Univ. Press, 1993).

70. For other important works interrogating these kinds of common categories, see Kabir Tambar, *The Reckoning of Pluralism: Political Belonging and the Demands of History in Turkey* (Stanford, CA: Stanford Univ. Press, 2014); Christopher Dole, *Healing Secular Life: Loss and Devotion in Modern Turkey* (Philadelphia: Univ. of Pennsylvania Press, 2012); Esra Özyürek, *Nostalgia for the Modern: State Secularism and Everyday Politics in Turkey* (Durham, NC: Duke Univ. Press, 2006).

71. Yılmaz, *Becoming Turkish*, 9. For important critical examples of this approach, see Kezer, *Building Modern Turkey*; Emir Kaya, *Secularism and State Religion in Modern Turkey: Law, Policy-Making, and the Diyanet* (New York: I. B. Tauris, 2017); Pınar Şenışık, "The Allied Occupation of İstanbul and the Construction of Turkish National Identity in the Early Twentieth Century," *Nationalities Papers* 46, no. 3 (2018): 501–13.

72. Yılmaz, *Becoming Turkish*; Döşemeci, *Debating Turkish Modernity*; Alexandros Lamprou, *Nation-Building in Modern Turkey: The "People's Houses," the State, and the Citizen* (New York: I. B. Tauris, 2015); Yiğit Akın, *When the War Came Home: The Ottomans' Great War and the Devastation of an Empire* (Stanford, CA: Stanford Univ. Press, 2018); Jordi Tejel Gorgas, "Making Borders from Below: The Emergence of the Turkish–Iraqi Frontier, 1918–1925," *Middle*

Eastern Studies 54, no. 5 (2018): 811–26; Ryan Gingeras, *Fall of the Sultanate: The Great War and the End of the Ottoman Empire, 1908–1922* (New York: Oxford Univ. Press, 2016); Ryan Gingeras, *Eternal Dawn: Turkey in the Age of Atatürk* (New York: Oxford Univ. Press, 2019); Uğur Ümit Üngör, *The Making of Modern Turkey: Nation and State in Eastern Anatolia, 1913–1950* (New York: Oxford Univ. Press, 2011); Gavin D. Brockett, *How Happy to Call Oneself a Turk: Provincial Newspapers and the Negotiation of a Muslim National Identity* (Austin: Univ. of Texas Press, 2011).

73. Perin Gürel, *The Limits of Westernization: A Cultural History of America in Turkey* (New York: Columbia Univ. Press, 2017); Begüm Adalet, *Hotels and Highways: The Construction of Modernization Theory in Cold War Turkey* (Stanford, CA: Stanford Univ. Press, 2018); Ali Bilgiç, *Turkey, Power, and the West: Gendered International Relations and Foreign Policy* (New York: I. B. Tauris, 2016).

74. E. Fuat Keyman, "Articulating Citizenship and Identity: The 'Kurdish Question' in Turkey," in *Citizenship in a Global World: European Questions and Turkish Experiences*, ed. E. Fuat Keyman and Ahmet İçduygu (New York: Routledge, 2005), 282.

75. Ronald Grigor Suny and Fatma Müge Göçek, "Introduction: Leaving It to the Historians," in *A Question of Genocide: Armenians and Turks at the End of the Ottoman Empire*, ed. Ronald Grigor Suny, Fatma Müge Göçek, and Norman M. Naimark (New York: Oxford Univ. Press, 2011), 3–12. Similar state-ideology-reaffirming styles of historical interpretation regarding Fethullah Gülen, Kurds, and international terrorism have flourished in Turkey and abroad following the attempted coup in July 2016.

76. Asad, *Formations of the Secular*, 17.

1. Figures of Nationalist Discourse in Atatürk's *Nutuk*

1. In this chapter, I refer to Mustafa Kemal Atatürk by his second name at the time he gave the speech: Kemal. In 1934, the Turkish Parliament passed a law requiring Turks to take surnames and offered Mustafa Kemal the surname "Atatürk," which means "Father/Leader of the Turks." I employ the surname "Atatürk" in this chapter only to refer to the more grandiose historical personage of the founding father or to his figure in discourse.

2. This chapter references three translations of *Nutuk*. First, I primarily cite the Leipzig English version of 1929, a translation from Ottoman Turkish to German to English that Erik J. Zürcher has called "unreliable": Mustafa Kemal Atatürk, *A Speech Delivered by Ghazi Mustapha Kemal, President of the Turkish Republic, October 1927* (Leipzig: Koehler, 1929); Zürcher, "The Politician as Historian, Historians in Politics," 9. Second, I reference an Ankara "update" of the

English text of 1929 published in 2008, which claims to substantially revise the earlier translation based on the Ottoman text but which seems only to correct the spelling of Turkish names: Mustafa Kemal Atatürk, *The Great Speech*, 2nd ed., ed. Neşe Özden and Richard Dietrich (Ankara: Erdal Basım Yayın Dağıtım, 2008). Finally, I refer to a modern Turkish translation based on the Ottoman text: Mustafa Kemal Atatürk, *Atatürk'ün bütün eserleri* [The complete works of Atatürk], vols. 19–20: *Nutuk I–II*, ed. M. Türker Acaroğlu, Feroz Ahmad, Sina Akşin, Talip Apaydın, Zeki Arıkan, İlhan Arsel, Hüsnü Baki, et al. (Istanbul: Kaynak Yayınları, 2006–7). Although each of these translations contains recognizable flaws, I reference them because they are part of how the text still circulates, making them important evidentiary bases for an analysis of discursive form. I most often refer to the English translation of 1929.

3. Erik J. Zürcher, *Turkey: A Modern History*, 3rd ed. (New York: I. B. Tauris, 2004), 133–63.

4. Zürcher, "Politician as Historian," 10–11.

5. For instance, *Atatürk'ün* Nutuk'ta *kullandığı belgeler* [Documents used in Atatürk's *Nutuk*], trans. Kemal Bek (Istanbul: Bordo Siyah Yayınlar, 2007).

6. Hanioğlu, *Atatürk*, 144.

7. Zürcher, "Politician as Historian"; Zürcher, *Turkey*; Adak, "National Myths and Self-Na(rra)tions"; Toni Alaranta, "Mustafa Kemal Atatürk's Six-Day Speech of 1927: Defining the Official Historical View of the Foundation of the Turkish Republic," *Turkish Studies* 9, no. 1 (Mar. 2008): 115–29; Aysel Morin and Ronald Lee, "Constitutive Discourse of Turkish Nationalism: Atatürk's *Nutuk* and the Rhetorical Construction of the 'Turkish People,'" *Communication Studies* 61, no. 5 (Nov.–Dec. 2010): 485–506.

8. For instance, Erik Jan Zürcher, *The Unionist Factor: The Role of the Committee of Union and Progress in the Turkish Nationalist Movement 1905–1926* (Leiden, Netherlands: Brill, 1984). See also Erik-Jan Zürcher, "Ottoman Sources of Kemalist Thought," in *Late Ottoman Society: The Intellectual Legacy*, ed. Elisabeth Özdalga (New York: Routledge, 2005), 14–27.

9. Hayden White, "The Value of Narrativity in the Representation of Reality," *Critical Inquiry* 7, no. 1 (1980): 5–27.

10. Süleyman İnan, "The First 'History of the Turkish Revolution' Lectures and Courses in Turkish Universities (1934–42)," *Middle Eastern Studies* 43, no. 4 (2007): 594.

11. Foucault, *Archaeology of Knowledge*, 127. See also Thomas Osborne, "The Ordinariness of the Archive," *History of the Human Sciences* 12, no. 2 (1999): 51–64; Stuart Hall, "Constituting an Archive," *Third Text* 15, no. 54 (2001): 89–92. Foucault's *historical a priori* is similar to Charles Taylor's *social imaginary* insofar as both terms refer to a vast background of social understandings that is

the precondition of the thinkable or sayable. See Charles Taylor, *Modern Social Imaginaries* (Durham, NC: Duke Univ. Press, 2004).

12. Jacques Derrida, "Declarations of Independence," *New Political Science* 7, no. 1 (1986): 10. See also Bonnie Honig, "Declarations of Independence: Arendt and Derrida on the Problem of Founding a Republic," *American Political Science Review* 85, no. 1 (Mar. 1991): 97–113.

13. "Figures," as outlined in the introduction, are not ideological statements or instrumental narratives and are not, therefore, analogous to the familiar "six arrows" of Kemalist ideology (republicanism, populism, secularism, reformism, nationalism, and statism) or to Morin and Lee's "political myths." See Munis Tekinalp, *Kemalizm*, trans. Çetin Yetkin (1936; reprint, Istanbul: Toplumsal Dünüşüm Yayınları, 2004); Morin and Lee, "Constitutive Discourse of Turkish Nationalism," 492.

14. Carter Vaughn Findley, *Turkey, Islam, Nationalism, and Modernity: A History, 1789–2007* (New Haven, CT: Yale Univ. Press, 2010). Many of these same criticisms were voiced when the first Ottoman Constitution was adopted in 1876.

15. Atatürk, *A Speech Delivered by Ghazi Mustapha Kemal*, 717. The Progressive Republican Party existed for seven months in 1924–25 until its activities were outlawed (Zürcher, "Politician as Historian," 12).

16. Quoted in Atatürk, *A Speech Delivered by Ghazi Mustapha Kemal*, 123; see also 125, 138, 227.

17. Distinguishing between the sultan and the cabinet also broadly describes the waning political influence of the sultan since at least the Second Constitutional Period (1908–13), when most political decisions began to run through the cabinet. Of course, Kemal himself was a Young Turk and member of the CUP, the group primarily responsible for this restriction of the sultan's authority (Findley, *Turkey, Islam, Nationalism, and Modernity*, 198–99).

18. Atatürk, *A Speech Delivered by Ghazi Mustapha Kemal*, 194, 223, 315. These sections of *Nutuk* refer to the aftermath of the Ottoman Empire's defeat in World War I, when the Allies forced the Istanbul government to relinquish the vast majority of Ottoman territory, so that it ended up maintaining sovereignty over only a small section of Anatolia and the Black Sea region. The rest of the territory was divided among French, British, Italian, and Greek zones; a much larger independent Armenia; and an internationalized zone administered by the British around Istanbul and the Dardanelles. See Findley, *Turkey, Islam, Nationalism, and Modernity*, 219–20.

19. For other characterizations of the nationalist movement as a defender of the sanctity of the caliph's seat, see Atatürk, *A Speech Delivered by Ghazi Mustapha Kemal*, 215, 315, 319, 363, 373, 572.

20. The term *nation* in *Nutuk* refers to an amorphous polity composed of somewhat contradictory features of republicanism, populism, democracy, and popular sovereignty. The valence of the term *nation* in the speech resembles Rousseau's "general will" and Jacobin constructions of the people. See Hanioğlu, *Atatürk*, 109–10.

21. Atatürk, *A Speech Delivered by Ghazi Mustapha Kemal*, 310; see also 308, 309.

22. Atatürk, *A Speech Delivered by Ghazi Mustapha Kemal*, 246–47. Kemal quotes a telegram he sent to the Ottoman minister of war Ahmed Cemal Paşa in 1919.

23. It is important to note that despite the use of terms such as *sacred* and *salvation* in Kemal's characterization of the nation, I do not argue that the nation became a substitute for religion through the use of metaphor or that it came to fill religion's place in society. See Asad, *Formations of the Secular.*

24. Atatürk, *A Speech Delivered by Ghazi Mustapha Kemal*, 378.

25. Findley, *Turkey, Islam, Nationalism, and Modernity*, 135–37.

26. As discussed later in this chapter, it is likely that any territory that came under the authority of the nationalist army during the war of 1919–23 would have been deemed "national" territory in 1927. See also Abu El-Haj, *Facts on the Ground.*

27. Atatürk, *A Speech Delivered by Ghazi Mustapha Kemal*, 481.

28. Not only does Kemal subvert the authority of the sultan to that of the Grand National Assembly by associating the latter with the "nation," but he also supports his argument with a number of other maneuvers in the text. For instance, he distinguishes between the person who is sultan and the authority of that office (*A Speech Delivered by Ghazi Mustapha Kemal*, 481, 580) and argues that the Ottoman family is corrupt, incapable of leadership, and unfit for that office (577, 578, 580, 581, 586, 670). These arguments also imply that the nationalist movement seems to defend the sanctity of the sultan's office and has a conflict only with the person currently in power.

29. For a detailed narrative of Mehmet IV's departure, see Gingeras, *Fall of the Sultanate*, 1–2. Most of the officers and soldiers of the regular Ottoman army had long ago continued to follow Kemal's orders rather than the War Ministry's (Erik J. Zürcher, "Young Turk Memoirs as a Historical Source: Kâzım Karabekir's *İstiklâl Harbimiz*," in *The Young Turk Legacy*, 23–24).

30. Although the terms *caliph* and *sultan* had referred to the same person since the Ottoman monarch Selim I in 1517, *caliph* technically describes a religious teacher and leader of the worldwide *umma* (the community of Muslims who practice sharia), whereas *sultan* describes a sovereign monarch with moral and religious authority within Islam. The separation of these two titles constitutes an amalgamation of modern secular reform and premodern vocabulary.

31. Quoted in Atatürk, *A Speech Delivered by Ghazi Mustapha Kemal*, 584.

32. The tension between local political representation and global religious authority had been debated since at least 1909 (Nurullah Ardıç, *Islam and the Politics of Secularism: The Caliphate and Middle Eastern Modernization in the Early 20th Century* [New York: Routledge 2012], 171–72).

33. Atatürk, *A Speech Delivered by Ghazi Mustapha Kemal*, 595.

34. Atatürk, *A Speech Delivered by Ghazi Mustapha Kemal*, 670; see also 667, 669, 675.

35. Atatürk, *A Speech Delivered by Ghazi Mustapha Kemal*, 684; see also 717. Kemal quotes a speech he gave on the "fifth anniversary" of the opening of the Grand National Assembly in 1924. As Zürcher notes, the retroactive establishment of the meeting at Sivas in 1919, which occurred in the midst of the Independence War (1919–22), as the first session of the Grand National Assembly and first meeting of the CHP served clear instrumental ends for Kemal, making his party in 1927 a single, continuous entity with the whole of the nationalist movement (*Turkey*, 175).

36. Michael E. Meeker demonstrates that local-government structures from the Ottoman Empire continued to operate through the 1960s and continue to organize much local and rural governance today (*A Nation of Empire: The Ottoman Legacy of Turkish Modernity* [Berkeley: Univ. of California Press, 2002], 30–33, 38). Zürcher makes a similar point in Erik-Jan Zürcher, "The Vocabulary of Muslim Nationalism," *International Journal of the Sociology of Language* 137 (1999): 82.

37. To my knowledge, no published version of *Nutuk* in any language divides the text by day or indicates where breaks in speaking were taken. Clues in the text about where speaking may have restarted after a break are inconclusive (typically taking the form "Gentlemen . . ."). According to Zürcher, presentation of the speech typically lasted for approximately three hours in the morning, followed by a long lunch break, and continued again for three hours in the afternoon ("Politician as Historian," 7).

38. Atatürk, *A Speech Delivered by Ghazi Mustapha Kemal*, 717; see also 718, 719, 722.

39. Kemal rarely refers to Islam negatively and suggests his own faith and respect for Islam, if infrequently. See Atatürk, *A Speech Delivered by Ghazi Mustapha Kemal*, 373–74, where Kemal quotes a complete telegram in which he gives orders to military commanders to read the Koran to troops and to say prayers for the sultan, the nation, and the empire.

40. Despite the fact that Mustafa Kemal did not receive the surname "Atatürk" until 1934 (see note 1), this surname better describes the valence of the *idea* of Kemal in post-Ottoman Turkey, and I therefore use it to refer to the function or status of Mustafa Kemal in discourse: the "figure of Atatürk."

41. Atatürk, *A Speech Delivered by Ghazi Mustapha Kemal*, 9.

42. Adak, "National Myths and Self-Na(rra)tions," 516.

43. In a telegram addressed to the press, local governors, and military leaders in 1920, Kemal declares, "We shall have won the applause of mankind and shall pave the road to liberation which the Islamic world is yearning for, if we deliver the seat of the Caliphate from foreign influence and defend it with religious fidelity in a manner worthy of our glory and realize the independence of the nation" (quoted in Atatürk, *A Speech Delivered by Ghazi Mustapha Kemal*, 363). The Khilafat Movement (1920–24) in India accounted for an especially significant portion of the Turkish nationalists' finances during the Independence War. See Hanioğlu, *Atatürk*, 140–41; M. Naem Qureshi, *Pan-Islam in British Indian Politics: A Study of the Khilafat Movement, 1918–1924* (Leiden, Netherlands: Brill, 1999).

44. See also Hanioğlu, *Atatürk*, 140–41.

45. Rauf Orbay, quoted in Atatürk, *A Speech Delivered by Ghazi Mustapha Kemal*, 704. When Orbay referred to people who granted "to some other authority" the right of dissolving the Assembly and vetoing its resolutions, he was referring to a complex series of political maneuvers by Kemal that preceded the declaration of the Republic by the Turkish Grand National Assembly. As described in *Nutuk*, in 1923 Kemal convinced a number of his comrades (including Orbay) to resign their cabinet-level positions in Parliament either out of loyalty to Kemal or because of threats from him. This then forced the Assembly to dissolve. Kemal then reconstituted the cabinet of ministers with his closest allies in order to ensure approval of a motion to declare Turkey a republic and elect Kemal as its president.

46. Numerous other indications of confusion about Kemal's future role in a post-Ottoman government are given in Atatürk, *A Speech Delivered by Ghazi Mustapha Kemal*, 66, 227, 347, 469, 472, 476, 499, 501, 506, 508, 549, 554–55, 578, 581–83, 675.

47. Atatürk, *A Speech Delivered by Ghazi Mustapha Kemal*, 581.

48. Atatürk, *A Speech Delivered by Ghazi Mustapha Kemal*, 583. The complexity of this political moment cannot be overstated: Abdülmecid II's appointment as caliph occurred days before the peace negotiations at Lausanne, France, which ended the Turkish Independence War in 1922. Clarity *within* Turkey about the balance of power was critical to a strong negotiating position (and a single Turkish delegation) at Lausanne. See Atatürk, *A Speech Delivered by Ghazi Mustapha Kemal*, 585–87.

49. Erik J. Zürcher, "The Ottoman Legacy of the Kemalist Republic," in *The Young Turk Legacy*, 142.

50. Atatürk, *A Speech Delivered by Ghazi Mustapha Kemal*, 660–61. Other quotations of seemingly reasonable criticisms of Kemal can be found on 658, 707–8, and 715.

51. The analogy to the American constitutional process could also be tinged with a number of other historically situated political judgments. For instance, following the successful campaigns of Kemal's nationalist army after World War I, some prominent members of the nationalist movement supported an American mandate to help establish modern Turkey. Kemal sternly opposes such an alternative in *Nutuk* (*A Speech Delivered by Ghazi Mustapha Kemal*, 86–88).

52. For instance, Kemal states, "With regard to the Ottoman Empire, I had been convinced for a long time that it had run its course. An idea so utterly foolish as that I should accept the post of Grand Vizier of the Ottoman Empire would, of course, never have entered my head. While I was calmly and deliberately watching the natural course of the revolution, I had thought of nothing but the plans that would be necessary to adopt in the future" (Atatürk, *A Speech Delivered by Ghazi Mustapha Kemal*, 347; see also 379–80, 675–76).

53. Esra Özyürek, "Introduction: The Politics of Public Memory in Turkey," in *The Politics of Public Memory in Turkey*, ed. Esra Özyürek (Syracuse, NY: Syracuse Univ. Press, 2007), 4–5; Alev Çınar, *Modernity, Islam, and Secularism in Turkey: Bodies, Places, and Time* (Minneapolis: Univ. of Minnesota Press, 2005), 14–15.

54. Adak, "National Myths and Self-Na(rra)tions," 515.

55. William Hale, *Turkish Politics and the Military* (New York: Routledge, 1994), 79.

56. Hale, *Turkish Politics and the Military*, 79–80, quoting a CHP poster from the 1930s. The Independence War produced recognized national heroes (such as Kemal, İsmet İnönü, Fevzi Çakmak, Kazım Karabekir, Ali Fuat Cebesoy, Refet Bele, and others) who were hailed in public, helping to produce national consciousness after 1922 (Hale, *Turkish Politics and the Military*, 70, 75; Atatürk, *A Speech Delivered by Ghazi Mustapha Kemal*, 74).

57. Zürcher, "Ottoman Legacy of the Kemalist Republic," 149. Enver Paşa stationed a mass of troops in eastern Anatolia in the closing weeks of World War I, where they would be relatively safe from attack. Enver planned to use these troops for Turanist campaigns into Central Asia following the war. See Dankwart A. Rustow, "The Army and the Founding of the Turkish Republic," *World Politics* 11, no. 4 (1959): 538, 541.

58. One well-known guerilla leader, Çerkes Ethem (Ethem the Circasian, discussed in Atatürk, *A Speech Delivered by Ghazi Mustapha Kemal*, 384, 424–27, 461–62), won a number of battles against both the Greeks and the sultan's army (which had been sent against the nationalists) and established a small fiefdom in western Anatolia by 1920. When Ethem refused to take orders from Kemal, he was forced out of his command (eventually joining the Greeks), and his soldiers joined the Turkish nationalist army in 1921. See Hale, *Turkish Politics and the Military*,

66; Rustow, "The Army and the Founding of the Turkish Republic," 546; Benjamin C. Fortna, *The Circassian: The Life of Eşref Bey, Late Ottoman Insurgent and Special Agent* (New York: Oxford Univ. Press, 2016).

59. Quoted in Atatürk, *A Speech Delivered by Ghazi Mustapha Kemal*, 45.

60. Kemal dismisses the commander of the Fifteenth Division in western Anatolia as "entertain[ing] strong feelings toward the Sultan" when the commander writes to Kemal: "I feel sure that on the day following the outbreak of hostilities there will not be a trace left of the national forces. With regard to the regular troops, desertions have already taken place. As there is no money forthcoming and as there is still a Government in Istanbul, I am very doubtful also about the officers" (Atatürk, *A Speech Delivered by Ghazi Mustapha Kemal*, 370, 371).

61. An assumed consistency between the military of 1919 and the military of 1927 could serve numerous instrumental purposes for Kemal, including reinforcing Kemal as the sole leader of the nationalist movement because he remained the leader of the Turkish Armed Forces in 1927; strengthening patriotism toward and support of the armed forces in 1927 because they liberated the Republic; continued marginalization of former generals who had fallen out with Kemal, left the military, and therefore weren't associated with the armed forces that defend the fatherland; and so on. Tracing broad instrumental purposes is methodologically suspect because it presumes access to the speaker's consciousness and unstated motives, and this section focuses on the textual rhetorical effect of the figure of the military.

62. Intellectual elites had debated Ottoman state identity since the late nineteenth century, with competing notions of Pan-Islamism, Ottomanism, Turanism, and Turkish nationalism as the primary ideologies. Pan-Islamism advocated a unification of the Muslim world under the sultan-caliph (Findley, *Turkey, Islam, Nationalism, and Modernity*, 149; see also Cemil Aydın, *The Idea of the Muslim World: A Global Intellectual History* [Cambridge, MA: Harvard Univ. Press, 2017]). Ottomanism sought community autonomy for the three main religious groups (Jews, Christians, and Muslims) subordinated to the authority of the sultan (Findley, *Turkey, Islam, Nationalism, and Modernity*, 100; M. Şükrü Hanioğlu, *A Brief History of the Late Ottoman Empire* [Princeton, NJ: Princeton Univ. Press, 2008], 188). Turanism, or pan-Turkism, advocated unifying "Turkic" peoples of Central Asia (Tatars, Azeris, Turkmen, Kyrgyz, Khazaks, and others) in an ideal future homeland: Turan (Hanioğlu, *Brief History*, 188). Turkish nationalism sought to unify a much smaller ethnoreligious community, which nevertheless included Kurds, Circasians, Alevis, and others (Findley, *Turkey, Islam, Nationalism, and Modernity*, 254–57). See also Kemal H. Karpat, *The Politicization of Islam: Reconstructing Identity, State, Faith, and Community in the Late Ottoman State* (New York: Oxford Univ. Press, 2001); Kemal H. Karpat, ed., *Ottoman Past and Today's Turkey* (Boston: Brill, 2000); Şerif Mardin, *The Genesis of Young*

Ottoman Thought: A Study in the Modernization of Turkish Political Ideas (Princeton, NJ: Princeton Univ. Press, 1962); and Zürcher, *The Young Turk Legacy*.

63. Findley, *Turkey, Islam, Nationalism, and Modernity*, 220. The location of the capital of Turkey at Ankara (a town of twenty thousand in 1923) is the result of a number of strategic considerations associated with this postwar power arrangement. Anatolia was relatively free from foreign-troop presence, thereby making it a safer location to organize a resistance movement than Istanbul, which was home to the sultan and occupied by the British. Ankara was also located along the route of the main rail and telegraph lines to Istanbul.

64. Atatürk, *A Speech Delivered by Ghazi Mustapha Kemal*, 24.

65. Quoted in Atatürk, *A Speech Delivered by Ghazi Mustapha Kemal*, 24.

66. Quoted in Atatürk, *A Speech Delivered by Ghazi Mustapha Kemal*, 25.

67. See Atatürk, *A Speech Delivered by Ghazi Mustapha Kemal*, 19, 60–61, 139, 217, 233, 411, 435, 522, 665–66.

68. Quoted in Atatürk, *A Speech Delivered by Ghazi Mustapha Kemal*, 146. Kastamonu Province extended along the Black Sea coast in northwestern Anatolia, bordering Istanbul Province to the west and Ankara Province to the south.

69. Atatürk, *A Speech Delivered by Ghazi Mustapha Kemal*, 146.

70. Other instances where Kemal quotes documents that suggest a simultaneity of address and constitution of a Turkish national people include pages 29, 192, 246–47, and 523 in *A Speech Delivered by Ghazi Mustapha Kemal*.

71. Derrida, "Declarations of Independence," 9–11. See also Louis Althusser, "Ideology and Ideological State Apparatus (Notes toward an Investigation)," in *Lenin and Philosophy and Other Essays*, trans. Ben Brewster (1971; reprint, New York: Monthly Review Press 2001), 85–126; and Maurice Charland, "Constitutive Rhetoric: The Case of the *Peuple Québécois*," *Quarterly Journal of Speech* 73, no. 2 (1987): 133–50.

72. Atatürk, *A Speech Delivered by Ghazi Mustapha Kemal*, 568; see also 55, 58, 120, 121, 138, 301, 320, 329, 342, 363, 580.

73. In a similar way, the presumed continuity between the Sivas Congress, the early legislative meetings in Ankara, and the Turkish Grand National Assembly helped mitigate the newness of the people by suggesting a consistent means of their representation (Zürcher, *Turkey*, 178; see also Atatürk, *A Speech Delivered by Ghazi Mustapha Kemal*, 168).

74. Atatürk, *A Speech Delivered by Ghazi Mustapha Kemal*, 521.

75. Atatürk, *A Speech Delivered by Ghazi Mustapha Kemal*, 349–51. Thrace encompasses all of contemporary European Turkey and parts of contemporary Greece and Bulgaria. Bulgaria became independent in 1908 after operating as an autonomous region of the Ottoman Empire since 1878 (Zürcher, *Turkey*, 75, 356–58; Findley, *Turkey, Islam, Nationalism, and Modernity*, 205).

76. Quoted in Atatürk, *A Speech Delivered by Ghazi Mustapha Kemal*, 351. *Nutuk* also details how Kemal insisted that the official title of the Turkish nationalist organizations include the name "Rumelia" (an area extending much farther west than Thrace)—for example, becoming "Union for the Defense of Rights of Anatolia and Rumelia" (Atatürk, *A Speech Delivered by Ghazi Mustapha Kemal*, 77). Rumelia historically refers to all Ottoman territories in Europe. Kemal was born in Thessaloniki (contemporary Greece) and participated in Young Turk political activities from there prior to 1908 (A. L. Macfie, *Atatürk* [New York: Longman, 1994], 11–35; Zürcher, *Turkey*, 9).

77. Military circumstances in eastern Anatolia also influenced national borders in eastern and southeastern Turkey, as Kemal insists on the national character and thus indivisibility of land occupied by the Armenian army but quickly cedes everything south and east of Hatay Province to France to avoid conflict (Atatürk, *A Speech Delivered by Ghazi Mustapha Kemal*, 333, 415).

78. See Abu El-Haj, *Facts on the Ground*; Sahlins, *Boundaries*; Aslı Gür, "Stories in Three Dimensions: Narratives of Nation and the Anatolian Civilizations Museum," in *Politics of Public Memory in Turkey*, ed. Özyürek, 40–69; Tuğba Tanyeri-Erdemir, "Archaeology as a Source of National Pride in the Early Years of the Turkish Republic," *Journal of Field Archaeology* 31, no. 4 (2006): 381–93.

79. As mentioned in note 35, Kemal retroactively claims the Sivas Congress as the first meeting of the CHP (the party he organized in 1924) (Zürcher, *Turkey*, 178).

80. Atatürk, *Nutuk I*, in *Atatürk'ün bütün eserleri*, 19:80, my translation; see the published translation in Atatürk, *Speech Delivered by Ghazi Mustapha Kemal*, 77.

81. Atatürk, *A Speech Delivered by Ghazi Mustapha Kemal*, 421.

82. Atatürk, *A Speech Delivered by Ghazi Mustapha Kemal*, 522.

83. Atatürk, *A Speech Delivered by Ghazi Mustapha Kemal*, 521, my emphasis.

84. Yakup Bektas, "The Sultan's Messenger: Cultural Constructions of Ottoman Telegraphy, 1847–1880," *Technology and Culture* 41, no. 4 (2000): 674. The railroad ran along a parallel route. This overland telegraph route was devised and constructed in part by the British and French in the mid–nineteenth century as a reliable method of connecting London and Paris to these empires' Indian and Southeast Asian colonies.

85. Bektas, "The Sultan's Messenger," 674.

86. The importance of telegraph operators' loyalty was not lost on Kemal; see Atatürk, *A Speech Delivered by Ghazi Mustapha Kemal*, 167. The everyday *telgrafçı* (telegraph operator) is a common supporting motif in the official history of the nationalist movement. See, for instance, A. Gökoğlu, *Inkilâbımızda posta ve telgrafçılar* [Postal and telegraph workers during our revolution] (Istanbul: N.p., 1938).

87. Atatürk, *A Speech Delivered by Ghazi Mustapha Kemal*, 187; see also 231. Regarding Kemal's control of the communications network, Roderic H. Davison quotes a *Chicago Daily News* correspondent who was traveling with Kemal in 1919: "I have never heard of more efficient communications than I witnessed that night. Within half an hour [Erzurum], [Erzincan], Mosul, [Diyarbakır], Samsun, [Trabzon], [Ankara], [Malatya], [Elazığ], [Konya], and [Bursa] were all in communication by wire with Sivas. [Mustafa] Kemal sat at one end of the wire leading to all these places and at the other end[s] sat the military commander and civil authorities of the respective cities and vilayets" (Lewis Edgar Browne, *Chicago Daily News*, Oct. 13, 1919, dispatch datelined Paris, Oct. 13, quoted in Roderic H. Davison, "The Advent of the Electric Telegraph in the Ottoman Empire," in *Essays in Ottoman and Turkish History, 1774–1923: The Impact of the West* [Austin: Univ. of Texas Press, 1990], 157).

88. Atatürk, *A Speech Delivered by Ghazi Mustapha Kemal*, 525; see also 212, 217–18.

89. Atatürk, *A Speech Delivered by Ghazi Mustapha Kemal*, 17.

90. In *The Origins of Totalitarianism* (New York: Harcourt, 1973), Hannah Arendt describes the "stateless people" after World War I, minorities without legal recourse to a "home" state, a nation, or a nationality (276). See also Asad, *Formations of the Secular*, 129. The concept of the peopleless state perhaps resembles the power described in Giorgio Agamben, *State of Exception*, trans. Kevin Attell (Chicago: Univ. of Chicago Press, 2005). Ryan Gingeras alludes to a similar understanding of Atatürk's Turkey, quoting President Recep Tayyip Erdoğan's critique in 2015 of the single-party era (1923–45) as "a democracy without the people" (*Eternal Dawn: Turkey in the Age of Atatürk* [New York: Oxford Univ. Press 2019], 13).

91. Atatürk, *A Speech Delivered by Ghazi Mustapha Kemal*, 20.

92. Quoted in Atatürk, *A Speech Delivered by Ghazi Mustapha Kemal*, 578.

93. Andrew Mango, *Atatürk* (London: John Murray, 1999), 461. Kemal probably made the selection of historical documents used in *Nutuk* during the summer of 1927 at Dolmabahçe Palace in Istanbul, his first return to the city since he left for Samsun in 1919.

94. Adak, "National Myths and Self-Na(rra)tions," 514.

95. Perhaps the most prominent scholarly example of a text that produces the authority of *Nutuk* by using it as an archive is Bernard Lewis, *The Emergence of Modern Turkey* (London: Oxford Univ. Press, 1961). Large portions of Lewis's text rely *only* on *Nutuk* as a source for information on the early nationalist movement. For a more thorough critique of Lewis's work, including the way his modernization paradigm helped reproduce Kemalist ideology, see Erik J. Zürcher, "The Rise and Fall of 'Modern' Turkey: Bernard Lewis's *Emergence* Fifty Years On," in *The*

Young Turk Legacy, 50–52. See also Edward W. Said, *Orientalism* (New York: Vintage Books, 1978), 314–21.

96. This resembles what Derrida calls "a sort of fabulous retroactivity" ("Declarations of Independence," 10).

2. The Figure of Religion in the Transition to Multiparty Democracy

1. Eve McPherson, "Political History and Embodied Identity Discourse in the Turkish Call to Prayer," *Music and Politics* 5, no. 1 (2011): 7; Geoffrey Lewis, *The Turkish Language Reform: A Catastrophic Success* (New York: Oxford Univ. Press, 1999), 46. Theoretically, the *ezan* in Turkey continues to be unique from the *ezan* in other regions because of its melodic style and notation.

2. McPherson, "Political History and Embodied Identity Discourse," 7.

3. Hidayet Aydar and Necmettin Gökkır, "Discussions on the Language of Prayer in Turkey: A Modern Version of the Classical Debate," *Turkish Studies* 8, no. 1 (2007): 129. The "enlightened" imams whom Mustafa Kemal put in charge of producing an authoritative Turkish translation of the Koran in 1932 were unable to make any progress by the following year, and so the translation efforts were abandoned.

4. Umut Azak, "Secularism in Turkey as a Nationalist Search for Vernacular Islam: The Ban on the Call to Prayer in Arabic (1932–1950)," *Revue des mondes Musulmans et de la Méditerranée* 124 (2008): 161–79. See also Aydar and Gökkır, "Discussions on the Language of Prayer in Turkey." In 1932, most Turks had a very rudimentary knowledge of Arabic, and therefore use of Arabic in Turkish mosques added a mystical quality to religious practice (Kemal H. Karpat, *Turkey's Politics: The Transition to a Multi-party System* [Princeton, NJ: Princeton Univ. Press, 1959], 286). According to the liberal Hanafi school of Sunni Islam (official Turkish Islam), translations of the Koran should be used only to aid worship before the believer knows Arabic fluently because these translations are only approximations of God's own words.

5. McPherson, "Political History and Embodied Identity Discourse," 7.

6. Some of these arrests led to hospitalization in the mental asylum as protesters were labeled *ezan çılgınları*, "call-to-prayer lunatics" (Azak, "Secularism in Turkey," 176; McPherson, "Political History and Embodied Identity Discourse," 7).

7. For instance, "Ramazanı şerif bugün başladı," *Yeni Sabah*, June 17, 1950; "Arabça [*sic*] ezan dün kabul edildi," *Yeni Sabah*, June 17, 1950; "Ezanı Arapça okuma yasağı kalktı," *Hürriyet*, June 17, 1950; "Meclis, Arapça ezanı kabul etti," *Vatan*, June 17, 1950; "Arapça ezan okuma yasağı kaldırıldı," *Ulus*, June 17, 1950. In 1950, *Ulus* was the official newspaper of the newly oppositional CHP.

8. Ufuk Ulutaş, "Religion and Secularism in Turkey: The Dilemma of the Directorate of Religious Affairs," *Middle Eastern Studies* 46, no. 3 (2010): 393; John M. VanderLippe, *The Politics of Turkish Democracy: İsmet İnönü and the Formation of the Multi-party System, 1938–1950* (Albany: State Univ. of New York Press, 2005), 192; Ahmet T. Kuru, *Secularism and State Policies toward Religion: The United States, France, and Turkey* (New York: Cambridge Univ. Press, 2009), 228.

9. Findley, *Turkey, Islam, Nationalism, Modernity*, 252–53. Mandates about women's clothing were deemed too risky to be codified into law at this time, although Atatürk repeatedly encouraged women to abandon head scarves and veils (Gingeras, *Eternal Dawn*, 163). Although this chapter discusses events both before and after the surname law in 1934, surnames adopted after the law are used.

10. McPherson, "Political History and Embodied Identity Discourse," 7. Penalties for reciting the Arabic *ezan* were not codified until 1941, at which point enforcement increased.

11. Lewis, *Turkish Language Reform*, 57. Although the Sun-Language Theory was not officially codified until 1936, some of its major themes were clear as early as 1923 (Lewis, *Turkish Language Reform*, 40–41).

12. Hannah Arendt, *On Revolution* (1963; reprint, New York: Penguin Books, 2006), 133. In Arendt's work, "freedom" refers to the ability of individuals to act together in public, to construct and enact a common world with one another. Therefore, the "foundation of freedom" references the political and juridical apparatuses that secure individuals' continuing ability to act in concert. See also Arendt, *On Revolution*, 167, and Hannah Arendt, *The Human Condition*, 2nd ed. (Chicago: Univ. of Chicago Press, 1998).

13. Michel Foucault, "Governmentality," in *The Foucault Effect: Studies in Governmentality: With Two Lectures and an Interview with Michel Foucault*, ed. Graham Burchell, Colin Gordon, and Peter Miller (Chicago: Univ. of Chicago Press, 1991), 97, 100.

14. Benjamin Moffit's theory of the "political style" of populism is analogous in some ways to my argument here. See Benjamin Moffitt, *The Global Rise of Populism: Performance, Political Style, and Representation* (Stanford, CA: Stanford Univ. Press, 2016). See also Hariman, *Political Style.*

15. Zürcher, *Turkey*, 168, 187.

16. Bryan S. Turner and Berna Zengin Arslan, "State and Turkish Secularism: The Case of the Diyanet," in Bryan S. Turner, *The Religious and the Political: A Comparative Sociology of Religion* (New York: Cambridge Univ. Press, 2013), 211–14. The directorate later became its own ministry with a corresponding name change: Diyanet İşleri Başkanlığı.

17. Turner and Arslan, "State and Turkish Secularism," 213–14.

18. Geoffrey Lewis, *Turkey*, 3rd ed. (London: Ernest Benn, 1965), 182.

19. Findley, *Turkey, Islam, Nationalism, and Modernity*, 252. As Findley notes (253), the title of the education law, Unification of Instruction Law (Tevhid-I Tedrisat), constituted a "materialist assault" on Islam because the term for unification used in the title of the law, *tevhid*, previously referred only to God's unity and believers' affirmation of that unity.

20. Findley, *Turkey, Islam, Nationalism, and Modernity*, 252. The Constitution of the Turkish Republic was not amended until 1928 to remove the statement that pledged government support of the *şeriat* courts. By 1928, this was essentially a pro forma amendment.

21. Umut Azak, *Islam and Secularism in Turkey: Kemalism, Religion, and the Nation State* (New York: I. B. Tauris, 2010), 51.

22. Yılmaz, *Becoming Turkish*, 143–49; Zürcher, *Turkey*, 188–89. The law required shop signs, newspapers, magazines, and ads to use the new letters by December 1928 and prohibited the use of all Arabic script in public beginning on January 1, 1929. Private correspondence with the government had to be adapted to Latin script by June 1929, when state employees also had to be literate in the new alphabet.

23. Lewis, *Turkish Language Reform*, 2. Although Western writers refer to the Turkish-language "reform," the Turkish phrase for this series of reforms is *dil devrimi*, "language revolution." The Turkish Language Society reforms abated in 1950 but resumed in the 1960s and continued through the 1980s. They technically continue today but at a much less aggressive pace.

24. Yılmaz, *Becoming Turkish*, 140–41. Many neologisms did not take root, and by 1935 the Turkish Language Society began inventing etymologies for commonly used Persian or Arabic words, arguing that these words had been originally borrowed by Arabic or Persian speakers from ancient Turkish, then borrowed back by Turkish speakers. This theory depended heavily on the influence of the Sun-Language Theory. See Soner Çağaptay, "Race, Assimilation, and Kemalism: Turkish Nationalism and the Minorities in the 1930s," *Middle East Studies* 40, no. 3 (2004): 91–92.

25. As the commission tasked with alphabet reform explained in 1928, "In order to save the nation from illiteracy and ignorance, there is no solution other than to abandon the Arab letters that do not suit her language and to adopt Turkish letters taken from the Latin alphabet" (translated and quoted in Yılmaz, *Becoming Turkish*, 144). To an appreciable extent, the Ottoman Turkish alphabet was indeed incomprehensible to a large majority of people in 1928 in a country with a 10 percent literacy rate (Findley, *Turkey, Islam, Nationalism, and Modernity*, 283).

26. Lewis, *Turkish Language Reform*, 3–4. In 1935, the Turkish Language Society produced the *Ottoman-Turkish Pocket Guide*, listing Turkish replacements for Arabic and Persian words (Çağaptay, "Race, Assimilation, and Kemalism," 91).

27. Senem Aslan, "'Citizen, Speak Turkish!': A Nation in the Making," *Nationalism and Ethnic Politics* 13, no. 2 (2007): 250–53. The Ministry of Education provided a thousand Turkish lira for this campaign. The Turkish Hearths (Türk Ocağı) were a network of state- and party-run civil associations originally founded in 1911 and revived in 1924, which consisted of meeting houses throughout the country and served a wide range of functions, including adult education in agricultural skills, literacy, and Kemalist and nationalist ideology. The Hearths were closed in 1931 and replaced with the People's Houses (Halk Evleri) and People's Rooms (Halk Odası), which were more directly controlled by Atatürk's CHP for the purpose of promoting national unity (and educating the adult population). The meeting houses were closed at the height of the Cold War, in 1950, owing both to opposition parties' complaints that they were institutions for controlling election results and to suspicion that they had begun to promote communism in the countryside. See Kemal H. Karpat, "The People's Houses in Turkey: Establishment and Growth," *Middle East Journal* 17, nos. 1–2 (1963): 55–67; VanderLippe, *The Politics of Turkish Democracy*, 17–18; Lamprou, *Nation-Building in Modern Turkey.*

28. Filiz Meşeci Giorgetti, "Nation-Building in Turkey through Ritual Pedagogy: The Late Ottoman and Early Turkish Republican Era," *History of Education* 49, no. 1 (2020): 77–103.

29. The development of nationalist-oriented academic disciplines and institutional organizations was significantly influenced by Ziya Gökalp's social theory, leading to a kind of parallelism in discipline-specific narratives of self-understanding. For instance, many social sciences and humanities disciplines focused on the Central Asian origin of their diverse objects of study. See Ziya Gökalp, *Turkish Nationalism and Western Civilization: Selected Essays of Ziya Gökalp*, trans. and ed. Niyazi Berkes (London: Allen and Unwin, 1959); Mardin, *The Genesis of Young Ottoman Thought*; Taha Parla, *Social and Political Thought of Ziya Gökalp, 1876–1924* (Leiden, Netherlands: Brill, 1985). See also Michel Foucault, *The Order of Things: An Archaeology of the Human Sciences* (1970; reprint, New York: Vintage Books, 1990).

30. John Morgan O'Connell, "Fine Art, Fine Music: Controlling Turkish Taste at the Fine Arts Academy in 1926," *Yearbook for Traditional Music* 32 (2000): 117; see also 118, 136. The classicization of Turkish folk music during this period relied heavily on Mahmud Ragip Gazimihâl's universalist theory of music history, which posited the Central Asian origin of all world folk musics, paralleling the Sun-Language Theory. See John Morgan O'Connell, "In the Time of Alaturka: Identifying Difference in Musical Discourse," *Ethnomusicology* 49, no. 2 (2005): 177–205.

31. Aslan, "'Citizen, Speak Turkish!,'" 246. Although the extent of reform efforts in the Republic's first decade is indeed vast, scholars have noted the ways in

which many state policies were designed to mitigate their own impact on the majority of the population (Anatolian villagers) through either lax enforcement or local reinterpretation. See, for example, Gavin D. Brockett, "Collective Action and the Turkish Revolution: Towards a Framework for the Social History of the Atatürk Era, 1923–38," *Middle Eastern Studies* 34, no. 4 (1998): 60–61.

32. McPherson, "Political History and Embodied Identity Discourse," 5. The chairman of the committee that issued these recommendations, Fuat Köprülü, was one of the founding members of the DP in 1946 (Azak, *Islam and Secularism in Turkey*, 53). A full translation of the committee's recommendations for religious reform as published in *Vakit* can be found in Lutfy Levonian, ed. and trans., *The Turkish Press: Selections from the Turkish Press Showing Events and Opinions, 1925–1932* (Athens: School of Religion, 1932), 124–26.

33. Azak, *Islam and Secularism in Turkey*, 52.

34. Azak, *Islam and Secularism in Turkey*, 54. *Hafız* is the honorific title for someone who has memorized the entire Koran.

35. "70 bin kisinin [*sic*] iştirak ettiği dinî merasim," *Cumhuriyet*, Feb. 4, 1932; "Dün geceki dinî ihtifal," *Akşam*, Feb. 4, 1932. *Cumhuriyet* reported forty thousand people inside Ayasofya and thirty thousand who could not get in and so filled the squares outside the mosque. See also Azak, *Islam and Secularism in Turkey*, 55. *Akşam* reported on numerous readings of the Turkish Koran in January and February 1932 both in Istanbul and elsewhere. See "İlk Türkçe Kuran dün Yerebatan Camiinde okundu," *Akşam*, Jan. 23, 1932; "Dün de bir çok camilerde Türkçe Kuran okundu," *Akşam*, Jan. 25, 1932; "Bugün hangi camilerde Türkçe Kur'an okunacak?," *Akşam*, Jan. 26, 1932; "Sultan Ahmet Camii erkenden dolmağa başladı," *Akşam*, Jan. 29, 1932.

36. Azak, *Islam and Secularism in Turkey*, 56–57.

37. Howard A. Reed, "Turkey's New İmam-Hatip Schools," *Die Welt des Islams* 4, nos. 2–3 (1955): 151. See also VanderLippe, *The Politics of Turkish Democracy*, 191. As discussed later in this chapter, the lack of religious education in Turkey from 1934 to 1948 led to a considerable personnel crisis for mosques in the countryside by 1950.

38. Necmeddin [*sic*] Sadık, "Taassup ve tesamüh," *Akşam*, July 3, 1929; unless otherwise noted, translations of Turkish text are my own.

39. Azak, "Secularism in Turkey," 177.

40. Findley, *Turkey, Islam, Nationalism, and Modernity*, 251. The Law for the Maintenance of Order came as a response to the separatist Kurdish Şeyh Said Rebellion, and it was used to justify mass arrests and consolidate Atatürk's power. See also Zürcher, *Turkey*, 171–73.

41. İsmet İnönü, speech, reprinted in "Başvekil Pş. Hazretlerinin nutku," *Hakimiyeti Milliye*, Mar. 5, 1929. Minister of Justice Mahmut Esat Bozkurt expressed

a similar sentiment in an editorial in 1928, where he argued that the "proper place" of religion is "the sanctuary of men's consciences" and that "the only way to safeguard religion . . . is to separate it totally from the affairs of the State" (Mahmut Esat Bozkurt, untitled article, *İkdam Gazetesi*, Mar. 27, 1928, in *The Turkish Press*, ed. Levonian, 129). See also İstar B. Gözaydın, "*Diyanet* and Politics," *Muslim World* 98, nos. 2–3 (2008): 217.

42. Azak, "Secularism in Turkey," 162. During the early Republic, Kemalist understanding of Islam heavily emphasized Ziya Gökalp's argument that the entire Protestant Reformation "imitated Islamic civilization and religion," especially in its rejection of the priesthood (quoted in Charles Kurzman and Michaelle Browers, "Introduction: Comparing Reformations," in *An Islamic Reformation?*, ed. Michaelle Browers and Charles Kurzman [Lanham, MD: Lexington Books, 2004], 4).

43. Aydar and Gökkir, "Discussions on the Language of Prayer in Turkey," 128, citing *İkdam Gazetesi*, Apr. 8, 1926. Similarly, Umut Azak argues that the concept of *irtica* (reactionary Islam) structured republican response to protest movements and the ulema (*Islam and Secularism in Turkey*, 14–16).

44. See also Mahmood Mamdani, *Good Muslim, Bad Muslim: America, the Cold War, and the Roots of Terror* (New York: Pantheon, 2004). Discouraging public expression of religion should not be understood as privatizing religion in Turkey. The activities of the Diyanet helped and continue to help maintain the distinction between legitimate and illegitimate religious expression. See Andrew Davison, "Turkey, a 'Secular' State? The Challenge of Description," *South Atlantic Quarterly* 102, nos. 2–3 (Spring–Summer 2003): 333–50.

45. Azak, "Secularism in Turkey," 165.

46. Yunus Nadi [Abalıoğlu], "Çok ruhanî bir kadir gecesi," *Cumhuriyet*, Feb. 4, 1932.

47. Nadi, "Çok ruhanî bir kadir gecesi."

48. Law 4055, translated and quoted in Azak, "Secularism in Turkey," 175. Until 1941, violations of the ban on the Arabic *ezan* were prosecuted according to a general law against breaking laws, and punishments were therefore very inconsistent.

49. Brockett, "Collective Action and the Turkish Revolution," 48. The Şeyh Said Rebellion of 1925 was a month-long separatist rebellion in southeastern Turkey led by a Kurdish religious leader that was quelled by the Turkish army through bombing campaigns and ground troops. The Menemen Incident is a highly contentious topic in Turkish historiography, and agreed-upon facts state that a crowd was led (or forced) through the streets of Menemen by Giritli (Cretan) Mehmet, who later decapitated a Turkish reserve officer in the square after one of Mehmet's accomplices shot and injured the officer. The prosecutions that followed this incident resulted in the execution of twenty-eight people, and the Menemen Incident was labeled an instance of the continuing radicalism of the Nakşibendi sect. The Bursa

protest followed the first recitation of the Turkish *ezan* in Bursa in 1933, when a group of people gathered outside the local office of the Directorate of Pious Foundations to register their disapproval of the *ezan* law. Numerous "reactionaries" were arrested following this event, and Mustafa Kemal personally visited Bursa in the days following the arrests.

50. *Vakit*, June 20, 1928, translated and reprinted in *The Turkish Press*, ed. Levonian, 124–26.

51. VanderLippe, *The Politics of Turkish Democracy*, 112. Statism was an early form of import substitution industrialization, which emphasized the development of state-owned or state-subsidized industry to encourage a "national economy." "Statism" is one of the six "arrows" of Kemalist ideology, along with republicanism, secularism, nationalism, populism, and reformism/revolutionism, which were codified in the CHP program in 1935. In accordance with the language reforms, the CHP also revised its name in 1935 from Cumhuriyet Halk Fırkası to Cumhuriyet Halk Partisi, to use the "modern" Turkish word for a political party. For the official English translation of the CHP program of 1935, see Suna Kili, *Kemalism* (Istanbul: Robert College School of Business Administration, 1969), 76–79.

52. VanderLippe, *The Politics of Turkish Democracy*, 83. Although Turkey did not declare war on Germany and Japan until February 1945 (when it was clear the Allies would win), and although Turkish troops did not fight in World War II, the Turkish government incurred the cost of the defensive mobilization of the Turkish army that began nearly at the outbreak of hostilities in Europe.

53. The Wealth Tax had devastating effects on minority businesses in Turkey. Among the numerous problems with the law, assessment methods were determined by local taxing authorities based on presumptions about each person's wealth, leading to widely varying assessments of tax burden and enforcement. Inability to pay fines led to imprisonment in a labor camp. The law was officially repealed in February 1944, but collection ceased and anyone imprisoned under the law was released in November 1943 (VanderLippe, *The Politics of Turkish Democracy*, 84–85; see also Seven Ağır and Cihan Artunç, "The Wealth Tax of 1942 and the Disappearance of Non-Muslim Enterprises in Turkey," *Journal of Economic History* 79, no. 1 [2019]: 201–43).

54. VanderLippe, *The Politics of Turkish Democracy*, 86.

55. VanderLippe, *The Politics of Turkish Democracy*, 86. Under the Land Products Tax, smaller farmers were often forced to take unrepayable loans from large landholders, which eventually meant that they had to sell their farms to the landowners who had made the loans.

56. VanderLippe, *The Politics of Turkish Democracy*, 115. By 1947, only a very small amount of private land had been redistributed under the law (the emphasis had been on distribution of public land), and the law was altered in 1947 to

meet the demands of newly formed opposition parties (VanderLippe, *The Politics of Turkish Democracy*, 121).

57. Feroz Ahmad, *The Turkish Experiment in Democracy, 1950–1975* (Boulder, CO: Westview Press, 1977), 8–10. Ahmad also suggests that the Land Reform Law of 1945 constituted a last-ditch effort by the conservative wing of the CHP to eliminate the only significant opposition to its policies, the Anatolian landholders.

58. VanderLippe, *The Politics of Turkish Democracy*, 120.

59. Karpat, *Turkey's Politics*, 145.

60. Karpat, *Turkey's Politics*, 146. The CHP Parliamentary Group rejected the memorandum, saying that it proposed the revision of existing law and therefore that the Assembly and not the Parliamentary Group was the appropriate place for the proposal. In a one-party system, the Assembly and the CHP Parliamentary Group were made up of the same people.

61. The DP was not the first opposition party formed in the multiparty period, nor was it the first opposition party in Turkey's history. The Progressive Republican Party (1924–25) and the Free Republican Party (Serbest Cumhuriyet Fırkası, 1930) were short-lived early attempts to establish a multiparty system, and the National Development Party (Millî Kalkınma Partisi, later the Nation Party, 1945–58) was formed five months before the DP and played an important role in the elections of 1950. See VanderLippe, *The Politics of Turkish Democracy*, 121, 175–76, 185.

62. VanderLippe, *The Politics of Turkish Democracy*, 141–43.

63. VanderLippe, *The Politics of Turkish Democracy*, 143. Bayar thought the DP actually won 279 seats.

64. Before 1950, there was no distinction between CHP officials and government election commissioners (or any other state official), especially after twenty-five years of single-party administration of the state. This led to widespread election fraud. In February 1950, however, a new election law created panels of judges and lawyers to oversee the election results all over the country (VanderLippe, *The Politics of Turkish Democracy*, 195).

65. Metin Heper, *İsmet İnönü: The Making of a Turkish Statesman* (Boston: Brill, 1998), 184, summarizing İsmet İnönü, "July 12 Declaration," July 11, 1947, (the declaration is named for the day of its publication in newspapers). The declaration marked İnönü's support for the existence of opposition parties.

66. As VanderLippe points out, one can easily correlate Turkish politicians' emphasis on democracy and free elections with the rapid escalation of the Cold War and Turkey's early commitment to the American side through a Treaty of Assistance in 1947 (signed one day after İnönü's "July 12 Declaration") (*The Politics of Turkish Democracy*, 151–87).

67. Ahmad, *The Turkish Experiment in Democracy*, 27. Beginning in 1946, to try to undercut support for the DP, the CHP argued that no difference existed

between it and the DP. Similarity of party platform resulted in part from the necessity that the DP include the "six arrows" of Kemalism (see note 51 in this chapter) in its party platform to avoid seeming treasonous (Ahmad, *The Turkish Experiment in Democracy*, 13–14). The ban on wearing turbans and fezzes in public resulted from a law passed in 1925 that banned religious clothing for men and mandated the use of the Western-style brimmed hat (Findley, *Turkey, Islam, Nationalism, and Modernity*, 252). In 1947, more than five hundred people were arrested for wearing illegal headgear (Mehmet Yaşar Geyikdağı, *Political Parties in Turkey: The Role of Islam* [New York: Praeger, 1984], 65; Yılmaz, *Becoming Turkish*, 22–77).

68. Ahmad, *The Turkish Experiment in Democracy*, 7.

69. Karpat, *Turkey's Politics*, 281; Reed, "Turkey's New İmam-Hatip Schools," 152; Geyikdağı, *Political Parties in Turkey*, 68. The Ministry of Education administered religious instruction in primary and secondary schools as well as in the Faculty of Divinity at Ankara University, and syllabi for religious courses in primary and secondary schools needed the ministry's prior approval. The accelerated İmam-Hatip Schools were replaced in 1951 by more sophisticated schools of religious vocational training.

70. Karpat, *Turkey's Politics*, 281. See also Mustafa Öcal, "From the Past to the Present: Imam and Preacher Schools in Turkey—an Ongoing Quarrel," *Religious Education* 102, no. 2 (2007): 193; Ahmet Hadi Adanalı, "The Presidency of Religious Affairs and the Principle of Secularism in Turkey," *Muslim World* 98, nos. 2–3 (2008): 229–30.

71. Azak, "Secularism in Turkey," 176.

72. Azak, "Secularism in Turkey," 176. For instance, during the celebration of the birth of the Prophet Muhammad, the Arabic phrase "Allahu ekber [God is great]" could be used in place of the "pure" Turkish phrase "Tanrı uludur."

73. Howard A. Reed argues that the only people in Turkey who knew Arabic in 1954 learned it in a *medrese* prior to 1924 or privately ("Revival of Islam in Secular Turkey," *Middle East Journal* 8, no. 3 [1954]: 280).

74. In the early 1950s, people frequently criticized the fact that the Directorate of Religious Affairs employed mosque officials but also criticized President Adnan Menderes when he was photographed with the Greek Orthodox patriarch and the chief Jewish rabbi in Istanbul but not with the Diyanet's president (Reed, "Revival of Islam in Secular Turkey," 278). Public understanding of the identity of this institution seems to have varied widely around this time because of the peculiar relationship between the Diyanet and its eponymous concept.

75. Azak, "Secularism in Turkey," 176.

76. *Ulus*, Feb. 5, 1949, translated and quoted in Geyikdağı, *Political Parties in Turkey*, 70, emphasis omitted; see also Azak, "Secularism in Turkey," 176.

77. VanderLippe, *The Politics of Turkish Democracy*, 202–3.

78. Karpat, *Turkey's Politics*, 285; VanderLippe, *The Politics of Turkish Democracy*, 203.

79. The DP's campaign advantage on the issue of the *ezan* resulted from general perception of the DP and from campaign promises rather than from the party's official policies. When Menderes presented the DP's official program on May 29, 1950, it included no references to the *ezan* or freedom of conscience. The primary difference between the DP's official program and the CHP's was that the DP supported extending the right of workers to strike (VanderLippe, *The Politics of Turkish Democracy*, 203).

80. Justifications for the education laws introduced in 1948 and 1949 specifically note the lack of village imams (Karpat, *Turkey's Politics*, 281).

81. The DP victory seems to have surprised numerous people inside and outside Turkey. İnönü, the CHP, and Western observers did not expect the result, and no procedure was in place for the transference of power between administrations (VanderLippe, *The Politics of Turkish Democracy*, 205–6). The DP won 53 percent of the vote, and the CHP got 40 percent, which, according to electoral law, gave the DP 408 seats in Parliament as opposed to the CHP's 69 seats (Findley, *Turkey, Islam, Nationalism, and Modernity*, 268).

82. The CHP had established optional religious education classes, and the DP eventually made these courses mandatory (Reed, "Turkey's New İmam-Hatip Schools," 152). For the full DP program, see Adnan Menderes, *Adnan Menderes'in konuşmaları, demeçleri, makaleleri*, vol. 2: *Mayıs 1950–Aralık 1951*, ed. Halûk Kılçık (Ankara: Demokratlar Kulübü Yayınları: 3, 1991), 15–29. As prime minister, Menderes was also the leader of the party.

83. "Hükûmet programını dün okudu: D.P. hükûmeti, programında ihtiyatlı dil kullandı," *Yeni Sabah*, May 30, 1950.

84. For İnönü's role in supporting the democratic transition, see Findley, *Turkey, Islam, Nationalism, and Modernity*, 268–69.

85. This interview is also the most calculated yet neutral of Menderes's statements on the *ezan* issue because he offered it in the DP's official newspaper as the first official statement of the intent to change the policy. Many of his later speeches regarding the *ezan* were consumed with responding to CHP accusations of the DP's antisecular stance.

86. Adnan Menderes, interview by *Zafer*, June 5, 1950, in Menderes, *Adnan Menderes'in konuşmaları, demeçleri, makaleleri*, 2:51. Unless otherwise noted, all translations from this interview are my own. Alternate translations of parts of the interview can be found in Azak, *Islam and Secularism in Turkey*, 74.

87. Menderes, interview by *Zafer*, June 5, 1950, in Menderes, *Adnan Menderes'in konuşmaları, demeçleri, makaleleri*, 2:51.

88. Menderes, interview by *Zafer*, June 5, 1950, in Menderes, *Adnan Menderes'in konuşmaları, demeçleri, makaleleri*, 2:51.

89. For instance, the United Nations General Assembly ratified the Universal Declaration of Human Rights on December 10, 1948, and Turkey was one of forty-eight countries voting to affirm it (United Nations, *Yearbook of the United Nations, 1948–49* [Lake Success, NY: United Nations Department of Public Information, 1950], 535), at https://www.unmultimedia.org/searchers/yearbook/page.jsp?volume=1948-49&page=1). Article 18 of the declaration states, "Everyone has the right to freedom of thought, conscience and religion; this right includes freedom to change his religion or belief, and freedom, either alone or in community with others and in public or private, to manifest his religion or belief in teaching, practice, worship and observance only with the permission of the person and not by force" (United Nations, "Universal Declaration of Human Rights," Dec. 10, 1948, at http://www.un.org/en/universal-declaration-human-rights/index.html).

90. United Nations, "Universal Declaration of Human Rights," Art. 18. In arguing that Menderes's use of the phrase "freedom of conscience" resembles international human rights discourse, I do not mean to suggest that Menderes or the DP developed policies that supported international human rights. For an explanation of the DP's involvement in encouraging a pogrom against the Istanbul Greek population, see Findley, *Turkey, Islam, Nationalism, and Modernity*, 308–10; Zürcher, *Turkey*, 230–31; Speros Vryonis Jr., *The Mechanism of Catastrophe: The Turkish Pogrom of September 6–7, 1955, and the Destruction of the Greek Community of Istanbul* (New York: Greekworks, 2005).

91. Menderes, interview by *Zafer*, June 5, 1950, in Menderes, *Adnan Menderes'in konuşmaları, demeçleri, makaleleri*, 2:52.

92. Menderes, interview by *Zafer*, June 5, 1950, in Menderes, *Adnan Menderes'in konuşmaları, demeçleri, makaleleri*, 2:52.

93. Menderes, interview by *Zafer*, June 5, 1950, in Menderes, *Adnan Menderes'in konuşmaları, demeçleri, makaleleri*, 2:51, my emphasis.

94. Adnan Menderes, remarks to the DP Parliamentary Group meeting, June 13, 1950, in Menderes, *Adnan Menderes'in konuşmaları, demeçleri, makaleleri*, 2:63.

95. Talal Asad, *Genealogies of Religion: Discipline and Reasons of Power in Christianity and Islam* (Baltimore: Johns Hopkins Univ. Press, 1993), 28–29.

3. Historical Revision and the Figure of the Military

1. Bayar and eleven others also received death sentences in 1961, but their sentences were commuted (Zürcher, *Turkey*, 248).

2. "27 Mayıs'ın 3 kurbanına 'itibar' iadesi," *Hürriyet*, May 23, 1987. Adnan Menderes was honored by having named after him a street in Istanbul, a highway in his hometown, and the newly built Izmir International Airport (only the second international airport in Turkey at the time, after Atatürk Airport in Istanbul). Fatin Rüştü Zorlu was honored by having a steel plant on the Black Sea coast named after him. The Sarıyar Dam (sixty miles west of Ankara and fifty miles northeast of Eskişehir) was renamed after Hasan Polatkan.

3. "3 naaşın İmralı'dan nakli 2 gün sürecek: Devlet törenine Özal da katılıyor," *Günaydın*, Sept. 13, 1990; "Cenaze törende naklen yayın yok," *Günaydın*, Sept. 14, 1990; "Adnan Menderes'in oğlu Aydın Menderes: 'Devlet, özür diledi,'" *Günaydın*, Sept. 15, 1990. *Günaydın İstanbul*, the Istanbul city insert of the national newspaper *Günaydın*, also ran numerous sensationalist cover stories preceding Monday, September 17, 1990, warning of the impending chaos of Istanbul traffic that would result from the confluence of the first day of public school, a rainy weather forecast, a taxi driver work stoppage (because of gas rationing), and the closure of Adnan Menderes Boulevard for the state funeral ("Pazartesi İstanbul felç," *Günaydın İstanbul*, Sept. 14, 1990). For the phrase "three martyrs" (*üç şehitler*), see "Aydın Menderes 'üç şehitler' konuştu 'Devlet töreni çok mu görülüyor,'" *Tercüman*, May 22, 1987. For the full text of Özal's speech, see Güner Sarısözen, ed., *Yassıada'dan Anıtmezar'a* (Ankara: Demokratlar Kulübü Yayınları: 1, 1991), 17–20 (Yassıada is the island where Menderes was tried following the coup; "Anıtmezar" is the name of his mausoleum).

4. "3 naaşın İmralı'dan nakli 2 gün sürecek."

5. The major military interventions in Turkish history are referenced in newspapers and colloquial speech by only the month and day on which they occurred. Thus, "May 27" (1960), "March 12" (1971), "September 12" (1980), and "February 28" (1997) have become the proper names of the military interventions that occurred on those dates.

6. Zürcher, *Turkey*, 248.

7. Quoted in "Devlet töreni istiyoruz," *Tercüman*, May 29, 1987; translations of quotations from newspaper articles are mine unless otherwise noted. Eskişehir is approximately sixty miles southwest of the Sarıyar Dam.

8. Hale, *Turkish Politics and the Military*, 142, quoting the oath of the Armed Forces Union (Silahlı Kuvvetler Birliği), an ultranationalist group within the army and air force.

9. This was a frequent criticism of Özal's treatment of the Menderes reburial. A political cartoon in 1990 in the centrist, mass-public-oriented newspaper *Günaydın* showed Özal and Demirel lifting up Menderes's mausoleum to reveal a label on the bottom of the monument that reads, "Expiration Date: 1992 General Elections"

(Nehar Tüblek, untitled political cartoon, in the series "Nehar Tüblek'in gözüyle," *Günaydın*, Sept. 20, 1990).

10. "Cenazeler devlet töreniyle anıt mezarda," *Cumhuriyet*, Sept. 18, 1990. Erdal İnönü visited the Menderes family on September 13 to pay his respects ahead of the reburial ("Cenaze törende naklen yayın yok," *Günaydın*, Sept. 14, 1990). The ceremony was carefully planned so that Demirel's visit to the Aksaray mosque happened after Özal had already left (Mehmed Kemal, "Oy mirasına oturmak," *Cumhuriyet*, Sept. 18, 1990).

11. Marvine Howe, "Ankara Abolishes 2 Holidays and Turks Ask Why," *New York Times*, Mar. 21, 1981.

12. Throughout this chapter, I maintain this distinction between the *figure* of the military as an ordering feature of political and national discourse and the *institution* of the Turkish Armed Forces or the *concept* of the army as a site within the figure of the military that helps to compose it.

13. The Susurluk Incident of 1996 commonly marks the birth of the term *deep state* in Turkey, but many scholars note a much longer history of underground networks that have manipulated politics in Turkey stretching back at least as far as the CUP and the Revolution of 1908 in the Ottoman Empire. See, for example, H. Akin Ünver, "Turkey's 'Deep-State' and the Ergenekon Conundrum," *Middle East Institute Policy Brief* 23 (Apr. 2009), at https://www.mei.edu/publications/turkeys-deep-state-and-ergenekon-conundrum; Serdar Kaya, "The Rise and Decline of the Turkish 'Deep State': The Ergenekon Case," *Insight Turkey* 11, no. 4 (2009): 99–113; Merve Kavakçi, "Turkey's Test with Its Deep State," *Mediterranean Quarterly* 20, no. 4 (2009): 83–97; Mehtap Söyler, *The Turkish Deep State: State Consolidation, Civil–Military Relations, and Democracy* (New York: Routledge, 2015). Since late 2013, President Recep Tayyip Erdoğan has deployed the terms *deep state* and *parallel state* to refer exclusively to Fethullah Gülen and the Gülen Movement, a significant reversal in the presumed political philosophy of this "deep state" ("MİT to Monitor All Religious Groups as Potential Parts of Parallel State," Cihan News Agency, Jan. 18, 2014).

14. By 2005, the term *deep state* was widely acknowledged in Turkey, even by prominent politicians such as former prime minister and former president Süleyman Demirel and former president Kenan Evren ("Süleyman Demirel: İki devlet var," NTVMSNBC, Nov. 16, 2005; Yavuz Donat, "Kenan Evren: Derin devlet . . . Evet . . . Var . . . Bir realite," *Sabah*, Apr. 4, 2005, at https://www.sabah.com.tr/yazarlar/donat/2005/04/04/kenan_evren_derin_devlet_evet_var_bir_r).

15. The military has intervened twice since 1990, in the "postmodern" or "soft" coup of 1997 and in the failed coup attempt in 2016. In 1997, the MGK wrote a memorandum requiring Prime Minister Necmettin Erbakan to implement a number of policies regarding religious practice and then to resign or face a military

coup (Gareth Jenkins, "Continuity and Change: Prospects for Civil–Military Relations in Turkey," *International Affairs* 83, no. 2 [Mar. 2007]: 345–46). In 2016, the Turkish Armed Forces occupied bridges in Istanbul and bombed the Parliament in Ankara, but military disorganization and active civilian resistance resulted in an abandoned coup effort within twenty-four hours. The coup attempt was followed by a vast government "countercoup," including nearly one hundred thousand arrests, purges of employees in all sectors of government and private industry, and significant limitations on the press. For updated information on the postputsch purge based on Turkish state media reports, see the website www.turkeypurge.com. For an excellent summary of the most popular explanatory narratives about the coup attempt in 2016, see Hakkı Taş, "The 15 July Abortive Coup and Post-truth Politics in Turkey," *Southeast European and Black Sea Studies* 18, no. 1 (2018): 1–19.

16. Gerassimos Karabelias, "The Evolution of Civil–Military Relations in Post-war Turkey, 1980–95," *Middle Eastern Studies* 35, no. 4 (Oct. 1999): 132.

17. Findley, *Turkey, Islam, Nationalism, and Modernity*, 306.

18. Hale, *Turkish Politics and the Military*, 94–95. Zürcher, *Turkey*, 235. Participation in the Korean War was a watershed event in Turkish national culture (and remains a source of pride) as a generation of Turks (1919–51) had had very little contact with foreign tourists and only very wealthy Turks traveled internationally.

19. Hale, *Turkish Politics and the Military*, 94; Karabelias, "Evolution of Civil–Military Relations in Post-war Turkey," 132. Karabelias argues that the declining economic status of junior officers led directly to the 1960 coup.

20. Hale summarizes continuing disagreement about the extent of the DP's knowledge of an impending coup (*Turkish Politics and the Military*, 111).

21. Kemal H. Karpat, "Military Interventions: Army–Civilian Relations in Turkey before and after 1980," in *State, Democracy, and the Military: Turkey in the 1980s*, ed. Metin Heper and Ahmet Evin (New York: De Gruyter, 1988), 140–41. Karpat argues that this back-and-forth between İnönü and Menderes was political bluster and that neither was interested in jailing or harming the other.

22. Hale, *Turkish Politics and the Military*, 104–7.

23. Hale, *Turkish Politics and the Military*, 107. A week before the coup, one thousand cadets marched in an orderly protest from the Ankara Military College to the Presidential Mansion in Çankaya, Ankara.

24. Hale, *Turkish Politics and the Military*, 100, 107.

25. The Constitution of 1961 also decreased the power of the president and established the Constitutional Courts to review the acts of Parliament, but these changes didn't directly affect public understanding of the military.

26. Hale, *Turkish Politics and the Military*, 138.

27. Semih Vaner, "The Army," trans. Rezan Benatar and İrvin C. Schick, in *Turkey in Transition: New Perspectives*, ed. İrvin C. Schick and Ertuğrul Ahmet

Tonak (New York: Oxford Univ. Press, 1987), 251; Hale, *Turkish Politics and the Military*, 175. See also Ordu Yardımlaşma Kurumu Kanunu [Law on Armed Forces Mutual Assistance Fund], Law No. 205, Jan. 9, 1961, at https://www.mevzuat.gov.tr/MevzuatMetin/1.4.205.pdf.

28. Karabelias, "Evolution of Civil–Military Relations in Post-war Turkey," 140.

29. Hale, *Turkish Politics and the Military*, 144; Vaner, "The Army," 253.

30. Temporary Law No. 1, June 14, 1960, quoted in Hale, *Turkish Politics and the Military*, 123. By the summer of 1961, this narrative justification for the coup, which needed defense by that time, became known as "the spirit of May 27" (Hale, *Turkish Politics and the Military*, 142).

31. Hale, *Turkish Politics and the Military*, 126–27.

32. Zürcher, *Turkey*, 248. The MBK dropped numerous cases for lack of evidence, and 123 people were eventually acquitted, but it persisted in pursuing bizarre or outlandish corruption trials, such as the accusation that former president Celâl Bayar had forced a zoo to buy a dog he was given as a gift by the king of Afghanistan.

33. Hale, *Turkish Politics and the Military*, 142.

34. Zürcher, *Turkey*, 248. The MBK commuted eleven of these sentences because the verdicts were not unanimous and commuted Bayar's unanimous verdict because of his old age. Hale argues that trials and executions proceeded out of fear that Menderes might arrest, try, and execute the leaders of the coup if he were ever freed (*Turkish Politics and the Military*, 145).

35. Hale, *Turkish Politics and the Military*, 144. Menderes was scheduled to be executed on September 16 along with Zorlu and Polatkan, but he attempted suicide on the night of September 15, and his execution was postponed until after his "recovery" (Nicole Pope and Hugh Pope, *Turkey Unveiled: A History of Modern Turkey* [Woodstock, NY: Overlook Press, 1997], 98).

36. Karpat, "Military Interventions," 143. The resulting coalition government did not include one of these DP successor parties, the New Turkey Party (Yeni Türkiye Partisi) because the JP and the CHP decided on a government with İnönü as prime minister.

37. Findley, *Turkey, Islam, Nationalism, and Modernity*, 315–16. At one point, riot police forced the closure of Istanbul University. Increasing violence included a politically motivated bank robbery and abduction of American military personnel.

38. A complete English translation of the military's statement in 1971 can be found in Hale, *Turkish Politics and the Military*, 184–85.

39. Hale, *Turkish Politics and the Military*, 193–94.

40. Hale, *Turkish Politics and the Military*, 196–97. Numerous reports of torture that were not investigated by the military authorities served to further undermine the legitimacy of the martial law period.

41. Hale, *Turkish Politics and the Military*, 186. Hale argues that armed intervention in 1971 was highly unlikely and not actually planned.

42. Hale, *Turkish Politics and the Military*, 198–201.

43. Hale, *Turkish Politics and the Military*, 209.

44. Hale, *Turkish Politics and the Military*, 195.

45. Hale, *Turkish Politics and the Military*, 203. İnönü was eighty-eight at the time of the vote.

46. Karpat, "Military Interventions," 147–48. CHP outreach to specific minority groups such as Alevis marked a significant departure from the republican concept of Turkishness as the unifying national identity category. See also Frank Tachau and Metin Heper, "The State, Politics, and the Military in Turkey," *Comparative Politics* 16, no. 1 (1983): 24.

47. Tachau and Heper, "The State, Politics, and the Military in Turkey," 24–25. Erim was assassinated on the street in Istanbul by two gunmen on July 19, 1980.

48. Hale, *Turkish Politics and the Military*, 240. The ineffectiveness of martial law prior to the 1980 coup is a topic of controversy. Martial law commanders claim they were stymied by bureaucracy, but Süleyman Demirel suggested in 1985 and has argued more forcefully since then that martial law commanders deliberately failed to restore order in order to increase public support for a military intervention (Kavakçi, "Turkey's Test with Its Deep State," 84; Karpat, "Military Interventions," 149).

49. Hale, *Turkish Politics and the Military*, 234. In a widely publicized event, Demirel and Ecevit were invited to the Presidential Mansion in Ankara on January 1, 1980, to discuss a letter from the chief of the General Staff, Kenan Evren, expressing concern about deteriorating public safety and urging a JP–CHP coalition government (Mehmet Ali Birand, *The Generals' Coup in Turkey: An Inside Story of 12 September 1980*, trans. M. A. Dikerdem [London: Brassey's Defense, 1987], 107–10; Hale, *Turkish Politics and the Military*, 235).

50. Hale, *Turkish Politics and the Military*, 229–31.

51. The Constitution of 1961 stipulated that the president was to be chosen by a two-thirds majority vote of Parliament. If a president was not elected on the first or second ballots, only a simple majority was required, and there was no procedure for breaking an intractable stalemate. Between April and September 1980, Parliament held more than one hundred ballots attempting to elect a president. The Constitution of 1982 mandated dissolving Parliament and snap general elections if

a president weren't chosen after four ballots (Hale, *Turkish Politics and the Military*, 236).

52. The entire military hierarchy and command structure remained intact from 1980 to 1983, without the general purge of officers that followed the 1960 coup (Hale, *Turkish Politics and the Military*, 248–49). Alparslan Türkeş, leader of the Nationalist Action Party and a prominent figure in the 1960 coup, evaded detention for twelve days after the 1980 coup (Hale, *Turkish Politics and the Military*, 247).

53. Zürcher, *Turkey*, 279–80; Hale, *Turkish Politics and the Military*, 251. Professors and journalists were commonly arrested without justification or on the basis that their employment was no longer desirable. Forty-three thousand people were arrested for the dubious charge of "political terrorism" (Hale, *Turkish Politics and the Military*, 252–53).

54. Hale, *Turkish Politics and the Military*, 247.

55. Hale, *Turkish Politics and the Military*, 252, 261. Both Alparslan Türkeş and Necmettin Erbakan were released in 1985.

56. Hale, *Turkish Politics and the Military*, 252–53.

57. Ümit Cizre Sakallioğlu, "The Anatomy of the Turkish Military's Political Autonomy," *Comparative Politics* 29, no. 2 (1997): 157.

58. Constitution of the Republic of Turkey, Art. 118, quoted in Gareth Jenkins, *Context and Circumstance: The Turkish Military and Politics* (New York: Routledge, 2001), 45.

59. Millî Güvenlik Kurulu ve Millî Güvenlik Kurulu Genel Sekreterliği Kanunu [National Security Council and General Secretariat of the National Security Council Law], Law no. 2945, Nov. 9, 1983, Art. 2a, quoted in Jenkins, *Context and Circumstance*, 46; Sakallioğlu, "Anatomy of the Turkish Military's Political Autonomy," 158; Findley, *Turkey, Islam, Nationalism, and Modernity*, 353.

60. The regulatory apparatus that resulted from the 1980 coup is too vast to be treated fully here. A second judicial system, the State Security Courts (Devlet Güvenlik Mahkemeleri), secured military authority over the judicial system after the return to civilian government (Sakallioğlu, "Anatomy of the Turkish Military's Political Autonomy," 157). These courts did not start using all civilian judges until 1999, a bid to increase the international legitimacy of the trial of Kurdistan Worker's Party (PKK) founder Abdullah Öcalan (Jenkins, *Context and Circumstance*, 54–55). Two other controversial aspects of the regulatory apparatus include: (1) the very high threshold for political parties in national elections, in which a party must receive 10 percent of the national vote to be eligible for Parliament; and (2) the Protocol on Cooperation for Security and Public Order (Emniyet Asayiş Yardımlaşma Protokolü, EMASYA Protokolü), which authorized the Turkish Armed Forces to conduct operations and intelligence on the domestic population and "internal

threats" without the civilian government's approval. The latter was repealed in 2010. See Kayhan Karaca, "Europe Remains Critical of Turkey's 10 Percent Election Threshold," *Hürriyet Daily News*, June 10, 2011; "Erdoğan Vows to Abolish EMASYA Protocol, Revise Security Priorities," *Today's Zaman*, Feb. 1, 2010; Söyler, *The Turkish Deep State*, 182.

61. Hale, *Turkish Politics and the Military*, 257. According to the Constitution of 1982, after Evren's term, the president of the Republic would be elected by the Parliament for a seven-year term without the possibility of reelection.

62. MGK decision, 1981, quoted in Hale, *Turkish Politics and the Military*, 262; Karabelias, "Evolution of Civil–Military Relations in Post-war Turkey," 145 n. 33.

63. Karabelias, "Evolution of Civil–Military Relations in Post-war Turkey," 145 n. 33; Ergun Özbudun, "The Status of the President of the Republic under the Turkish Constitution of 1982: Presidentialism or Parliamentarism?," in *State, Democracy, and the Military*, ed. Heper and Evin, 44–45.

64. Karabelias, "Evolution of Civil–Military Relations in Post-war Turkey," 137.

65. The MGK issued a law just after the elections in 1983 forbidding criticism of the military's activities between 1980 and 1983 (Hale, *Turkish Politics and the Military*, 269). Hale states that the law was seriously enforced only until 1984 (275).

66. Hale, *Turkish Politics and the Military*, 268–69. Hale argues that the Motherland Party's unexpected dramatic victory indicates a public desire for the military to remove itself from politics.

67. Karabelias, "Evolution of Civil–Military Relations in Post-war Turkey," 137.

68. Karabelias, "Evolution of Civil–Military Relations in Post-war Turkey," 146 n. 48.

69. Karabelias, "Evolution of Civil–Military Relations in Post-war Turkey," 146 n. 48.

70. Karpat, "Military Interventions," 149.

71. Karpat, "Military Interventions," 147–48. As Taha Parla and Andrew Davison note in *Corporatist Ideology in Kemalist Turkey: Progress or Order?* (Syracuse, NY: Syracuse Univ. Press, 2004), scholarly reference to "Kemalism" frequently reinscribes official state discourse (7). I use this term precisely to refer to the military's official ideological characterization of its relationship to the nation's founding.

72. Feroz Ahmad, *The Making of Modern Turkey* (New York: Routledge, 1993), 131–32; Sakallioğlu, "Anatomy of the Turkish Military's Political Autonomy," 157; Vaner, "The Army," 251.

73. Hale reproduces this official narrative in *Turkish Politics and the Military*, 232, 233, 238. Opponents of the coup, such as Demirel, even repeated the basic contours of this narrative, trying to blame the "anarchy" on the military. See also Karpat, "Military Interventions," 149. For the phrase "chaotic days," see Kenan Evren, preface to General Secretariat of the National Security Council, *12 September in Turkey: Before and After* (Ankara: Ongun Kardeşler Printing House, 1982), xi. This text is the official English (propaganda) account of the coup.

74. Kenan Evren, "Speech Delivered by General Evren at the War Academy," Sept. 30, 1980, in General Secretariat, *12 September in Turkey*, 301. See also Hale, *Turkish Politics and the Military*, 250. The idea that the 1980 coup was a "last resort" is reinforced in Evren's five-volume memoir: Kenan Evren, *Kenan Evren'in anıları* (Istanbul: Milliyet Yayınları, 1991–92).

75. Sakallioğlu, "Anatomy of the Turkish Military's Political Autonomy," 162.

76. Evren, preface to General Secretariat, *12 September in Turkey*, xi.

77. The MGK also removed May 27 from the register of Turkish holidays, a date celebrated since 1961 to commemorate the 1960 coup (Zürcher, *Turkey*, 278).

78. Restrictions on speech also made this narrative the only possible public account of the coup for nearly a decade after 1980.

79. George Harris, "Celal Bayar: Conspiratorial Democrat," in *Political Leaders and Democracy in Turkey*, ed. Metin Heper and Sabri Sarayı (Lanham, MD: Lexington Books, 2002), 53.

80. Zürcher, *Turkey*, 251.

81. Associated Press, "Once Scorned Former President to Receive State Funeral," Aug. 23, 1986; Harris, "Celal Bayar," 53.

82. "Aydın Menderes 'Üç Şehitler' konuştu 'Devlet töreni çok mu görülüyor'" (interview), *Tercüman*, May 22, 1987.

83. Quoted in "Menderes İmralı'da kalıyor," *Tercüman*, May 28, 1987.

84. "İtibarların iadesi," *Cumhuriyet*, Apr. 18, 1990; "Vatan Caddesi'nin adı 'Menderes Caddesi' oldu," *Tercüman*, June 7, 1987.

85. "Devlet töreni istiyoruz," *Tercüman*, May 29, 1987.

86. Quoted in "Menderes'e Boğaz'da anıt mezar," *Cumhuriyet*, June 1, 1987.

87. "27 Mayıs'ın 3 kurbanına 'itibar' iadesi," *Hürriyet*, May 23, 1987.

88. *Tercüman* was a moderate conservative and religious intellectual newspaper, its title referencing the first independent Ottoman newspaper *Tercüman-ı hakikat* (Interpreter of Truth). For the contemporary political significance of appropriated Ottoman symbols, see Çınar, *Modernity, Islam, and Secularism in Turkey.*

89. The continued public criticism of 1980 coup leaders by 1960 coup leaders, such as Alparslan Türkeş, also reinforces the ideological separation of these two coups. (Türkeş was jailed following the 1980 coup.)

90. Metin Heper, "Turgut Özal's Presidency: Crisis and the Glimmerings of Consensus," in *Politics in the Third Turkish Republic*, ed. Metin Heper and Ahmet Evin (Boulder, CO: Westview Press, 1994), 192. A close associate of Özal and a former Speaker of Parliament, Yıldırım Akbulut, became prime minister.

91. "Demokrasi şehitleri için devlet töreni," *Tercüman*, Apr. 12, 1990; "Menderes'in itibarı hukuken iade edildi," *Hürriyet*, Apr. 12, 1990; "Menderes'in mezarı," *Cumhuriyet*, Apr. 12, 1990. For the full text of both laws, see *Yassıada'dan Anıtmezar'a*, ed. Sarısözen, 47–51, 151–52.

92. "İmralı'dan . . . Anıtmezar'a . . . ," *Günaydın*, Sept. 18, 1990.

93. Quoted in "Adnan Menderes'in oğlu Aydın Menderes."

94. "Adnan Menderes'in oğlu Aydın Menderes."

95. Quoted in "Artık Anıtmezar'dalar . . . ," *Hürriyet*, Sept. 18, 1990, and "Aydın Menderes: İdamlar cinayetti," *Cumhuriyet*, Sept. 18, 1990, respectively.

96. "Cenazeler devlet töreniyle Anıt Mezarda," *Cumhuriyet*, Sept. 18, 1990. In the funeral procession for Menderes, four police officers and four soldiers carried each coffin, and a line that alternated policeman and soldier one after the other flanked each side of the procession ("1.5 saatlık yürüyüş," *Cumhuriyet*, Sept. 18, 1990).

97. Hugh Pope, "Hanged PM Has 'Honour Restored' by State Burial," *Independent*, Sept. 18, 1990.

98. *Tercüman*, Sept. 17, 1990.

99. "Menderes'i hangi Türkiye yarattı?," *Cumhuriyet*, Sept. 16, 1990; "İkinci Dünya Savaşı yıllarında faşist dalgaya karşı 'buyurun Adnan Bey, söz sizin,'" *Cumhuriyet*, Sept. 16, 1990.

100. "Tek Partiye karşı populism silahı," *Cumhuriyet*, Sept. 18, 1990; "'Milletten devlete' Demokrat Parti," *Cumhuriyet*, Sept. 18, 1990.

101. "Menderes demokrasisi," *Cumhuriyet*, Sept. 19, 1990; "DP ve parlamenter diktatörlük," *Cumhuriyet*, Sept. 20, 1990.

102. As Findley notes, the tactics employed by the DP to marginalize the CHP had been pioneered by the CHP itself in the mid-1940s for use against the DP (*Turkey, Islam, Nationalism, and Modernity*, 308).

103. "Adnan Menderes'in oğlu Aydın Menderes."

104. "27 Mayıs'ın lideri Gürsel anıldı," *Günaydın*, Sept. 15, 1990. Gürsel died on September 14, 1966.

105. Mehmed Kemal, "Oy mirasına oturmak," *Cumhuriyet*, Sept. 18, 1990.

106. Later in the 1990s, organizations such as the May 27th National Revolution Association began to be thought of as centers of "deep-state" activity. Güler's association currently occupies the margins of Turkish political thought.

107. "27 Mayısçılardan orduya teşekkür," *Günaydın*, Sept. 18, 1990.

108. Quoted in Pope, "Hanged PM Has 'Honour Restored' by State Burial."

109. Numerous scholars have noted the nondemocratic nature of the MGK. See, for instance, Ümit Cizre, "Problems of Democratic Governance of Civil–Military Relations in Turkey and the European Union Enlargement Zone," *European Journal of Political Research* 43, no. 1 (2004): 107–25; Tim Jacoby, "For the People, of the People, and by the Military: The Regime Structure of Modern Turkey," *Political Studies* 51, no. 4 (2003): 669–85; Nilüfer Narlı, "Civil–Military Relations in Turkey," *Turkish Studies* 1, no. 1 (2000): 107–27.

110. See Kavakçi, "Turkey's Test with Its Deep State."

4. Article 301 and the Oscillations of the Figure of the Minority

1. Türk Büyük Millet Meclisi [Turkish Grand National Assembly], Kanun No. 5237, Türk Ceza Kanunu [Law No. 5237, Turkish Penal Law], Sept. 26, 2004 (effective June 1, 2005), at http://www.tbmm.gov.tr/kanunlar/k5237.html.

2. Bülent Algan, "The Brand New Version of Article 301 of Turkish Penal Code and the Future of Freedom of Expression Cases in Turkey," *German Law Journal* 9, no. 12 (2008): 2237. The revised Penal Code of 2005 was one of a number of harmonization packages adopted by the Turkish Parliament prior to formal EU accession talks. See Baskın Oran, "The Minority Concept and Rights in Turkey: The Lausanne Peace Treaty and Current Issues," in *Human Rights in Turkey*, ed. Zehra F. Kabasakal Arat (Philadelphia: Univ. of Pennsylvania Press, 2007), 53–55; Marlies Casier, "The Politics of Solidarity: The Kurdish Question in the European Parliament," in *Nationalisms and Politics in Turkey: Political Islam, Kemalism, and the Kurdish Issue*, ed. Marlies Casier and Joost Jongerden (New York: Routledge, 2011), 197–98.

3. Maureen Freely, "Why They Killed Hrant Dink," *Index on Censorship* 36, no. 2 (2007): 17.

4. Mücahit Bilici, "Black Turks, White Turks: On the Three Requirements of Turkish Citizenship," *Insight Turkey* 11, no. 3 (2009): 26; Jenny White, *Muslim Nationalism and the New Turks* (Princeton, NJ: Princeton Univ. Press, 2013), 6–11.

5. Dink was prosecuted numerous times under Articles 301 and 159 for various statements beginning in 2002. This chapter focuses only on the investigation in 2004 and the trial in 2005, the only charge that resulted in his conviction.

6. The phrase *Türklüğü aşağılama*, "insulting Turkishness," is also sometimes translated as "denigrating Turkishness." Many NGO and official EU documents focus on Article 301. See Amnesty International, "Turkey: Article 301: How the Law on 'Denigrating Turkishness' Is an Insult to Free Expression," Mar. 1, 2006, at https://www.amnesty.org/en/documents/eur44/003/2006/en/; European Commission, *Turkey 2011 Progress Report*, Commission Staff Working Paper

(Brussels: European Commission, 2011), at http://ec.europa.eu/enlargement/pdf/key_documents/2011/package/tr_rapport_2011_en.pdf, 25; European Commission, *Enlargement Strategy and Main Challenges 2011–2012*, Communication from the Commission to the European Parliament and the Council (Brussels: European Commission, 2011), at http://ec.europa.eu/enlargement/pdf/key_documents/2011/package/strategy_paper_2011_en.pdf; Miklos Haraszti, *Review of the Draft Turkish Penal Code: Freedom of Media Concerns*, Report of the Organization for Security and Co-operation in Europe (Vienna: Organization for Security and Co-operation in Europe, 2005), at http://www.osce.org/fom/14672. Algan also proposes extensive revision of Article 301 and other laws to secure freedom of speech ("Brand New Version of Article 301").

7. Constitution of the Republic of Turkey, Art. 66, in English at https://global.tbmm.gov.tr/docs/constitution_en.pdf, in Turkish at https://www.mevzuat.gov.tr/MevzuatMetin/1.5.2709.pdf.

8. As discussed later in this chapter, policies of "assimilation" have been the primary means by which the Turkish state has addressed its Muslim minorities, especially Kurds. See Mesut Yeğen, "The Kurdish Question in Turkey: Denial to Recognition," in *Nationalisms and Politics in Turkey*, ed. Casier and Jongerden, 72.

9. Quoted in Ayşegül Aydıngün and İsmail Aydıngün, "The Role of Language in the Formation of Turkish National Identity and Turkishness," *Nationalism and Ethnic Politics* 10, no. 3 (2004): 426.

10. Aydıngün and Aydıngün, "The Role of Language," 426.

11. My emphasis.

12. Mustafa Kemal Atatürk, "Onuncu yıl nutku," Oct. 29, 1933, in *Atatürk'ün bütün eserleri*, vol. 26: *2 Ekim 1932–27 Eylül 1934* [The complete works of Atatürk, vol. 26: October 2, 1932–September 27, 1934], ed. Rifat N. Bali, Elif Ertan, Süha Göney, Firdevs Kıral, Kiraz Perinçek, Sabri Sayarı, and Martı Şahin (Istanbul: Kaynak Yayınları, 2009), 268. English translations are easily accessible online; see, for instance, Mustafa Kemal Atatürk, "Atatürk's Speech at the 10th Anniversary of the Turkish Republic," Oct. 29, 1933, Atatürk Society of America, at http://www.ataturksociety.org/about-ataturk/ataturks-speech-at-the-10th-anniversary-of-the-turkish-republic/.

13. Kenan Evren, "Cumhuriyet Bayramı mesajı," Oct. 29, 1981, in Kenan Evren, *Türkiye Cumhuriyeti devlet başkanı orgeneral Kenan Evren'in söylev ve demeçleri*, vol. 2: *12 Eylül 1981–12 Eylül 1982*, ed. K. Ali Baransel (Ankara: Başbakanlık Basımevi, 1982), 82, quoted and translated in Tachau and Heper, "The State, Politics, and the Military in Turkey," 27.

14. According to Ergun Özbudun, the phrase "indivisible unity of the State with its territory and nation" appears sixteen times in the Constitution of 1982 ("The Turkish Constitutional Court and Political Crisis," in *Democracy, Islam,*

and Secularism in Turkey, ed. Ahmet T. Kuru and Alfred Stepan [New York: Columbia Univ. Press, 2012], 150).

15. Oran argues that the idea of the indivisibility of the nation in the Turkish Constitution is "contrary to the very essence of democracy" ("The Minority Concept and Rights in Turkey," 45).

16. For instance, Atatürk, *A Speech Delivered by Ghazi Mustapha Kemal*, 93. For more on the operation of the phrase "external and internal enemies" in *Nutuk*, see Alaranta, "Mustafa Kemal Atatürk's Six-Day Speech of 1927."

17. Millî Güvenlik Kurulu ve Millî Güvenlik Kurulu Genel Sekreterliği Kanunu [National Security Council and General Secretariat of the National Security Council Law], Law no. 2945, Nov. 9, 1983, Art. 2a, quoted in Jenkins, *Context and Circumstance*, 46.

18. The categories "external threats" and "internal threats" are also explicitly developed in Turkish primary and secondary textbooks. See Kaplan, *The Pedagogical State*, 195–96.

19. Keyman, "Articulating Citizenship and Identity," 269.

20. As discussed earlier in this chapter, the "indivisible unity of the State with its territory and nation" (Constitution of the Republic of Turkey, Art. 3) is integral to understanding the category "Turk."

21. B. Ali Soner, "Citizenship and the Minority Question in Turkey," in *Citizenship in a Global World*, ed. Keyman and İçduygu, 303. See also Oran, "The Minority Concept and Rights in Turkey," 52; Taner Akçam, *From Empire to Republic: Turkish Nationalism and the Armenian Genocide* (New York: Zed Books, 2004), 230. The "Syndrome" can also refer to Kurdish separatist violence.

22. Oran, "The Minority Concept and Rights in Turkey," 35–37. Although common understanding of the Treaty of Lausanne suggests that rights were granted to specific groups (Greek Orthodox, Armenian Christians, and Jews, the three largest religious minorities in the late Ottoman Empire), the treaty refers to these minorities only as "non-Muslims" (Oran, "The Minority Concept and Rights in Turkey," 38).

23. As Oran notes, contemporary Turkish courts also continue to invoke the Treaty of Lausanne in human rights cases because "it is legally correct for Turkey to consider only non-Muslims as minorities" ("The Minority Concept and Rights in Turkey," 37, emphasis omitted).

24. Many Turkish politicians made this comparison explicit, especially as France prepared to prohibit denying the Armenian Genocide in October 2006 and after Dink's assassination in 2007. See "AK Parti: 301 yasa değil, kafa işidir," *Dünya*, Sept. 23, 2006; "Tartışılan madde bir kez daha gündemde," Haber 7, Jan. 24, 2007, at https://www.haber7.com/guncel/haber/213912-tartisilan-madde-bir-kez-daha-gundemde.

25. This translation is from Algan, "Brand New Version of Article 301," 2238. As Algan explains, Article 301 was revised in 2008 to remove the third point, to change "Turkishness" to "the Turkish nation," and to necessitate approval by the minister of justice for all prosecutions under the article (2239–40). The text of Article 301 quoted here is the older version of the law under which Dink, Pamuk, and Şafak were indicted.

26. The revision of Article 301 in 2008 to read "Turkish nation" rather than "Turkishness" was "copied from the penal codes of several EU member states. For that reason, it is difficult for the EU to criticize the new formulation" (Joost Lagendijk, "Turkey's Accession to the European Union and the Role of the Justice and Development Party," in *Democracy, Islam, and Secularism in Turkey*, ed. Kuru and Stepan, 176–77).

27. There is a dearth of academic research on the cultural history, linguistic roots, and religious practices of the Zaza people, and there are disputes about their status as either Alevi or Kurdish. See Mehmed S. Kaya, *The Zaza Kurds of Turkey: A Middle Eastern Minority in a Globalised Society* (New York: I. B. Tauris, 2011); Paul J. White, "The Debate on the Identity of 'Alevi Kurds,'" in *Turkey's Alevi Enigma: A Comprehensive Overview*, ed. Paul J. White and Joost Jongerden (Leiden: Brill, 2003), 17–29.

28. Yeğen, "The Kurdish Question in Turkey," 73. Yeğen notes that according to a report issued by the Turkish Parliament, more than three thousand Kurdish villages in mountainous areas of southeastern Turkey were "evacuated" in the late 1990s, which typically meant that the people were removed and the villages burned.

29. Keyman, "Articulating Citizenship and Identity," 277. See also Yeğen, "The Kurdish Question in Turkey," 71. Keyman also argues that emphasis on the backwardness of Kurds helped efface the "Kurdishness" of the "Kurdish Question," and a policy of assimilation and modernization became the natural solution to a problem of an underdeveloped, premodern people ("Articulating Citizenship and Identity," 277–78).

30. On the concept of "mountain Turks," see Bilici, "Black Turks, White Turks," 30. On the Şeyh Said Rebellion, see Yeğen, "The Kurdish Question in Turkey," 69.

31. Keyman, "Articulating Citizenship and Identity," 282–83; Casier, "The Politics of Solidarity," 201.

32. Markus Dressler, "Public–Private Distinctions, the Alevi Question, and the Headscarf: Turkish Secularism Revisited," in *Comparative Secularisms in a Global Age*, ed. Linell E. Cady and Elizabeth Shakman Hurd (New York: Palgrave, 2010), 126. Alevi groups disagree on the advantages of being officially designated a religious minority because the Sunni state would dictate the terms of this status and

establish rules of practice for Alevis. See Kabir Tambar, "The Aesthetics of Public Visibility: Alevi *Semah* and the Paradoxes of Pluralism in Turkey," *Comparative Studies in Society and History* 52, no. 3 (2010): 652–79.

33. Markus Dressler, "Making Religion through Secularist Legal Discourse: The Case of Turkish Alevism," in *Secularism and Religion-Making*, ed. Markus Dressler and Arvind-Pal S. Mandair (New York: Oxford Univ. Press, 2011), 195.

34. Dressler, "Making Religion through Secularist Legal Discourse," 198.

35. Esra Özyürek, "Beyond Integration and Recognition: Diasporic Constructions of Alevi Muslim Identity between Germany and Turkey," in *Transnational Transcendence: Essays on Religion and Globalization*, ed. Thomas J. Csordas (Berkeley: Univ. of California Press, 2009), 131.

36. Akçam, *From Empire to Republic*, 221; Oran, "The Minority Concept and Rights in Turkey," 52; Özyürek, "Beyond Integration and Recognition," 136.

37. Özyürek, "Beyond Integration and Recognition," 136.

38. Oran, "The Minority Concept and Rights in Turkey," 44.

39. Oran, "The Minority Concept and Rights in Turkey," 44.

40. Constitution of the Republic of Turkey, Art. 134.

41. This translation of Pamuk's statement is from Freely, "Why They Killed Hrant Dink," 27.

42. Kaplan, *The Pedagogical State*, 198–99; Akçam, *From Empire to Republic*, 208.

43. Ministry of Education report from 1982, quoted in Kaplan, *The Pedagogical State*, 195–96.

44. Murat Belge, "'Love Me, or Leave Me?': The Strange Case of Orhan Pamuk," Open Democracy, Oct. 17, 2005, at https://www.opendemocracy.net/en/orhan_pamuk_2935jsp.

45. Akçam, *From Empire to Republic*, 208–9.

46. This is not to suggest a binary understanding of histories produced in Turkey as opposed to histories produced outside of Turkey. Turkish state historians do not account for all histories produced in Turkey, and British and American historians of Turkey have been equally complicit in Armenian Genocide denial. For an account of American scholars' complicity, see Howard Eissenstat, "Children of Özal: The New Face of Turkish Studies," *Journal of the Ottoman and Turkish Studies Association* 1, nos. 1–2 (2014): 24–26. For the history of some American institutions' relationship to the production of knowledge about the Armenian Genocide, see Richard G. Hovannisian, ed., *Remembrance and Denial: The Case of the Armenian Genocide* (Detroit: Wayne State Univ. Press, 1999).

47. Suny, Göçek, and Naimark, eds., *A Question of Genocide*. Ronald Grigor Suny and Fatma Müge Göçek note in their introduction to this volume that among the members of their working group the term *genocide* is still not agreed upon as

a descriptor, with some members preferring the phrase *ethnic cleansing* because *genocide* can silence productive discussion of the massacres of 1915 ("Introduction," 9–10).

48. Norman M. Naimark, preface to *A Question of Genocide*, ed. Suny, Göçek, and Naimark, xv.

49. Suny and Göçek, "Introduction," 10.

50. The precise number of Armenian deaths in 1915–20 is difficult to determine because historical documentation is sparse and frequently housed in closed Turkish archives and because many deaths (potentially half of the total) resulted from a lack of food and water in relocation caravans that were sent to locations without resources to support the deportees. See Taner Akçam, *A Shameful Act: The Armenian Genocide and the Question of Turkish Responsibility* (New York: Holt, 2006), 5.

51. Naimark, preface to *A Question of Genocide*, xviii.

52. Suny and Göçek, "Introduction," 6. For Suny and Göçek, the Armenian Genocide reflects a "propensity for violent repression" of this population by the Ottomans, but the events of 1915 are not directly related to massacres of Armenians in the 1890s and 1909.

53. Richard G. Hovannisian, "Introduction: The Armenian Genocide: Remembrance and Denial," in *Remembrance and Denial*, ed. Hovannisian, 15; Erik Jan Zürcher, "Renewal and Silence: Postwar Unionist and Kemalist Rhetoric on the Armenian Genocide," in *A Question of Genocide*, ed. Suny, Göçek, and Naimark, 314.

54. Much of the evidence from these trials was destroyed (Akçam, *A Shameful Act*, 5; see also Vahakn N. Dadrian and Taner Akçam, *Judgment at Istanbul: The Armenian Genocide Trials* [New York: Berghahn Books, 2011]).

55. Akçam, *From Empire to Republic*, 21.

56. Zürcher, "Renewal and Silence," 313–14.

57. The significant number of Muslim civilian deaths at the hands of Armenians is a major point of emphasis in Turkish official histories of the "Armenian Question." This point is on gruesome display in the state Military Museum in Harbiye, Istanbul, in a room entitled "The Armenian Question" (as of November 2009). Muslim civilians suffered approximately 5 percent of the number of casualties of Armenians in Anatolia during 1915–20.

58. Zürcher, "Renewal and Silence," 313–14.

59. Akçam notes that the failure of the Istanbul trials also resulted from the Entente Powers' competing interests and inadequate international law, which covered only crimes committed by one state against the people of another state rather than crimes of a state committed against its own people (*A Shameful Act*, 3). See also, Arendt, *Origins of Totalitarianism*, 267–302.

60. Hovannisian, "Introduction," 16.

61. Hovannisian, "Introduction," 16.

62. Akçam, *A Shameful Act*, 10–11. Another possible motivation for Turkish state denial of genocide involves potential reparations that would result from an acknowledgment of these events as genocide.

63. People directly involved in the massacres, such as the chief architect of the genocide, Bahaeddin Şakir, remained close to Mustafa Kemal Atatürk throughout Atatürk's lifetime (Zürcher, "Renewal and Silence," 313, 315).

64. Zürcher, "Renewal and Silence," 313. According to Suny and Göçek, the consensus among their international group of scholars is that no civil war between Muslims and Armenians occurred in eastern Anatolia ("Introduction," 5).

65. M. Hakan Yavuz and Nihat Ali Özcan, "The Kurdish Question and Turkey's Justice and Development Party," *Middle East Policy* 13, no. 1 (2006): 102. Tension between Kurds and the Turkish state existed well before 1984, but this chapter focuses on events since that time given their relevance to Pamuk's statement.

66. Kemal Kirişci and Gareth M. Winrow, *The Kurdish Question and Turkey: An Example of a Trans-state Ethnic Conflict* (London: Frank Cass, 1997), 110–11. Identification with a Kurdish ethnicity category that conflicted with Turkish ethnicity was rare until the late 1970s and especially the mid-1980s.

67. Kirişci and Winrow, *The Kurdish Question and Turkey*, 149. Kirişci and Winrow emphasize that the vast majority of Turkish Kurds living in the Southeast wish to remain citizens of Turkey and support governmental reforms of laws limiting Kurdish political expression.

68. Kirişci and Winrow, *The Kurdish Question and Turkey*, 129. The Village Guard system was also intended to provide economic support to a depressed region of the country.

69. H. Ayla Kiliç, "Democratization, Human Rights, and Ethnic Policies in Turkey," *Journal of Muslim Minority Affairs* 18, no. 1 (1998): 91–110; Joost Jongerden, "Resettlement and Reconstruction of Identity: The Case of the Kurds in Turkey," *Global Review of Ethnopolitics* 1, no. 1 (2001): 83.

70. Kirişci and Winrow, *The Kurdish Question and Turkey*, 130. Blaming the PKK for razed villages does accurately describe PKK activity in the Southeast, but the Turkish military has used this explanation even when witnesses have reported Turkish Armed Forces helicopters instigating the fires (Kirişci and Winrow, *The Kurdish Question and Turkey*, 131). Yeğen cites a Turkish Parliamentary report stating that more than three thousand villages were evacuated and one million people displaced during the conflict ("The Kurdish Question in Turkey," 73).

71. Kirişci and Winrow, *The Kurdish Question and Turkey*, 135.

72. Kirişci and Winrow, *The Kurdish Question and Turkey*, 135.

73. Yavuz and Özcan, "The Kurdish Question and Turkey's Justice and Development Party," 102.

74. Kirişci and Winrow, *The Kurdish Question and Turkey*, 127.

75. Belge, "'Love Me, or Leave Me?'"

76. This assessment of intensified media criticism of Dink following his article on Gökçen is Dink's own. See Hrant Dink, "Niçin hedef seçildim?" [Why was I chosen as a target?], *Agos*, Jan. 12, 2007, at http://www.agos.com.tr/tr/yazi/14049/agos-un-arsivinden-nicin-hedef-secildim. See also Daniella Kuzmanovic, "Dead Bodies, Affective States, and Volatile Icons: An Iconology of Hrant Dink," *Middle East Journal of Culture and Communication* 8, no. 1 (2015): 94. Gökçen is often referred to as Atatürk's "spiritual daughter" to emphasize the way she embodied the ideal Turkish nationalist woman.

77. Hrant Dink, "Sabiha-Hatun'un sırrı," *Agos*, Feb. 6, 2004, at http://www.agos.com.tr/tr/yazi/17528/sabiha-hatunun-sirri. I use the awkward phrasing "Turkish woman of Armenian descent" because the category "Turk" does not formally admit of compound names relating to nationality, such as "Armenian Turkish." Dink was charged in 2002 for insulting Turkishness because he advocated use of "Türkiyeli," "from (*-li*) Turkey (Türkiye)," to mirror the Turkish linguistic construction of other nationalities rather than using the ethnic category "Türk" that is in the Constitution. For instance, "Amerikalı" is used for US nationality and literally means "from (*-lı*) America (Amerika)." See Freely, "Why They Killed Hrant Dink," 16; Ioannis N. Grigoriadis, "*Türk* or *Türkiyeli*? The Reform of Turkey's Minority Legislation and the Rediscovery of Ottomanism," *Middle Eastern Studies* 43, no. 3 (2007): 423–38.

78. Ersin Kalkan, "Sabiha Gökçen'in 80 yıllık sırrı," *Hürriyet*, Feb. 21, 2004. See also Ersin Kalkan, "Sabiha Gökçen mi Hatun Sebilciyan mı," *Hürriyet*, Feb. 21, 2004, at https://www.hurriyet.com.tr/gundem/sabiha-gokcen-mi-hatun-sebilciyan-mi-204239. Gökçen died two years prior to the publication of this article series.

79. "Genelkurmay: Gökçen Ata'nın armağanıdır," *Hürriyet*, Feb. 22, 2004, at https://www.hurriyet.com.tr/gundem/genelkurmay-gokcen-atanin-armaganidir-204466. For a full English translation of this government press release, see Fatma Ulgen, "'Sabiha Gökçen's 80-Year-Old Secret': Kemalist Nation Formation and the Ottoman Armenians," PhD diss., Univ. of California–San Diego, 2010, 131–32.

80. "Genelkurmay." Dink details other aspects of his persecution by government officials at this time, including a warning "interview" at the Istanbul Governor's Office on February 23, 2004, attended by two national intelligence officers (Dink, "Niçin hedef seçildim?").

81. Hrant Dink, "Ermeni kimliği üzerine (6) Ermeni'nin 'Türk'ü," *Agos*, Jan. 23, 2004, at http://www.agos.com.tr/tr/yazi/17527/ermeni-kimligi-uzerine-6-ermeninin-turku. For full (if awkward) English translations of the sixth, seventh,

and eighth articles in this series (the subject of Dink's trial), see "About Armenian Identity," Turquie Européenne, July 15, 2006, at http://turquieeuropeenne.eu/about-armenian-identity.html.

82. Hrant Dink, "Ermeni kimliği üzerine (8) Ermenistan'la tanışmak," *Agos*, Feb. 13, 2004, at http://www.agos.com.tr/tr/yazi/17525/ermeni-kimligi-uzerine-8-ermenistanla-tanismak. The translation in the chapter text is based on a translation given in Gülay Türkmen-Dervişoğlu, "Coming to Terms with a Difficult Past: The Trauma of the Assassination of Hrant Dink and Its Repercussions on Turkish National Identity," *Nations and Nationalism* 19, no. 4 (2013): 681. A more literal translation might begin "The clean blood that will replace the poisonous blood emptied from 'the Turk,'" but Türkmen-Dervişoğlu's rendering is more faithful to the contextual meaning of the sentence in this article and in Dink's article series, whereas a more literal translation sounds like the ultranationalist intentional misreading (especially if the quotation marks around "the Turk" are dropped). In either case, the phrase is provocative as a means of gaining reader attention at the start of a column.

83. Deniz Som, "Sabiha Gökçen," for the column "Vaziyet," *Cumhuriyet*, Feb. 24, 2004. See also Ulgen, "'Sabiha Gökçen's 80-Year-Old Secret,'" 127–28.

84. Emin Çölaşan, "Ufak ufak, yavaş yavaş . . . ," *Hürriyet*, Feb. 28, 2004. "Imam marriage" in this quote refers to a proposal that imams should be able to perform legally binding marriage ceremonies without further involvement of (secular) state officials.

85. Dink, "Niçin hedef seçildim?" See also "A Chronology: Hrant Dink's Murder," Bianet, June 27, 2007, at https://bianet.org/bianet/politics/98382-a-chronology-hrant-dinks-murder.

86. Quoted in Arda Uskan, "Apo'ya neden 'Kürt dölü' değil de 'Ermeni dölü' deniyor?," *Vatan*, Oct. 1, 2005, at http://www.gazetevatan.com/-apo-ya-neden--kurt-dolu--degil-de--ermeni-dolu--deniyor---61569-roportajlar/; Üstün Bilgen-Reinart, "Hrant Dink: Forging an Armenian Identity in Turkey," Open Democracy, Feb. 7, 2006, at https://www.opendemocracy.net/en/dink_3246jsp/. See also Dink, "Niçin hedef seçildim?" For a review of media attacks on Dink, see Türkmen-Dervişoğlu, "Coming to Terms with a Difficult Past," 682.

87. Jenny White argues that "Turkish blood represents the nation and is surrounded by taboos" (*Muslim Nationalism and the New Turks*, 6).

88. Kerinçsiz and his group were responsible for nearly sixty cases brought to court under Article 301, including those against Dink, Pamuk, and Şafak. He also repeatedly fought to prevent the major international academic conference "The Ottoman Armenians in the Era of Ottoman Decline," which was finally held at Istanbul Bilgi University on September 24–25, 2005, and at which Dink presented. As Fatma Müge Göçek explains, this historic conference was the first conference in

Turkey on Armenians in general, and organizers faced fierce resistance when they would not include official state historians who denied the fact of collective violence against Armenians in 1915. The conference followed a series of workshops in the United States and Europe and was originally planned for May 2005 before Kerinçsiz intervened (Fatma Müge Göçek, *Denial of Violence: Ottoman Past, Turkish Present, and Collective Violence against the Armenians, 1789–2009* [New York: Oxford Univ. Press, 2015], 388–89). See also "'Dönüm noktası'," *Milliyet*, Sept. 27, 2005, at https://www.milliyet.com.tr/siyaset/donum-noktasi-129605.

89. Quoted in "'Hrant Dink milletin değerlerini aşağıladı,'" *Hürriyet*, Oct. 19, 2005, at https://www.hurriyet.com.tr/gundem/hrant-dink-milletin-degerlerini-asagiladi-3405993.

90. Dink himself speculated in 2007 that the only reason his trial went forward was that he (in contrast to Pamuk and Şafak) was Armenian (Dink, "Niçin hedef seçildim?"; see also Kuzmanovic, "Dead Bodies, Affective States, and Volatile Icons," 92).

91. Quoted in "Hrant Dink'e hapis cezası," *Milliyet*, Oct. 8, 2005, at https://www.milliyet.com.tr/gundem/hrant-dinke-hapis-cezasi-253901.

92. "Address to the Turkish Youth" is the peroration of *Nutuk*, and the excerpt relevant to Dink's case is the very last line of *Nutuk*.

93. Atatürk, *The Great Speech*, 716.

94. Quoted in Ayşegül Usta, "Ata'nın sözlerini çarpıttı," *Hürriyet*, Oct. 20, 2005, at https://www.hurriyet.com.tr/gundem/ata-nin-sozlerini-carpitti-3409519; "'Hrant Dink milletin değerlerini aşağıladı.'"

95. Kerinçsiz also unsuccessfully appealed Dink's original six-month suspended sentence, arguing that a harsher penalty was necessary. See "Hrant Dink aleyhine temyiz davası," Haber 7, Oct. 12, 2005, at https://www.haber7.com/guncel/haber/116213-hrant-dink-aleyhine-temyiz-davasi.

96. Derya Sazak, "Soykırım değil 'karşılıklı kırım'" (interview with Mehmet Perinçek), *Milliyet*, May 8, 2006, at https://www.milliyet.com.tr/siyaset/soykirim-degil-karsilikli-kirim-156117. This account is one of a number of variations on the official Turkish state explanation of the genocide as a localized "civil war" started by Armenian forces backed by an alliance with Russia.

97. Kuzmanovic, "Dead Bodies, Affective States, and Volatile Icons," 93.

98. Türkmen-Dervişoğlu, "Coming to Terms with a Difficult Past," 683.

99. Türkmen-Dervişoğlu, "Coming to Terms with a Difficult Past," 686; Dilaver Arıkan Açar and İnan Rüma, "External Pressure and Turkish Discourse on 'Recognition of the Armenian Genocide,'" *Southeast European and Black Sea Studies* 7, no. 3 (2007): 456.

100. Peer Teuwsen, "Der meistgehasste Türke" [The most hated Turk], interview of Orhan Pamuk, *Das Magazin*, Feb. 5, 2005.

101. Pamuk interview quoted in İsmail Erel, "Kimse söylemiyor, bari ben söyleyeyim," *Hürriyet*, Feb. 9, 2005, at http://webarsiv.hurriyet.com.tr/2005/02/09/596844.asp. This article is a Turkish translation of excerpts of the *Das Magazin* interview. Translations into Turkish of Pamuk's brief statement varied in important ways in Turkish newspapers, and the English translation given in the chapter text is based on the *Hürriyet* translation of the excerpted interview.

102. Alper Uruş, "1 milyon Ermeni'yi ve 30 bin Kürt'ü kestik mi?" [Did we slaughter 1 million Armenians and 30 thousand Kurds?], *Vatan*, Feb. 9, 2005, at http://haber.gazetevatan.com/Haber/46650/1/Gundem; Belge, "'Love Me, or Leave Me?'"; Murat İri and H. Esra Arcan, "The Orhan Pamuk Case: How Mainstream Turkish Media Framed His Freedom of Speech," *Sosyal bilimler dergisi* 9, no. 18 (2007): 18; Oran, "The Minority Concept and Rights in Turkey," 53–55; Freely, "Why They Killed Hrant Dink," 16.

103. As mentioned at the beginning of this chapter and in note 101, quotations of Pamuk's statement varied in Turkish newspapers. This common formulation is from Ahmet Hakan, "Orhan Pamuk üzerine tezler," *Hürriyet*, Feb. 16, 2005, at https://www.hurriyet.com.tr/orhan-pamuk-uzerine-tezler-296882.

104. "Ermeniler kahraman ilan etti," *Hürriyet*, Feb. 27, 2005, at https://www.hurriyet.com.tr/gundem/ermeniler-kahraman-ilan-etti-299862.

105. Ardıç Aytalar, "Sözlerine öfke," *Hürriyet*, Feb. 15, 2005, at https://www.hurriyet.com.tr/gundem/sozlerine-ofke-296710. When Pamuk won the Nobel Prize for Literature in 2006, becoming Turkey's first recipient of the Nobel Prize in any category, this basic criticism circulated again, and the Nobel became "the prize for which Pamuk had sold his country to the Europeans" (Freely, "Why They Killed Hrant Dink," 28).

106. M. Hakan Yavuz, "Cleansing Islam from the Public Sphere," *Journal of International Affairs* 54, no. 1 (2000): 22; Bilici, "Black Turks, White Turks," 23.

107. Fatih Altaylı, "Kara yazar" [Black writer], *Hürriyet*, Feb. 11, 2005, at https://www.hurriyet.com.tr/kara-yazar-295790.

108. Altaylı, "Kara yazar."

109. Uruş, "1 milyon Ermeni'yi ve 30 bin Kürt'ü kestik mi?" As mentioned earlier in the chapter, the Turkish Historical Society is a state institution and primary purveyor of official state histories that deny the Armenian Genocide of 1915.

110. Suzan Fraser, "Şafak Recounts Struggles with Ultranationalists," *Turkish Daily News*, Sept. 9, 2006.

111. This is not to discount the very real silencing effect that Kerinçsiz's lawsuits have, especially on people less internationally famous than Şafak, Dink, and Pamuk. Şafak has noted this inequity and the silencing effect of Article 301 prosecutions. See "Elif Şafak'tan La Repubblica'ya demeç: '301. Maddeyi destekleyenler,

Türkiye'nin AB'yle bütünleşme sürecinin raydan çıkmasını sağlama peşindeler,'" Anadolu Ajansı, Sept. 23, 2006.

112. Elif Shafak, *The Bastard of Istanbul* (New York: Penguin, 2007), 53–54. (Şafak spells her name in English phonetically as "Shafak.") See also "Elif Şafak'ın 'Baba ve Piç'ine soruşturma," *Milliyet*, July 5, 2006, at https://www.milliyet.com.tr/gundem/elif-safakin-baba-ve-picine-sorusturma-248047.

113. Ayşe Özgün, "The Pope and Elif Şafak," *Turkish Daily News*, Sept. 24, 2006. This question also informed the judge's decision to dismiss the charges against Şafak. See Kemal Göktaş, "Roman kahramanı suç işlemez," *Vatan*, Oct. 4, 2006, at http://www.gazetevatan.com/-roman-kahramani-suc-islemez--89244-gundem/.

114. Quoted in Ivan Watson, "Schism: Free Speech vs. 'Insulting Turkishness,'" *All Things Considered*, NPR, Oct. 4, 2006, at https://www.npr.org/templates/story/story.php?storyId=6196764. The charges made against Şafak in July 2006 resulted from an appeal Kerinçsiz filed after the initial investigation into Şafak was dismissed in June 2006 because the statements at issue had been uttered by fictional characters. See Susanne Fowler, "Turkey, a Touchy Critic, Plans to Put a Novel on Trial," *New York Times*, Sept. 15, 2006, at https://www.nytimes.com/2006/09/15/world/europe/15turkey.html.

115. Quoted in "Yazar Elif Şafak'a jet beraat," *Hürriyet*, Sept. 21, 2006, at https://www.hurriyet.com.tr/gundem/yazar-elif-safaka-jet-beraat-5122371. *Ağa* is an Ottoman civilian and military honorific for officers and other influential functionaries.

116. Quoted in "Turkish Union of Jurists Calls for Writer Acquittal to Be Overturned," BBC, Sept. 26, 2006.

117. For a detailed analysis of the way Kerinçsiz's Article 301 cases helped make Article 301 a pivotal issue in EU preaccession negotiations that affected domestic politics as well, see Semih İdiz, "The Cur May Bay, but the Caravan Moves On," *Turkish Daily News*, Sept. 21, 2006.

118. Quoted in Göksel Bozkurt, "Article 301 Changes Fall Victim to Domestic Political Machinations," *Turkish Daily News*, Oct. 1, 2006.

119. Kemal Çiftçi, "The Kemalist Hegemony in Turkey and the Justice and Development Party (AKP) as an 'Other,'" *L'Europe en formation: Revue d'études sur la construction européenne et le fédéralisme* 367, no. 1 (2013): 143–69.

120. Quoted in "Elif Şafak'tan La Repubblica'ya demeç." See also Göçek, *Denial of Violence*, 388.

121. Quoted in "Elif Şafak beraat etti," *Yeni Şafak*, Sept. 21, 2006, at https://www.yenisafak.com/gundem/elif-safak-beraat-etti-6537.

122. Quoted in "Elif Şafak'la ilgili karar," Anadolu Ajansı, Sept. 21, 2006.

123. Cüneyt Ülsever, "301. Madde," *Hürriyet*, Sept. 21, 2006, at https://www.hurriyet.com.tr/301-madde-5122280.

124. Thomas K. Nakayama and Robert L. Krizek, "Whiteness: A Strategic Rhetoric," *Quarterly Journal of Speech* 81, no. 3 (1995): 302, 295.

5. Reflections of Liminality in the Figure of Europe

1. *Hürriyet*, Sept. 13, 1963, translated and quoted in Selim İlkin, "A Short History of Turkey's Association with the European Community," in *Turkey and the European Community*, ed. Ahmet Evin and Geoffrey Denton (Opladen, Germany: Leske und Budrich, 1990), 35–49.

2. Döşemeci, *Debating Turkish Modernity*, 218; Anneli Albi, *EU Enlargement and the Constitutions of Central and Eastern Europe* (New York: Cambridge Univ. Press, 2005), 45–46.

3. "Turkey's Full EU Membership Negotiations Start," *Today's Zaman*, Oct. 4, 2005; Selçuk Gültaşlı, "Gül: Rocky Road Awaits Us," *Today's Zaman*, Oct. 5, 2005; "Baykal Blasts Negotiating Mandate, Says Will Not Lead to Full Membership," *Hürriyet Daily News*, Oct. 6, 2005.

4. Gürel, *The Limits of Westernization*, 2–3.

5. Gürel, *The Limits of Westernization*, 4.

6. Andrew Davison, "Ziya Gökalp and Provincializing Europe," *Comparative Studies of South Asia, Africa, and the Middle East* 26, no. 3 (2006): 377–90. For a detailed account of another early Turkish nationalist theory of hybrid modernization, see Mushirul Hasan, *Between Modernity and Nationalism: Halide Edip's Encounter with Ghandhi's India* (New York: Oxford Univ. Press, 2010).

7. Adalet, *Hotels and Highways*, 13.

8. Jacques Derrida, *The Other Heading: Reflections on Today's Europe*, trans. Pascale-Anne Brault and Michael B. Naas (Bloomington: Indiana Univ. Press, 1992).

9. Chakrabarty, *Provincializing Europe*; Étienne Balibar, "Ideas of Europe: Civilization and Constitution," *Iris* 1, no. 1 (2009): 3–17.

10. For the concept "alternative modernity," see Dilip Parameshwar Gaonkar, ed., *Alternative Modernities* (Durham, NC: Duke Univ. Press, 2001); Dipesh Chakrabarty, *Habitations of Modernity: Essays in the Wake of Subaltern Studies* (Chicago: Univ. of Chicago Press, 2002).

11. Özyürek, "Beyond Integration and Recognition"; Tambar, *The Reckoning of Pluralism*.

12. Henri Barkey, "The Transformation of Turkey's Kurdish Question," in *The Kurdish Question Revisited*, ed. Gareth Stansfield and Mohammed Shareef

(New York: Oxford Univ. Press, 2017), 219; Ayhan Kaya, *Europeanization and Tolerance in Turkey: The Myth of Toleration* (New York: Palgrave, 2013), 125.

13. Meltem Ahıska, "Occidentalism: The Historical Fantasy of the Modern," *South Atlantic Quarterly* 102, nos. 2–3 (2003): 353. See also Meltem Ahıska, *Occidentalism in Turkey: Questions of Modernity and National Identity in Turkish Radio Broadcasting* (London: I. B. Tauris, 2010).

14. Deniz Vardar, "European Union–Turkish Relations and the Question of Citizenship," in *Citizenship in a Global World*, ed. Keyman and İçduygu, 87–102; Ziya Öniş, "Domestic Politics, International Norms, and Challenges to the State: Turkey–EU Relations in the Post-Helsinki Era," *Turkish Studies* 4, no. 1 (2003): 9–34; Firat Cengiz and Lars Hoffman, eds., *Turkey and the European Union: Facing New Challenges and Opportunities* (New York: Routledge, 2014); Catherine MacMillan, *Discourse, Identity, and the Question of Turkish Accession to the EU: Through the Looking Glass* (2013; reprint, New York: Routledge, 2016); Meltem Müftüler-Baç, "Turkish Foreign Policy, Its Domestic Determinants, and the Role of the European Union," in *Turkey and the EU: Accession and Reform*, ed. Gamze Avcı and Ali Çarkoğlu (New York: Routledge, 2013), 71–83.

15. Findley, *Turkey, Islam, Nationalism, and Modernity*, 33.

16. Findley, *Turkey, Islam, Nationalism, and Modernity*, 43.

17. The phrase is a misquote of Tsar Nicholas I in 1853, who described the Ottoman Empire as "a sick man—a very sick man." The phrase thus seems to originate in circulation. See Dimitris Livanios, "The 'Sick Man' Paradox: History, Rhetoric, and the 'European Character' of Turkey," *Journal of Southern Europe and the Balkans* 8, no. 3 (2006): 299–300. See also Aslı Çırakman, *From the "Terror of the World" to the "Sick Man of Europe": European Images of Ottoman Empire and Society from the Sixteenth Century to the Nineteenth* (New York: Peter Lang, 2002).

18. The narrative of decline presumes a perspective temporally removed from the nineteenth-century Ottoman Empire and can efface alternative intellectual trends of the time. This narrative nevertheless is what continues to circulate in contemporary Turkey. See Renée Worringer, "'Sick Man of Europe' or 'Japan of the Near East'? Constructing Ottoman Modernity in the Hamidian and Young Turk Eras," *International Journal of Middle East Studies* 36, no. 2 (2004): 207–30.

19. A related set of fictions circulates in Europe as well, but their function is frequently defined by the absence of definition of "Europe." See Paul T. Levin, *Turkey and the European Union: Christian and Secular Images of Islam* (New York: Palgrave, 2011).

20. Findley, *Turkey, Islam, Nationalism, and Modernity*, 220. As mentioned in note 63 in chapter 1, the location of Turkey's current capital in Ankara was a strategic response to this envisioned partition of the Ottoman Empire.

21. Findley, *Turkey, Islam, Nationalism, and Modernity*, 223–26.

22. Soner, "Citizenship and the Minority Question in Turkey."

23. Scholarship on the Tanzimat constitutes a major subfield in Ottoman history, and this brief account is meant to provide vague historical background of this period akin to that which circulates in Turkey through the figure of Europe. For a more detailed account, see Hanioğlu, *A Brief History of the Late Ottoman Empire*.

24. As part of the military reorganization, new "European-style" uniforms were instituted that incorporated the fez, and the turban was banned throughout the empire. The fez was in turn banned in 1925 by the Turkish nationalists and replaced with the Western hat. See Yılmaz, *Becoming Turkish*, 22–77; Selim Deringil, "The Invention of Tradition as Public Image in the Late Ottoman Empire, 1808 to 1908," *Comparative Studies in Society and History* 35, no. 1 (1993): 3–29; Findley, *Turkey, Islam, Nationalism, and Modernity*, 40, 252.

25. Esra Akcan, "Off the Frame: The Panoramic City Albums of Istanbul," in *Photography's Orientalism: New Essays on Colonial Representation*, ed. Ali Behdad and Luke Gartlan (Los Angeles: Getty Research Institute, 2013), 95.

26. Mary Roberts argues that concern about Orientalist visual representations of the Ottoman Empire predates the invention of photography ("The Limits of Circumscription," in *Photography's Orientalism*, ed. Behdad and Gartlan, 58, 69–70).

27. Nancy Micklewright argues that the "harem scene" had become standard to the point of being cliché by the late nineteenth century, and Ottoman families began to stage sarcastic "harem scenes" in Istanbul photography studios using familiar props such as water pipes and coffee sets ("Alternative Histories of Photography in the Ottoman Middle East," in *Photography's Orientalism*, ed. Behdad and Gartlan, 87–88).

28. Döşemeci, *Debating Turkish Modernity*, 44.

29. Döşemeci, *Debating Turkish Modernity*, 45.

30. Turkey's EEC Association Agreement is known as the "Ankara Agreement" in Turkey.

31. "Ortak Pazara girdik: Dün anlaşma imzalandı," *Cumhuriyet*, Sept. 13, 1963.

32. Shortly after the Ankara Agreement was signed in 1963, the sole representative of the Workers Party of Turkey (Türkiye İşçi Partisi) spoke to the Turkish Parliament about the possibility of significant harm to Turkish industry and economic development if the Ankara Agreement were ratified by the Parliament. His thorough criticism of EEC membership was received with loud boos and protests from members of other parties, received nearly no coverage in Turkish media, and gained traction with other parties only near the end of the first phase of the EEC

Association Agreement in 1968 (Döşemeci, *Debating Turkish Modernity*, 56–57; "İşçi Partisi 'Ortak Pazara hayır' diyor," *Cumhuriyet*, Sept. 15, 1963).

33. *Cumhuriyet*, June 1, 1963.

34. *Milliyet*, Sept. 13, 1963.

35. "Türkiye'nin, Avrupanın bir cüz'ü olduğu tesçil edildi," *Milliyet*, Sept. 13, 1963.

36. "175 milyon dolar YARDIM ALIYORUZ," *Milliyet*, May 10, 1963.

37. Döşemeci, *Debating Turkish Modernity*, 10.

38. "175 milyon dolar YARDIM ALIYORUZ."

39. See, for instance, Anne O. Krueger, "Turkey's Trade and Payments Regime in the Light of Integration with the EEC," in *Economic Relations between Turkey and the EEC: Proceedings of a Seminar Held in Antalya on October 11–14, 1976*, ed. Osman Okyar and Okan H. Aktan (Antalya, Turkey: Hacettepe Institute for Economic and Social Research on Turkey and the Middle East, 1976), 149–51. The minutes of the conference discussion following Krueger's paper in the volume *Economic Relations between Turkey and the EEC* provide a fascinating glimpse of Turkish nationalist rejection of the idea that transitioning from a planned economy to a liberal market economy would be good for Turkey. Professor V. Savaş, secretary-general of the Economic Development Foundation in Istanbul, argued that the transition from a state-planned economy to a liberal market economy that Krueger advocated was attempted in South Korea and resulted in an economy that was no longer owned by the Koreans but instead by foreign investors ("Discussion" (minutes), in *Economic Relations between Turkey and the EEC*, ed. Okyar and Aktan, 166).

40. *Cumhuriyet*, July 6, 1963.

41. Incidentally, the prime minister depicted in 1963 as eating from the plate of the Common Market was İsmet İnönü, who was also the first prime minister of Turkey in 1923 and the second president of Turkey in 1938 after Atatürk's death and who is colloquially referred to as "the Second Man (İkinci Adam)" of Turkey, where Atatürk is the "First Man (Tek Adam)." İnönü is officially remembered in Atatürk's *Nutuk* as a uniquely talented negotiator vis-à-vis western Europe and is characterized as being almost single-handedly responsible for the successful negotiations that annulled the Treaty of Sèvres of 1920 and replaced it with the Treaty of Lausanne of 1923, which enabled the territorial security of contemporary Turkey.

42. Osman Okyar, "Düşünceler: Müşterek Pazara girmeli miyiz?," *Cumhuriyet*, May 2, 1963.

43. Hulusi Sidal, "Düşünenlerin düşünceleri: Türkiye ve Ortak Pazar," *Milliyet*, Sept. 12, 1963.

44. Kayhan Sağlamer, "Dünyada bugün: Müşterek Pazar ve biz," *Cumhuriyet*, Sept. 9, 1963.

45. "Durum: İktisadî ayatımızda dönüm noktası," *Milliyet*, Sept. 12, 1963.

46. Both Luns and Hallstein quoted in "Türkiye'nin, Avrupanın bir cüz'ü olduğu tesçil edildi."

47. "Ortak Pazara girdik."

48. Quoted in "Millet Meclisi Ortak Pazar anlaşmasını dün onayladı," *Cumhuriyet*, Jan. 15, 1964.

49. By the time the Turkish Parliament ratified the Ankara Agreement, Turkish foreign relations were at a crisis point over violence in Cyprus that had begun on December 21, 1963, and had killed dozens of Turkish Cypriots. Numerous papers carried no coverage of the Ankara Agreement ratification, devoting almost all news space to developments in Cyprus and to the emergency conference taking place in London to stem the violence.

50. The notable exception is the criticism by the Workers Party of Turkey described earlier, a criticism that was all but marginalized in 1963. As Döşemeci argues, beginning in 1968, opposition to the EEC that characterized it as a neoimperialist mode of economic subjugation of Turkey became much more mainstream in Turkish political discourse (*Debating Turkish Modernity*, 56–57).

51. Albi, *EU Enlargement and the Constitutions of Central and Eastern Europe*, 45–46.

52. Austria raised the idea of a "privileged partnership" for Turkey late in September 2005 (just prior to the October accession decision date), leading to an emergency conference in Luxembourg involving the US secretary of state. The idea still circulates in contemporary negotiations and has been advocated by different countries at different times, most recently by German chancellor Angela Merkel. *Privileged partnership* is also the phrase used to describe the current treaties between Tunisia and the EU and between Russia and the EU. See Birol Yeşilada, *EU–Turkey Relations in the 21st Century* (New York: Routledge, 2013), 19–20.

53. According to Tony Barber, Turkey's chief negotiator to the EU, Egemen Bağış, responded to the idea of a "privileged partnership," "You are either in the EU or not in the EU. You cannot be half-pregnant" (quoted in "Sarkozy Ponders a Turkey Downgrade," *Financial Times*, Oct. 16, 2009).

54. In a different tripartite description of Turkish political discourse about EU accession, Bernard Steunenberg, Simay Petek, and Christiane Rüth distinguish between two different pro-EU themes (both of which correspond to AKP themes addressed later in the chapter) and one anti-EU theme that conflates CHP and MHP opposition to the AKP ("Between Reason and Emotion: Popular Discourses on Turkey's Membership of the EU," in *Turkey and the EU*, ed. Avcı and Ali Çarkoğlu, 246).

55. European Commission, "European Neighbourhood Policy and Enlargement Negotiations: Turkey," n.d., at https://ec.europa.eu/neighbourhood-enlargement/countries/detailed-country-information/turkey_en.

56. Translated and quoted in "Erdoğan: Clash of Civilizations Can Be Prevented by Our EU Membership," *Today's Zaman*, Oct. 11, 2004.

57. Just hours before the decision on October 3, 2005, that accession negotiations would begin with Turkey, Erdoğan made a similar statement about Turkey's independent political strength vis-à-vis Europe, arguing that "the EU will either show the political maturity to become a global actor on October 3, or it will become a Christian club" (quoted in Yusuf Kanlı, "PM Erdoğan: Reforms Will Go On, with or without EU," *Hürriyet Daily News*, Oct. 3, 2005).

58. "Turkish Accession Conference Statement Delivered by Foreign Minister Abdullah Gül," *Hürriyet Daily News*, Oct. 5, 2005.

59. Mehmet Döşemeci argues that the AKP attempted to "reclaim" EU-mandated reforms as motivated domestically and consistent with earlier nationalist narratives of reform (*Debating Turkish Modernity*, 220).

60. "Turkish Accession Conference Statement Delivered by Foreign Minister Abdullah Gül."

61. Quoted in "Baykal Blasts Negotiating Mandate, Says Will Not Lead to Full Membership," *Hürriyet Daily News*, Oct. 6, 2005. Turkey's accession document is silent on the term *privileged partnership*.

62. Quoted in "Baykal Blasts Negotiating Mandate."

63. Ödül Celep offers a detailed account of the CHP's "ideological U-turn" toward EU accession in the 2000s, focusing on CHP leaders' distrust of the AKP as the motivating factor for this policy change ("The Republican People's Party and Turkey's EU Membership," in *Turkey and the EU*, ed. Avcı and Çarkoğlu, 215–26).

64. Zeki Sezer, leader of the Democratic Left Party (Demokratik Sol Parti), which ran a coalition slate of candidates with the CHP in 2007, accused Baykal of collaborating with the AKP to hide details of the EU accession negotiations ("Frosty Reception from Opposition Awaits Gül Back in Turkey," *Hürriyet Daily News*, Oct. 4, 2005).

65. Quoted in "MHP Calls on Turkish Withdrawal from EU Talks," *Hürriyet Daily News*, Oct. 3, 2005. See chapter 4 regarding the presumed danger to contemporary Turkey of recognizing the Ottoman and Turkish nationalist role in the Armenian Genocide.

66. Quoted in "Kutan: EU Has Set Traitorous Traps for Turkey," *Hürriyet Daily News*, Oct. 3, 2005.

67. Quoted in "Okuyan Claims December 17 Agreement Was Sèvres Treaty Revisited," *Hürriyet Daily News*, Oct. 5, 2005.

68. For a review of AKP domestic political motivations for supporting EU accession, including discussion of how EU reforms have benefited the party in

national elections, see Gamze Avcı, "The Justice and Development Party and the EU: Political Pragmatism in a Changing Environment," in *Turkey and the EU*, ed. Avcı and Ali Çarkoğlu, 201–13.

69. Jonathan Spicer, "Lira Wobbles as U.S. Ties with Turkey Fray," Reuters, Mar. 29, 2019, at https://www.reuters.com/article/us-turkey-economy-crisis-analysis/lira-wobbles-as-u-s-ties-with-turkey-fray-idUSKCN1RA0FV.

70. See, for instance, David Jones and Dorian Jones, "Turkish President Stokes Anti-Western Rhetoric over New Zealand Killings," Voice of America, Mar. 19, 2019, at https://www.voanews.com/world-news/middle-east-dont-use/turkish-president-stokes-anti-western-rhetoric-over-new-zealand.

71. "Turkish President Erdoğan Launches War on Food Price 'Terror,'" *Hürriyet Daily News*, Feb. 11, 2019, at http://www.hurriyetdailynews.com/turkish-president-erdogan-launches-war-on-food-price-terror-141168.

72. "George and Hans Cannot Defeat Us, says Erdoğan," *Hürriyet Daily News*, May 28, 2018, at http://www.hurriyetdailynews.com/george-and-hans-cannot-defeat-us-says-erdogan-132506.

73. "Erdoğan: CHP Sides with Those Who Want to Divide Turkey," *Daily Sabah*, Feb. 28, 2019, at https://www.dailysabah.com/elections/2019/02/25/erdogan-chp-sides-with-those-who-desire-to-divide-turkey.

74. For another consideration of the contemporary significance of the figure of "Europe" in Turkey, see Matthew deTar, "Representation from the Margins: Brexit, Turkey, and the Idea of 'Europe,'" in *Negotiating Identity and Transnationalism: Middle Eastern and North African Communication and Critical Cultural Studies*, ed. Haneen Ghabra, Fatima Zahrae Chrifi Alaoui, Shadee Abdi, and Bernadette Marie Calafell (New York: Peter Lang, 2020), 91–103.

75. The scope of the post-2016 purge cannot be understated and has touched every sector of Turkish society. For updated statistics, see the website www.turkeypurge.com.

76. For this "turning away from the West" frame, see Soner Çağaptay, "Turkey's New Old Friends," *Wall Street Journal*, Dec. 30, 2015, at http://www.wsj.com/articles/turkeys-new-old-friends-1451502979; Ziya Öniş and Şuhnaz Yılmaz, "Between Europeanization and Euro-Asianism: Foreign Policy Activism in Turkey during the AKP Era," *Turkish Studies* 10, no. 1 (2009): 7–24; Bahar Rumelili, "Liminality and Perpetuation of Conflicts: Turkish–Greek Relations in the Context of Community-Building by the EU," *European Journal of International Relations* 9, no. 2 (2003): 213–48.

77. Merve Şebnem Oruç, "External Agendas in Turkey's Local Elections," *Daily Sabah*, Mar. 29, 2019, at https://www.dailysabah.com/columns/merve-sebnem-oruc/2019/03/30/external-agendas-in-turkeys-local-elections.

Epilogue

1. Fevzi Bilgin, "Sledgehammer (Balyoz): How Turkey Averted a Coup in 2003," *Washington Review of Turkish and Eurasian Affairs*, July 2010, at https://www.thewashingtonreview.org/articles/sledgehammer.html.

2. "Sledgehammer Plan Suggests Coup Was to Start at 3 a.m.," *Today's Zaman*, Jan. 27, 2010. Evidence included the five-thousand-page Sledgehammer Security Operation Plan, which consisted of PowerPoint slides supposedly used at the March 2003 meeting discussing the plan, video and audio recordings of that meeting, as well as a number of other documents, letters, and computer files.

3. Büşra Erdal and Kadir Kökten, "Turkey Challenges Sledgehammer Coup Plot in Historic Trial," *Today's Zaman*, Dec. 17, 2010; "Newly Exposed Coup Planned to Turn the Clock Back to 1923," *Today's Zaman*, Jan. 22, 2010. The revelation of military plans to carry out simultaneous bombings in Istanbul led many newspapers to wonder whether the military had played a role in the coordinated bombings by al-Qaeda in Istanbul in 2003 that killed fifty people and injured seven hundred.

4. "Subversive Sledgehammer Plot against AK Party Exposed," *Today's Zaman*, Jan. 20, 2010.

5. Erdal and Kökten, "Turkey Challenges Sledgehammer Coup Plot in Historic Trial."

6. Erdal and Kökten, "Turkey Challenges Sledgehammer Coup Plot in Historic Trial."

7. "Newly Exposed Coup Planned to Turn the Clock Back to 1923," quoting PowerPoint slides revealed by *Taraf*.

8. Bilgin, "Sledgehammer (Balyoz)."

9. Bilgin, "Sledgehammer (Balyoz)."

10. Dani Rodrik and Pınar Doğan, "Turkey's Other Dirty War: The Horrifying Legal Drama That Gives Lie to the Idea of a Democratic Turkey," *New Republic*, May 24, 2010, at https://newrepublic.com/article/75123/turkeys-other-dirty-war.

11. Mustafa Aykol, "What to Make of Turkey's First 'Coup Trial'?," *Hürriyet Daily News*, Sept. 26, 2012, at https://www.hurriyetdailynews.com/opinion/mustafa-akyol/what-to-make-of-turkeys-first-coup-trial-31007; Emre Peker, "Convictions Mostly Upheld in Turkish 'Sledgehammer' Coup-Plot Trial," *Wall Street Journal*, Oct. 9, 2013, at https://www.wsj.com/articles/convictions-mostly-upheld-in-turkish-8216sledgehammer8217-coup-trial-1381325265; Dani Rodrik, "Turkey's Miscarriage of Justice," *Washington Post*, Sept. 21, 2012, at https://www.washingtonpost.com/opinions/turkeys-miscarriage-of-justice/2012/09/21/e2125276-033d-11e2-8102-ebee9c66e190_story.html.

12. "Turkish Court Acquits Hundreds in 'Sledgehammer' Case," Anadolu Agency, Mar. 31, 2015, at https://www.aa.com.tr/en/turkey/turkish-court-acquits-hundreds-in-sledgehammer-case/61933. Eighty-eight of the defendants had already been released as a result of an appeal submitted on October 9, 2013.

13. "Balyoz Suspect Engin Alan to Receive Record Damages of over TL 1.3 Mln," *Today's Zaman*, Dec. 2, 2015; "Three Ex-colonels to Be Compensated over Unfair Arrest in Coup Plot Case," *Hürriyet Daily News*, Feb. 22, 2016, at https://www.hurriyetdailynews.com/three-ex-colonels-to-be-compensated-over-unfair-arrest-in-coup-plot-case-95555.

14. Mustafa Aykol articulated this concern as early as 2012 in "What to Make of Turkey's First 'Coup Trial'?"

15. Lale Kemal, "Betrayal of the Turkish Public," *Today's Zaman*, Feb. 29, 2016.

16. I continue to leave open the possibility that the meeting at which officers developed the Sledgehammer coup plot did, in fact, imagine the real overthrow of the AKP because significant evidence (such as audio recordings of this meeting) has not been determined to be fabricated and officers' explanations sound thin. Aykol's nuanced evaluation of what is plausible and implausible about Sledgehammer prior to the revelation of forgery remains an important assessment of this case ("What to Make of Turkey's First 'Coup Trial'?").

17. Olson, *Constitutive Visions*.

18. The downing of a Russian jet by the Turkish air force in November 2015 when the Russian jet violated Turkish airspace resonates too closely with what seemed like a farcical action plan in 2010 for a coup. See "Turkey Shoots Down Russian Warplane on Syria Border," *BBC News*, Nov. 24, 2015, at https://www.bbc.com/news/world-middle-east-34907983.

19. Peter J. Steinberger's project is precisely to argue for the state as an ontological entity with a discreet essence (*The Idea of the State* [New York: Cambridge Univ. Press, 2004]).

20. Navaro-Yashin, *Faces of the State*, 10.

21. See Butler, *Undoing Gender*.

22. For an excellent critique of the relationship between narrative and history, see White, "The Value of Narrativity in the Representation of Reality."

23. Erik Jan Zürcher's first groundbreaking work challenging the official history of Turkey as presented in *Nutuk* is *Political Opposition in the Early Turkish Republic: The Progressive Republican Party, 1924–1925* (New York: Brill, 1991).

24. Zürcher develops an important critique of Bernard Lewis's work along these lines. See Zürcher, "The Rise and Fall of 'Modern' Turkey."

25. Sakallioğlu, "The Anatomy of the Turkish Military's Political Autonomy"; M. Hakan Yavuz, "Turkey's Fault Lines and the Crisis of Kemalism," *Current History* 99, no. 633 (2000): 33–38.

26. Ali Bardakoğlu, "'Moderate Perception of Islam' and the Turkish Model of the Diyanet: The President's Statement," *Journal of Muslim Minority Affairs* 24, no. 2 (2004): 367–74; David Ghanim, "Turkish Democracy and Political Islam," *Middle East Policy* 16, no. 1 (2009): 75–84; Meliha Benli Altunışık, "The Turkish Model and Democratization in the Middle East," *Arab Studies Quarterly* 27, nos. 1–2 (2005): 45–63. See also Cihan Tuğal, *The Fall of the Turkish Model: How the Arab Uprisings Brought Down Islamic Liberalism* (New York: Verso, 2016).

27. Toygar Sinan Baykan, *The Justice and Development Party in Turkey: Populism, Personalism, Organization* (New York: Cambridge Univ. Press, 2018); Antonino Castaldo, "Populism and Competitive Authoritarianism in Turkey," *Southeast European and Black Sea Studies* 18, no. 4 (2018): 467–87; Ihsan Yilmaz and Galib Bashirov, "The AKP after 15 Years: Emergence of Erdoğanism in Turkey," *Third World Quarterly* 39, no. 9 (2018): 1812–30.

28. There are exceptions to this consensus. Enno Maessen sees continuities between Kemalism and the AKP ("Reassessing Turkish National Memory: An Analysis of the Representation of Turkish National Memory by the AKP," *Middle Eastern Studies* 50, no. 2 [2014]: 309–24).

29. White, *Muslim Nationalism and the New Turks*; Freely, "Why They Killed Hrant Dink."

30. This account of trends is overly reductive in order to briefly highlight "figures" in scholarship. For more thorough reviews of Turkish studies, see Eissenstat, "Children of Özal"; Nicholas Danforth, "The Writing of Modern Turkey," *Nationalities Papers* 41, no. 6 (2013): 1136–46.

Bibliography

Abbott, Don Paul. "The Genius of the Nation: Rhetoric and Nationalism in Eighteenth-Century Britain." *Rhetoric Society Quarterly* 40, no. 2 (2010): 105–27.

Abu El-Haj, Nadia. *Facts on the Ground: Archaeological Practice and Territorial Self-Fashioning in Israeli Society*. Chicago: Univ. of Chicago Press, 2001.

Açar, Dilaver Arıkan, and İnan Rüma. "External Pressure and Turkish Discourse on 'Recognition of the Armenian Genocide.'" *Southeast European and Black Sea Studies* 7, no. 3 (2007): 449–65.

Adak, Hülya. "National Myths and Self-Na(rra)tions: Mustafa Kemal's *Nutuk* and Halide Edib's *Memoirs* and *The Turkish Ordeal*." *South Atlantic Quarterly* 102, nos. 2–3 (Spring–Summer 2003): 509–27.

Adalet, Begüm. *Hotels and Highways: The Construction of Modernization Theory in Cold War Turkey*. Stanford, CA: Stanford Univ. Press, 2018.

Adanalı, Ahmet Hadi. "The Presidency of Religious Affairs and the Principle of Secularism in Turkey." *Muslim World* 98, nos. 2–3 (2008): 228–41.

Agamben, Giorgio. *State of Exception*. Translated by Kevin Attell. Chicago: Univ. of Chicago Press, 2005.

Ağır, Seven, and Cihan Artunç. "The Wealth Tax of 1942 and the Disappearance of Non-Muslim Enterprises in Turkey." *Journal of Economic History* 79, no. 1 (2019): 201–43.

Ahıska, Meltem. "Occidentalism: The Historical Fantasy of the Modern." *South Atlantic Quarterly* 102, nos. 2–3 (2003): 351–79.

———. *Occidentalism in Turkey: Questions of Modernity and National Identity in Turkish Radio Broadcasting*. London: I. B. Tauris, 2010.

Ahmad, Feroz. *The Making of Modern Turkey*. New York: Routledge, 1993.

———. *The Turkish Experiment in Democracy, 1950–1975*. Boulder, CO: Westview Press, 1977.

Ahmed, Sara. "Affective Economies." *Social Text* 22, no. 2 (2004): 117–39.

———. "Atmospheric Walls." feministkilljoys, Sept. 15, 2014. At https://feministkilljoys.com/2014/09/15/atmospheric-walls/.

———. *The Cultural Politics of Emotion*. Edinburgh: Edinburgh Univ. Press, 2004.

Akçam, Taner. *From Empire to Republic: Turkish Nationalism and the Armenian Genocide*. New York: Zed Books, 2004.

———. *A Shameful Act: The Armenian Genocide and the Question of Turkish Responsibility*. New York: Holt, 2006.

Akcan, Esra. "Off the Frame: The Panoramic City Albums of Istanbul." In *Photography's Orientalism: New Essays on Colonial Representation*, edited by Ali Behdad and Luke Gartlan, 93–114. Los Angeles: Getty Research Institute, 2013.

Akın, Yiğit. *When the War Came Home: The Ottomans' Great War and the Devastation of an Empire*. Stanford, CA: Stanford Univ. Press, 2018.

Alaranta, Toni. "Mustafa Kemal Atatürk's Six-Day Speech of 1927: Defining the Official Historical View of the Foundation of the Turkish Republic." *Turkish Studies* 9, no. 1 (Mar. 2008): 115–29.

Albi, Anneli. *EU Enlargement and the Constitutions of Central and Eastern Europe*. New York: Cambridge Univ. Press, 2005.

Alcoff, Linda. "The Problem of Speaking for Others." *Cultural Critique* 20 (1991–92): 5–32.

Algan, Bülent. "The Brand New Version of Article 301 of Turkish Penal Code and the Future of Freedom of Expression Cases in Turkey." *German Law Journal* 9, no. 12 (2008): 2237–252.

Althusser, Louis. "Ideology and Ideological State Apparatus (Notes toward an Investigation)." In *Lenin and Philosophy and Other Essays*, translated by Ben Brewster, 85–126. 1971. Reprint. New York: Monthly Review Press, 2001.

Altunışık, Meliha Benli. "The Turkish Model and Democratization in the Middle East." *Arab Studies Quarterly* 27, nos. 1–2 (2005): 45–63.

Anderson, Benedict. *Imagined Communities: Reflections on the Origins and Spread of Nationalism*. Rev. ed. New York: Verso, 1991.

Ardıç, Nurullah. *Islam and the Politics of Secularism: The Caliphate and Middle Eastern Modernization in the Early 20th Century*. New York: Routledge, 2012.

Arendt, Hannah. *The Human Condition*. 2nd ed. Chicago: Univ. of Chicago Press, 1998.

———. *On Revolution*. 1963. Reprint. New York: Penguin Books, 2006.

———. *The Origins of Totalitarianism*. New York: Harcourt, 1973.

Aristotle. *Aristotle on Rhetoric: A Theory of Civic Discourse*. 2nd ed. Translated by George A. Kennedy. New York: Oxford Univ. Press, 2007.

Asad, Talal. *Formations of the Secular: Christianity, Islam, Modernity*. Stanford, CA: Stanford Univ. Press, 2003.

———. *Genealogies of Religion: Discipline and Reasons of Power in Christianity and Islam*. Baltimore: Johns Hopkins Univ. Press, 1993.

Aslan, Senem. "'Citizen, Speak Turkish!': A Nation in the Making." *Nationalism and Ethnic Politics* 13, no. 2 (2007): 245–72.

Atatürk, Mustafa Kemal. *Atatürk'ün bütün eserleri*. Vols. 19–20: *Nutuk I–II*. Edited by M. Türker Acaroğlu, Feroz Ahmad, Sina Akşin, Talip Apaydın, Zeki Arıkan, İlhan Arsel, Hüsnü Baki, et al. Istanbul: Kaynak Yayınları, 2006–7.

———. *Atatürk'ün bütün eserleri*. Vol. 26: *2 Ekim 1932–27 Eylül 1934*. Edited by Rifat N. Bali, Elif Ertan, Süha Göney, Firdevs Kıral, Kiraz Perinçek, Sabri Sayarı, and Martı Şahin. Istanbul: Kaynak Yayınları, 2009.

———. *The Great Speech*. 2nd ed. Edited by Neşe Özden and Richard Dietrich. Ankara: Erdal Basım Yayın Dağıtım, 2008.

———. *A Speech Delivered by Ghazi Mustapha Kemal, President of the Turkish Republic, October 1927*. Leipzig, Germany: Koehler, 1929.

Atatürk'ün Nutuk'ta *kullandığı belgeler*. Translated by Kemal Bek. Istanbul: Bordo Siyah Yayınlar, 2007.

Atwill, Janet M. *Rhetoric Reclaimed: Aristotle and the Liberal Arts Tradition*. Ithaca, NY: Cornell Univ. Press, 1998.

Avcı, Gamze. "The Justice and Development Party and the EU: Political Pragmatism in a Changing Environment." In *Turkey and the EU: Accession and Reform*, edited by Gamze Avcı and Ali Çarkoğlu, 201–13. New York: Routledge, 2013.

Avcı, Gamze, and Ali Çarkoğlu, eds. *Turkey and the EU: Accession and Reform*. New York: Routledge, 2013.

Aydar, Hidayet, and Necmettin Gökkır. "Discussions on the Language of Prayer in Turkey: A Modern Version of the Classical Debate." *Turkish Studies* 8, no. 1 (2007): 121–36.

Aydın, Cemil. *The Idea of the Muslim World: A Global Intellectual History*. Cambridge, MA: Harvard Univ. Press, 2017.

Aydıngün, Ayşegül, and İsmail Aydıngün. "The Role of Language in the Formation of Turkish National Identity and Turkishness." *Nationalism and Ethnic Politics* 10, no. 3 (2004): 415–32.

Azak, Umut. *Islam and Secularism in Turkey: Kemalism, Religion, and the Nation State*. New York: I. B. Tauris, 2010.

———. "Secularism in Turkey as a Nationalist Search for Vernacular Islam: The Ban on the Call to Prayer in Arabic (1932–1950)." *Revue des mondes Musulmans et de la Méditerranée* 124 (2008): 161–79.

Balibar, Étienne. "Ideas of Europe: Civilization and Constitution." *Iris: European Journal of Philosophy and Public Debate* 1, no. 1 (2009): 3–17.

Bardakoğlu, Ali. "'Moderate Perception of Islam' and the Turkish Model of the Diyanet: The President's Statement." *Journal of Muslim Minority Affairs* 24, no. 2 (2004): 367–74.

Barkey, Henri. "The Transformation of Turkey's Kurdish Question." In *The Kurdish Question Revisited*, edited by Gareth Stansfield and Mohammed Shareef, 211–24. New York: Oxford Univ. Press, 2017.

Baykan, Toygar Sinan. *The Justice and Development Party in Turkey: Populism, Personalism, Organization*. New York: Cambridge Univ. Press, 2018.

Beasley, Vanessa B. *You, the People: American National Identity in Presidential Rhetoric*. College Station: Texas A&M Univ. Press, 2004.

Behdad, Ali, and Luke Gartlan, eds. *Photography's Orientalism: New Essays on Colonial Representation*. Los Angeles: Getty Research Institute, 2013.

Bektas, Yakup. "The Sultan's Messenger: Cultural Constructions of Ottoman Telegraphy, 1847–1880." *Technology and Culture* 41, no. 4 (2000): 669–96.

Belge, Murat. "'Love Me, or Leave Me?': The Strange Case of Orhan Pamuk." Open Democracy, Oct. 17, 2005. At https://www.opendemocracy.net/en/orhan_pamuk_2935jsp.

Biesecker, Barbara A. "Rethinking the Rhetorical Situation from within the Thematic of 'Différance.'" *Philosophy and Rhetoric* 22, no. 2 (1989): 110–30.

Bilgen-Reinart, Üstün. "Hrant Dink: Forging an Armenian Identity in Turkey." Open Democracy, Feb. 7, 2006. At https://www.opendemocracy.net/en/dink_3246jsp/.

Bilgiç, Ali. *Turkey, Power, and the West: Gendered International Relations and Foreign Policy*. New York: I. B. Tauris, 2016.

Bilgin, Fevzi. "Sledgehammer (Balyoz): How Turkey Averted a Coup in 2003." *Washington Review of Turkish and Eurasian Affairs*, July 2010. At https://www.thewashingtonreview.org/articles/sledgehammer.html.

Bilici, Mücahit. "Black Turks, White Turks: On the Three Requirements of Turkish Citizenship." *Insight Turkey* 11, no. 3 (2009): 23–35.

Birand, Mehmet Ali. *The Generals' Coup in Turkey: An Inside Story of 12 September 1980*. Translated by M. A. Dikerdem. London: Brassey's Defense, 1987.

Brennan, Theresa. *The Transmission of Affect*. Ithaca, NY: Cornell Univ. Press, 2004.

Brockett, Gavin D. "Collective Action and the Turkish Revolution: Towards a Framework for the Social History of the Atatürk Era, 1923–38." *Middle Eastern Studies* 34, no. 4 (1998): 44–66.

———. *How Happy to Call Oneself a Turk: Provincial Newspapers and the Negotiation of a Muslim National Identity*. Austin: Univ. of Texas Press, 2011.

Browers, Michaelle, and Charles Kurzman, eds. *An Islamic Reformation?* Lanham, MD: Lexington Books, 2004.

Brubaker, Rogers. "Categories of Analysis and Categories of Practice: A Note on the Study of Muslims in European Countries of Immigration." *Ethnic and Racial Studies* 36, no. 1 (2013): 1–8.

———. *Nationalism Reframed: Nationhood and the National Question in the New Europe*. New York: Cambridge Univ. Press, 1996.

Bruner, M. Lane. *Strategies of Remembrance: The Rhetorical Dimensions of National Identity Construction*. Columbia: Univ. of South Carolina Press, 2002.

Butler, Judith. *Frames of War: When Is Life Grievable?* New York: Verso, 2010.

———. *Undoing Gender*. New York: Routledge, 2004.

Butler, Judith, Ernesto Laclau, and Slavoj Žižek. *Contingency, Hegemony, Universality: Contemporary Dialogues on the Left*. New York: Verso, 2000.

Çağaptay, Soner. "Race, Assimilation, and Kemalism: Turkish Nationalism and the Minorities in the 1930s." *Middle East Studies* 40, no. 3 (2004): 86–101.

Calhoun, Craig. *Nationalism*. Minneapolis: Univ. of Minnesota Press, 1997.

Casier, Marlies. "The Politics of Solidarity: The Kurdish Question in the European Parliament." In *Nationalisms and Politics in Turkey: Political Islam, Kemalism, and the Kurdish Issue*, edited by Marlies Casier and Joost Jongerden, 197–217. New York: Routledge, 2011.

Casier, Marlies, and Joost Jongerden, eds. *Nationalisms and Politics in Turkey: Political Islam, Kemalism, and the Kurdish Issue*. New York: Routledge, 2011.

Castaldo, Antonino. "Populism and Competitive Authoritarianism in Turkey." *Southeast European and Black Sea Studies* 18, no. 4 (2018): 467–87.

Celep, Ödül. "The Republican People's Party and Turkey's EU Membership." In *Turkey and the EU: Accession and Reform*, edited by Gamze Avcı and Ali Çarkoğlu, 215–26. New York: Routledge, 2013.

Cengiz, Firat, and Lars Hoffman, eds. *Turkey and the European Union: Facing New Challenges and Opportunities*. New York: Routledge, 2014.

Chakrabarty, Dipesh. *Habitations of Modernity: Essays in the Wake of Subaltern Studies*. Chicago: Univ. of Chicago Press, 2002.

———. *Provincializing Europe: Postcolonial Thought and Historical Difference*. Princeton, NJ: Princeton Univ. Press, 2000.

Chaput, Catherine. "Rhetorical Circulation in Late Capitalism: Neoliberalism and the Overdetermination of Affective Energy." *Philosophy and Rhetoric* 43, no. 1 (2010): 1–25.

Charland, Maurice. "Constitutive Rhetoric: The Case of the *Peuple Québécois*." *Quarterly Journal of Speech* 73, no. 2 (1987): 133–50.

Chatterjee, Partha. *The Nation and Its Fragments*. Princeton, NJ: Princeton Univ. Press, 1993.

Cheah, Pheng, and Jonathan Culler, eds. *Grounds of Comparison: Around the Work of Benedict Anderson*. New York: Routledge, 2003.

Çiftçi, Kemal. "The Kemalist Hegemony in Turkey and the Justice and Development Party (AKP) as an 'Other.'" *L'Europe en formation: Revue d'études sur la construction européenne et le fédéralisme* 367, no. 1 (2013): 143–69.

Çınar, Alev. *Modernity, Islam, and Secularism in Turkey: Bodies, Places, and Time*. Minneapolis: Univ. of Minnesota Press, 2005.

Çırakman, Aslı. *From the "Terror of the World" to the "Sick Man of Europe": European Images of Ottoman Empire and Society from the Sixteenth Century to the Nineteenth*. New York: Peter Lang, 2002.

Cizre, Ümit. "Problems of Democratic Governance of Civil–Military Relations in Turkey and the European Union Enlargement Zone." *European Journal of Political Research* 43, no. 1 (2004): 107–25.

Clark, Gregory. *Rhetorical Landscapes in America: Variations on a Theme from Kenneth Burke*. Columbia: Univ. of South Carolina Press, 2004.

Dadrian, Vahakn N., and Taner Akçam. *Judgment at Istanbul: The Armenian Genocide Trials*. New York: Berghahn Books, 2011.

Danforth, Nicholas. "The Writing of Modern Turkey." *Nationalities Papers* 41, no. 6 (2013): 1136–46.

Davison, Andrew. "Turkey, a 'Secular' State? The Challenge of Description." *South Atlantic Quarterly* 102, nos. 2–3 (Spring–Summer 2003): 333–50.

———. "Ziya Gökalp and Provincializing Europe." *Comparative Studies of South Asia, Africa, and the Middle East* 26, no. 3 (2006): 377–90.

Davison, Roderic H. "The Advent of the Electric Telegraph in the Ottoman Empire." In *Essays in Ottoman and Turkish History, 1774–1923: The Impact of the West*, 133–65. Austin: Univ. of Texas Press, 1990.

De los Santos, René Augustín. "'The Future of Our History': Rhetorics of Transformation and Power in Plutarco Elías Calles' 1928 *Informe*." *Rhetoric Society Quarterly* 45, no. 3 (2015): 199–211.

De Man, Paul. *The Rhetoric of Romanticism*. New York: Columbia Univ. Press, 1984.

———. "Semiology and Rhetoric." In *Allegories of Reading: Figural Language in Rousseau, Nietzsche, Rilke, and Proust*, 3–19. New Haven, CT: Yale Univ. Press, 1979.

Deringil, Selim. "The Invention of Tradition as Public Image in the Late Ottoman Empire, 1808 to 1908." *Comparative Studies in Society and History* 35, no. 1 (1993): 3–29.

Derrida, Jacques. "Declarations of Independence." *New Political Science* 7, no. 1 (1986): 7–15.

———. *Margins of Philosophy*. Translated by Alan Bass. Chicago: Univ. of Chicago Press, 1982.

———. *The Other Heading: Reflections on Today's Europe*. Translated by Pascale-Anne Brault and Michael B. Naas. Bloomington: Indiana Univ. Press, 1992.

———. "Signature Event Context." In *Margins of Philosophy*, translated by Alan Bass, 307–30. Chicago: Univ. of Chicago Press, 1982.

———. "White Mythology: Metaphor in the Text of Philosophy." In *Margins of Philosophy*, translated by Alan Bass, 207–71. Chicago: Univ. of Chicago Press, 1982.

DeTar, Matthew. "Absence of the Present: The Reburial of Adnan Menderes and the Condition of Possibility of Public Memory in Turkey." *Communication and Critical/Cultural Studies* 13, no. 1 (2016): 93–108.

———. "Decolonizing Rhetorical History." In *Reframing Rhetorical History: Cases, Theories, and Methodologies*, edited by Jason Edward Black and Kathleen J. Turner. Tuscaloosa: Univ. of Alabama Press, forthcoming.

———. "Figures of Nationalist Speech in Atatürk's *Great Speech*." In *History, Politics, and Foreign Policy in Turkey*, edited by Kılıç Buğra Kanat, Kadir Üstün, and Nuh Yılmaz, 3–25. Ankara: SETA Foundation, 2012.

———. "Nationalism, Rhetoric, and Discursive Form." *Journal of Contemporary Thought* 44 (2016): 15–26.

———. "Representation from the Margins: Brexit, Turkey, and the Idea of 'Europe.'" In *Negotiating Identity and Transnationalism: Middle Eastern and North African Communication and Critical Cultural Studies*, edited by Haneen Ghabra, Fatima Zahrae Chrifi Alaoui, Shadee Abdi, and Bernadette Marie Calafell, 91–103. New York: Peter Lang, 2020.

Dole, Christopher. *Healing Secular Life: Loss and Devotion in Modern Turkey*. Philadelphia: Univ. of Pennsylvania Press, 2012.

Döşemeci, Mehmet. *Debating Turkish Modernity: Civilization, Nationalism, and the EEC*. New York: Cambridge Univ. Press, 2013.

Dressler, Markus. "Making Religion through Secularist Legal Discourse: The Case of Turkish Alevism." In *Secularism and Religion-Making*, edited by Markus Dressler and Arvind-Pal S. Mandair, 187–208. New York: Oxford Univ. Press, 2011.

———. "Public–Private Distinctions, the Alevi Question, and the Headscarf: Turkish Secularism Revisited." In *Comparative Secularisms in a Global Age*, edited by Linell E. Cady and Elizabeth Shakman Hurd, 121–41. New York: Palgrave, 2010.

Drzewiecka, Jolanta A. "Reinventing and Contesting Identities in Constitutive Discourses: Between Diaspora and Its Others." *Communication Quarterly* 50, no. 1 (2002): 1–23.

Edbauer, Jenny. "Unframing Models of Public Distribution: From Rhetorical Situation to Rhetorical Ecologies." *Rhetoric Society Quarterly* 35, no. 4 (2005): 5–24.

Edwards, Brian T. "*Tahrir*: Ends of Circulation." *Public Culture* 23, no. 3 (2011): 493–504.

Eissenstat, Howard. "Children of Özal: The New Face of Turkish Studies." *Journal of the Ottoman and Turkish Studies Association* 1, nos. 1–2 (2014): 23–35.

Ertürk, Nergis. *Grammatology and Literary Modernity in Turkey*. New York: Oxford Univ. Press, 2011.

Evren, Kenan. *Kenan Evren'in anıları*. Istanbul: Milliyet Yayınları, 1991–92.

———. *Türkiye Cumhuriyeti devlet başkanı orgeneral Kenan Evren'in söylev ve demeçleri*. Vol. 2: *12 Eylül 1981–12 Eylül 1982*. Edited by K. Ali Baransel. Ankara: Başbakanlık Basımevi, 1982.

Fahnestock, Jeanne. "Aristotle and Theories of Figuration." In *Rereading Aristotle's* Rhetoric, edited by Alan G. Gross and Arthur E. Walzer, 166–84. Carbondale: Southern Illinois Univ. Press, 2000.

———. *Rhetorical Figures in Science*. New York: Oxford Univ. Press, 1999.

Farrell, Thomas B. *Norms of Rhetorical Culture*. New Haven, CT: Yale Univ. Press, 1993.

Findley, Carter Vaughn. *Turkey, Islam, Nationalism, and Modernity: A History, 1789–2007*. New Haven, CT: Yale Univ. Press, 2010.

Finnegan, Cara A. "Doing Rhetorical History of the Visual: The Photograph and the Archive." In *Defining Visual Rhetorics*, edited by Charles A. Hill and Marguerite Helmers, 195–214. Mahwah, NJ: Lawrence Erlbaum, 2004.

Fortna, Benjamin C. *The Circassian: The Life of Eşref Bey, Late Ottoman Insurgent and Special Agent*. New York: Oxford Univ. Press, 2016.

Foucault, Michel. *The Archaeology of Knowledge and The Discourse on Language*. Translated by A. M. Sheridan Smith. New York: Harper Colophon, 1976.

———. "Governmentality." In *The Foucault Effect: Studies in Governmentality: With Two Lectures and an Interview with Michel Foucault*, edited by Graham Burchell, Colin Gordon, and Peter Miller, 87–104. Chicago: Univ. of Chicago Press, 1991.

———. "Nietzsche, Genealogy, History." Translated by Donald F. Bouchard and Sherry Simon. Edited by Donald F. Bouchard. In *The Foucault Reader*, edited by Paul Rabinow, 76–100. 1984. Reprint. New York: Vintage Books, 2010.

———. *The Order of Things: An Archaeology of the Human Sciences*. 1970. Reprint. New York: Vintage Books, 1990.

Freely, Maureen. "Why They Killed Hrant Dink." *Index on Censorship* 36, no. 2 (2007): 15–29.

Gaonkar, Dilip Parameshwar, ed. *Alternative Modernities*. Durham, NC: Duke Univ. Press, 2001.

———. "Foucault on Discourse: Methods and Temptations." *Journal of the American Forensic Association* 18, no. 4 (1982): 246–57.

———. "The Idea of Rhetoric in the Rhetoric of Science." In *Rhetorical Hermeneutics: Invention and Interpretation in the Age of Science*, edited by Alan G. Gross and William M. Keith, 25–85. Albany: State Univ. of New York Press, 1997.

Gaonkar, Dilip Parameshwar, and Elizabeth A. Povinelli. "Technologies of Public Forms: Circulation, Transfiguration, Recognition." *Public Culture* 15, no. 3 (2003): 385–97.

Garver, Eugene. *Aristotle's* Rhetoric: *An Art of Character*. Chicago: Univ. of Chicago Press, 1994.

Gellner, Ernest. *Nations and Nationalism*. Ithaca, NY: Cornell Univ. Press, 1983.

General Secretariat of the National Security Council. *12 September in Turkey: Before and After*. Ankara: Ongun Kardeşler Printing House, 1982.

Geyikdağı, Mehmet Yaşar. *Political Parties in Turkey: The Role of Islam*. New York: Praeger, 1984.

Ghanim, David. "Turkish Democracy and Political Islam." *Middle East Policy* 16, no. 1 (2009): 75–84.

Gingeras, Ryan. *Eternal Dawn: Turkey in the Age of Atatürk*. New York: Oxford Univ. Press, 2019.

———. *Fall of the Sultanate: The Great War and the End of the Ottoman Empire, 1908–1922*. New York: Oxford Univ. Press, 2016.

Giorgetti, Filiz Meşeci. "Nation-Building in Turkey through Ritual Pedagogy: The Late Ottoman and Early Turkish Republican Era." *History of Education* 49, no. 1 (2020): 77–103.

Göçek, Fatma Müge. *Denial of Violence: Ottoman Past, Turkish Present, and Collective Violence against the Armenians, 1789–2009*. New York: Oxford Univ. Press, 2015.

Gökalp, Ziya. *Turkish Nationalism and Western Civilization: Selected Essays of Ziya Gökalp*. Translated and edited by Niyazi Berkes. London: Allen and Unwin, 1959.

Gökoğlu, A. *Inkilâbımızda posta ve telgrafçılar*. Istanbul: N.p., 1938.

Gorgas, Jordi Tejel. "Making Borders from Below: The Emergence of the Turkish–Iraqi Frontier, 1918–1925." *Middle Eastern Studies* 54, no. 5 (2018): 811–26.

Goswami, Manu. *Producing India: From Colonial Economy to National Space*. Chicago: Univ. of Chicago Press, 2004.

Gözaydın, İstar B. "*Diyanet* and Politics." *Muslim World* 98, nos. 2–3 (2008): 216–27.

Grigoriadis, Ioannis N. "*Türk* or *Türkiyeli*? The Reform of Turkey's Minority Legislation and the Rediscovery of Ottomanism." *Middle Eastern Studies* 43, no. 3 (2007): 423–38.

Gross, Alan G., and Marcelo Dascal. "The Conceptual Unity of Aristotle's *Rhetoric*." *Philosophy and Rhetoric* 34, no. 4 (2001): 275–91.

Gross, Alan G., and Arthur E. Walzer, eds. *Rereading Aristotle's* Rhetoric. Carbondale: Southern Illinois Univ. Press, 2000.

Gür, Aslı. "Stories in Three Dimensions: Narratives of Nation and the Anatolian Civilizations Museum." In *The Politics of Public Memory in Turkey*, edited by Esra Özyürek, 40–69. Syracuse, NY: Syracuse Univ. Press, 2007.

Gürel, Perin. *The Limits of Westernization: A Cultural History of America in Turkey*. New York: Columbia Univ. Press, 2017.

Hale, William. *Turkish Politics and the Military.* New York: Routledge, 1994.

Hall, Stuart. "Constituting an Archive." *Third Text* 15, no. 54 (2001): 89–92.

Hanioğlu, M. Şükrü. *Atatürk: An Intellectual Biography.* Princeton, NJ: Princeton Univ. Press, 2011.

———. *A Brief History of the Late Ottoman Empire.* Princeton, NJ: Princeton Univ. Press, 2008.

Hariman, Robert. *Political Style: The Artistry of Power.* Chicago: Univ. of Chicago Press, 1995.

———. "Prudence/Performance." *Rhetoric Society Quarterly* 21, no. 2 (1991): 26–35.

———. "Theory without Modernity." In *Prudence: Classical Virtue, Postmodern Practice,* edited by Robert Hariman, 1–32. University Park: Pennsylvania State Univ. Press, 2003.

Harris, George. "Celal Bayar: Conspiratorial Democrat." In *Political Leaders and Democracy in Turkey,* edited by Metin Heper and Sabri Sarayı, 45–63. Lanham, MD: Lexington Books, 2002.

Hasan, Mushirul. *Between Modernity and Nationalism: Halide Edip's Encounter with Ghandhi's India.* New York: Oxford Univ. Press, 2010.

Hawhee, Debra, and Christa J. Olson. "Pan-historiography: The Challenges of Writing History across Time and Space." In *Theorizing Histories of Rhetoric,* edited by Michelle Ballif, 90–105. Carbondale: Southern Illinois Univ. Press, 2013.

Heper, Metin. *İsmet İnönü: The Making of a Turkish Statesman.* Boston: Brill, 1998.

———. "Turgut Özal's Presidency: Crisis and the Glimmerings of Consensus." In *Politics in the Third Turkish Republic,* edited by Metin Heper and Ahmet Evin, 187–98. Boulder, CO: Westview Press, 1994.

Heper, Metin, and Ahmet Evin, eds. *State, Democracy, and the Military: Turkey in the 1980s.* New York: De Gruyter, 1988.

Hobsbawm, E. J. *Nations and Nationalism since 1780: Programme, Myth, Reality.* 2nd ed. New York: Cambridge Univ. Press, 1993.

Honig, Bonnie. "Declarations of Independence: Arendt and Derrida on the Problem of Founding a Republic." *American Political Science Review* 85, no. 1 (Mar. 1991): 97–113.

Hovannisian, Richard G. "Introduction: The Armenian Genocide: Remembrance and Denial." In *Remembrance and Denial: The Case of the Armenian Genocide*, ed. Richard G. Hovannisian, 13–21. Detroit: Wayne State Univ. Press, 1999.

———, ed. *Remembrance and Denial: The Case of the Armenian Genocide*. Detroit: Wayne State Univ. Press, 1999.

İlkin, Selim. "A Short History of Turkey's Association with the European Community." In *Turkey and the European Community*, edited by Ahmet Evin and Geoffrey Denton, 35–49. Opladen, Germany: Leske und Budrich, 1990.

İnan, Süleyman. "The First 'History of the Turkish Revolution' Lectures and Courses in Turkish Universities (1934–42)." *Middle Eastern Studies* 43, no. 4 (2007): 593–609.

İri, Murat, and H. Esra Arcan. "The Orhan Pamuk Case: How Mainstream Turkish Media Framed His Freedom of Speech." *Sosyal bilimler dergisi* 9, no. 18 (2007): 17–24.

Jacoby, Tim. "For the People, of the People, and by the Military: The Regime Structure of Modern Turkey." *Political Studies* 51, no. 4 (2003): 669–85.

JanMohamed, Abdul. "Between Speaking and Dying: Some Imperatives in the Emergence of the Subaltern in the Context of US Slavery." In *Can the Subaltern Speak? Reflections on the History of an Idea*, edited by Rosalind C. Morris, 139–55. New York: Columbia Univ. Press, 2010.

Jenkins, Gareth. *Context and Circumstance: The Turkish Military and Politics*. New York: Routledge, 2001.

———. "Continuity and Change: Prospects for Civil–Military Relations in Turkey." *International Affairs* 83, no. 2 (Mar. 2007): 339–55.

Jongerden, Joost. "Resettlement and Reconstruction of Identity: The Case of the Kurds in Turkey." *Global Review of Ethnopolitics* 1, no. 1 (2001): 80–86.

Kaplan, Sam. *The Pedagogical State: Education and the Politics of National Culture in Post-1980 Turkey*. Stanford, CA: Stanford Univ. Press, 2006.

Karabelias, Gerassimos. "The Evolution of Civil–Military Relations in Post-war Turkey, 1980–95." *Middle Eastern Studies* 35, no. 4 (Oct. 1999): 130–51.

Karpat, Kemal H. "Military Interventions: Army–Civilian Relations in Turkey before and after 1980." In *State, Democracy, and the Military: Turkey in the 1980s*, edited by Metin Heper and Ahmet Evin, 137–58. New York: De Gruyter, 1988.

———, ed. *Ottoman Past and Today's Turkey*. Boston: Brill, 2000.

———. "The People's Houses in Turkey: Establishment and Growth." *Middle East Journal* 17, nos. 1–2 (1963): 55–67.

———. *The Politicization of Islam: Reconstructing Identity, State, Faith, and Community in the Late Ottoman State*. New York: Oxford Univ. Press, 2001.

———. *Turkey's Politics: The Transition to a Multi-party System*. Princeton, NJ: Princeton Univ. Press, 1959.

Kavakçı, Merve. "Turkey's Test with Its Deep State." *Mediterranean Quarterly* 20, no. 4 (2009): 83–97.

Kaya, Ayhan. *Europeanization and Tolerance in Turkey: The Myth of Toleration*. New York: Palgrave, 2013.

Kaya, Emir. *Secularism and State Religion in Modern Turkey: Law, Policy-Making, and the Diyanet*. New York: I. B. Tauris, 2017.

Kaya, Mehmed S. *The Zaza Kurds of Turkey: A Middle Eastern Minority in a Globalised Society*. New York: I. B. Tauris, 2011.

Kaya, Serdar. "The Rise and Decline of the Turkish 'Deep State': The Ergenekon Case." *Insight Turkey* 11, no. 4 (2009): 99–113.

Kennedy, George A. *A New History of Classical Rhetoric*. Princeton, NJ: Princeton Univ. Press, 1994.

Keyman, E. Fuat. "Articulating Citizenship and Identity: The 'Kurdish Question' in Turkey." In *Citizenship in a Global World: European Questions and Turkish Experiences*, edited by E. Fuat Keyman and Ahmet İçduygu, 267–88. New York: Routledge, 2005.

Keyman, E. Fuat, and Ahmet İçduygu, eds. *Citizenship in a Global World: European Questions and Turkish Experiences*. New York: Routledge, 2005.

Kezer, Zeynep. *Building Modern Turkey: State, Space, and Ideology in the Early Republic*. Pittsburgh: Univ. of Pittsburgh Press, 2015.

Kili, Suna. *Kemalism*. Istanbul: Robert College School of Business Administration, 1969.

Kiliç, H. Ayla. "Democratization, Human Rights, and Ethnic Policies in Turkey." *Journal of Muslim Minority Affairs* 18, no. 1 (1998): 91–110.

Kirby, John T. "Aristotle on Metaphor." *American Journal of Philology* 118, no. 4 (1997): 517–54.

Kirişci, Kemal, and Gareth M. Winrow. *The Kurdish Question and Turkey: An Example of a Trans-state Ethnic Conflict.* London: Frank Cass, 1997.

Krueger, Anne O. "Turkey's Trade and Payments Regime in the Light of Integration with the EEC." In *Economic Relations between Turkey and the EEC: Proceedings of a Seminar Held in Antalya on October 11–14, 1976*, edited by Osman Okyar and Okan H. Aktan, 145–71. Antalya, Turkey: Hacettepe Institute for Economic and Social Research on Turkey and the Middle East, 1976.

Kuru, Ahmet T. *Secularism and State Policies toward Religion: The United States, France, and Turkey.* New York: Cambridge Univ. Press, 2009.

Kuru, Ahmet T., and Alfred Stepan, eds. *Democracy, Islam, and Secularism in Turkey.* New York: Columbia Univ. Press, 2012.

Kurzman, Charles, and Michaelle Browers. "Introduction: Comparing Reformations." In *An Islamic Reformation?*, edited by Michaelle Browers and Charles Kurzman, 1–17. Lanham, MD: Lexington Books, 2004.

Kuzmanovic, Daniella. "Dead Bodies, Affective States, and Volatile Icons: An Iconology of Hrant Dink." *Middle East Journal of Culture and Communication* 8, no. 1 (2015): 85–101.

Lagendijk, Joost. "Turkey's Accession to the European Union and the Role of the Justice and Development Party." In *Democracy, Islam, and Secularism in Turkey*, edited by Ahmet T. Kuru and Alfred Stepan, 166–88. New York: Columbia Univ. Press, 2012.

Lamprou, Alexandros. *Nation-Building in Modern Turkey: The "People's Houses," the State, and the Citizen.* New York: I. B. Tauris, 2015.

Lee, Benjamin, and Edward LiPuma. "Cultures of Circulation: The Imaginations of Modernity." *Public Culture* 14, no. 1 (2002): 191–213.

Levin, Paul T. *Turkey and the European Union: Christian and Secular Images of Islam.* New York: Palgrave, 2011.

Levonian, Lutfy, ed. and trans. *The Turkish Press: Selections from the Turkish Press Showing Events and Opinions, 1925–1932.* Athens: School of Religion, 1932.

Lewis, Bernard. *The Emergence of Modern Turkey.* London: Oxford Univ. Press, 1961.

Lewis, Geoffrey. *Turkey*. 3rd ed. London: Ernest Benn, 1965.

———. *The Turkish Language Reform: A Catastrophic Success*. New York: Oxford Univ. Press, 1999.

Livanios, Dimitris. "The 'Sick Man' Paradox: History, Rhetoric, and the 'European Character' of Turkey." *Journal of Southern Europe and the Balkans* 8, no. 3 (2006): 299–311.

Lyotard, Jean-François. *The Différend: Phrases in Dispute*. Translated by Georges Van Den Abbeele. Minneapolis: Univ. of Minnesota Press, 1988.

Macfie, A. L. *Atatürk*. New York: Longman, 1994.

MacMillan, Catherine. *Discourse, Identity, and the Question of Turkish Accession to the EU: Through the Looking Glass*. 2013. Reprint. New York: Routledge, 2016.

Maessen, Enno. "Reassessing Turkish National Memory: An Analysis of the Representation of Turkish National Memory by the AKP." *Middle Eastern Studies* 50, no. 2 (2014): 309–24.

Mamdani, Mahmood. *Good Muslim, Bad Muslim: America, the Cold War, and the Roots of Terror*. New York: Pantheon, 2004.

Mango, Andrew. *Atatürk*. London: John Murray, 1999.

Mao, LuMing. "Beyond Bias, Binary, and Border: Mapping Out the Future of Comparative Rhetoric." *Rhetoric Society Quarterly* 43, no. 3 (2013): 209–25.

Mardin, Şerif. *The Genesis of Young Ottoman Thought: A Study in the Modernization of Turkish Political Ideas*. Princeton, NJ: Princeton Univ. Press, 1962.

McPherson, Eve. "Political History and Embodied Identity Discourse in the Turkish Call to Prayer." *Music and Politics* 5, no. 1 (2011).

Meeker, Michael E. *A Nation of Empire: The Ottoman Legacy of Turkish Modernity*. Berkeley: Univ. of California Press, 2002.

Menderes, Adnan. *Adnan Menderes'in konuşmaları, demeçleri, makaleleri*. Vol. 2: *Mayıs 1950–Aralık 1951*. Edited by Halûk Kılçık. Ankara: Demokratlar Kulübü Yayınları: 3, 1991.

Micklewright, Nancy. "Alternative Histories of Photography in the Ottoman Middle East." In *Photography's Orientalism: New Essays on Colonial Representation*, edited by Ali Behdad and Luke Gartlan, 75–92. Los Angeles: Getty Research Institute, 2013.

Miller, Carolyn R. "The Aristotelian *Topos*: Hunting for Novelty." In *Rereading Aristotle's* Rhetoric, edited by Alan G. Gross and Arthur E. Walzer, 130–46. Carbondale: Southern Illinois Univ. Press, 2000.

Moffitt, Benjamin. *The Global Rise of Populism: Performance, Political Style, and Representation*. Stanford, CA: Stanford Univ. Press, 2016.

Moran, Richard. "Artifice and Persuasion: The Work of Metaphor in the *Rhetoric*." In *Essays on Aristotle's* Rhetoric, edited by Amélie Oksenberg Rorty, 385–98. Berkeley: Univ. of California Press, 1996.

Morin, Aysel, and Ronald Lee. "Constitutive Discourse of Turkish Nationalism: Atatürk's *Nutuk* and the Rhetorical Construction of the 'Turkish People.'" *Communication Studies* 61, no. 5 (2010): 485–506.

Morris, Rosalind C., ed. *Can the Subaltern Speak? Reflections on the History of an Idea*. New York: Columbia Univ. Press, 2010.

Müftüler-Baç, Meltem. "Turkish Foreign Policy, Its Domestic Determinants, and the Role of the European Union." In *Turkey and the EU: Accession and Reform*, edited by Gamze Avcı and Ali Çarkoğlu, 71–83. New York: Routledge, 2013.

Naimark, Norman M. Preface to *A Question of Genocide: Armenians and Turks at the End of the Ottoman Empire*, edited by Ronald Grigor Suny, Fatma Müge Göçek, and Norman M. Naimark, xiii–xix. New York: Oxford Univ. Press, 2011.

Nakayama, Thomas K., and Robert L. Krizek. "Whiteness: A Strategic Rhetoric." *Quarterly Journal of Speech* 81, no. 3 (1995): 291–309.

Narlı, Nilüfer. "Civil–Military Relations in Turkey." *Turkish Studies* 1, no. 1 (2000): 107–27.

Navaro-Yashin, Yael. *Faces of the State: Secularism and Public Life in Turkey*. Princeton, NJ: Princeton Univ. Press, 2002.

Öcal, Mustafa. "From the Past to the Present: Imam and Preacher Schools in Turkey—An Ongoing Quarrel." *Religious Education* 102, no. 2 (2007): 191–205.

O'Connell, John Morgan. "Fine Art, Fine Music: Controlling Turkish Taste at the Fine Arts Academy in 1926." *Yearbook for Traditional Music* 32 (2000): 117–42.

———. "In the Time of Alaturka: Identifying Difference in Musical Discourse." *Ethnomusicology* 49, no. 2 (2005): 177–205.

Olson, Christa J. *Constitutive Visions: Indigeneity and Commonplaces of National Identity in Republican Ecuador.* University Park: Pennsylvania State Univ. Press, 2014.

Olson, Christa J., and René Augustín De los Santos. "Expanding the Idea of América." *Rhetoric Society Quarterly* 45, no. 3 (2015): 193–98.

Öniş, Ziya. "Domestic Politics, International Norms, and Challenges to the State: Turkey–EU Relations in the Post-Helsinki Era." *Turkish Studies* 4, no. 1 (2003): 9–34.

Öniş, Ziya, and Şuhnaz Yılmaz. "Between Europeanization and Euro-Asianism: Foreign Policy Activism in Turkey during the AKP Era." *Turkish Studies* 10, no. 1 (2009): 7–24.

Oran, Baskın. "The Minority Concept and Rights in Turkey: The Lausanne Peace Treaty and Current Issues." In *Human Rights in Turkey*, edited by Zehra F. Kabasakal Arat, 35–56. Philadelphia: Univ. of Pennsylvania Press, 2007.

Osborne, Thomas. "The Ordinariness of the Archive." *History of the Human Sciences* 12, no. 2 (1999): 51–64.

Özbudun, Ergun. "The Status of the President of the Republic under the Turkish Constitution of 1982: Presidentialism or Parliamentarism?" In *State, Democracy, and the Military: Turkey in the 1980s*, edited by Metin Heper and Ahmet Evin, 37–46. New York: De Gruyter, 1988.

———. "The Turkish Constitutional Court and Political Crisis." In *Democracy, Islam, and Secularism in Turkey*, edited by Ahmet T. Kuru and Alfred Stepan, 149–65. New York: Columbia Univ. Press, 2012.

Özdalga, Elisabeth, ed. *Late Ottoman Society: The Intellectual Legacy.* New York: Routledge, 2005.

Özyürek, Esra. "Beyond Integration and Recognition: Diasporic Constructions of Alevi Muslim Identity between Germany and Turkey." In *Transnational Transcendence: Essays on Religion and Globalization*, edited by Thomas J. Csordas, 121–44. Berkeley: Univ. of California Press, 2009.

———. "Introduction: The Politics of Public Memory in Turkey." In *The Politics of Public Memory in Turkey*, edited by Esra Özyürek, 1–15. Syracuse, NY: Syracuse Univ. Press, 2007.

———. *Nostalgia for the Modern: State Secularism and Everyday Politics in Turkey.* Durham, NC: Duke Univ. Press, 2006.

———, ed. *The Politics of Public Memory in Turkey.* Syracuse, NY: Syracuse Univ. Press, 2007.

Parker, Patricia. "Metaphor and Catachresis." In *The Ends of Rhetoric: History, Theory, Practice*, edited by John Bender and David E. Wellbery, 60–73. Stanford, CA: Stanford Univ. Press, 1990.

Parla, Taha. *Social and Political Thought of Ziya Gökalp, 1876–1924.* Leiden, Netherlands: Brill, 1985.

Parla, Taha, and Andrew Davison. *Corporatist Ideology in Kemalist Turkey: Progress or Order?* Syracuse, NY: Syracuse Univ. Press, 2004.

Parry-Giles, Trevor, and Shawn J. Parry-Giles. *The Prime-Time Presidency:* The West Wing *and U.S. Nationalism.* Chicago: Univ. of Illinois Press, 2006.

Pitkin, Hanna Fenichel. *The Concept of Representation.* Berkeley: Univ. of California Press, 1967.

Pocock, J. G. A. *The Machiavellian Moment: Florentine Political Thought and the Atlantic Republican Tradition.* 2nd ed. Princeton, NJ: Princeton Univ. Press, 2003.

Pope, Nicole, and Hugh Pope. *Turkey Unveiled: A History of Modern Turkey.* Woodstock, NY: Overlook Press, 1997.

Poster, Carol. "Being, Time, and Definition: Toward a Semiotics of Figural Rhetoric." *Philosophy and Rhetoric* 33, no. 2 (2000): 116–36.

Qureshi, M. Naem. *Pan-Islam in British Indian Politics: A Study of the Khilafat Movement, 1918–1924.* Leiden, Netherlands: Brill, 1999.

Reed, Howard A. "Revival of Islam in Secular Turkey." *Middle East Journal* 8, no. 3 (1954): 267–82.

———. "Turkey's New İmam-Hatip Schools." *Die Welt des Islams* 4, nos. 2–3 (1955): 150–63.

Rice, Jenny. "From Architectonic to Tectonics: Introducing Regional Rhetorics." *Rhetoric Society Quarterly* 42, no. 3 (2012): 201–13.

Roberts, Mary. "The Limits of Circumscription." In *Photography's Orientalism: New Essays on Colonial Representation*, edited by Ali Behdad and Luke Gartlan, 53–74. Los Angeles: Getty Research Institute, 2013.

Rorty, Amélie Oksenberg, ed. *Essays on Aristotle's* Rhetoric. Berkeley: Univ. of California Press, 1996.

Rumelili, Bahar. "Liminality and Perpetuation of Conflicts: Turkish–Greek Relations in the Context of Community-Building by the EU." *European Journal of International Relations* 9, no. 2 (2003): 213–48.

Rustow, Dankwart A. "The Army and the Founding of the Turkish Republic." *World Politics* 11, no. 4 (1959): 513–52.

Sahlins, Peter. *Boundaries: The Making of France and Spain in the Pyrenees.* Berkeley: Univ. of California Press, 1989.

Said, Edward W. *Orientalism.* New York: Vintage Books, 1978.

Sakallioğlu, Ümit Cizre. "The Anatomy of the Turkish Military's Political Autonomy." *Comparative Politics* 29, no. 2 (1997): 151–66.

Sarısözen, Güner, ed. *Yassıada'dan Anıtmezar'a.* Ankara: Demokratlar Kulübü Yayınları: 1, 1991.

Şenışık, Pınar. "The Allied Occupation of İstanbul and the Construction of Turkish National Identity in the Early Twentieth Century." *Nationalities Papers* 46, no. 3 (2018): 501–13.

Shafak, Elif. *The Bastard of Istanbul.* New York: Penguin, 2007.

Soner, B. Ali. "Citizenship and the Minority Question in Turkey." In *Citizenship in a Global World: European Questions and Turkish Experiences*, edited by E. Fuat Keyman and Ahmet İçduygu, 289–311. New York: Routledge, 2005.

Söyler, Mehtap. *The Turkish Deep State: State Consolidation, Civil–Military Relations, and Democracy.* New York: Routledge, 2015.

Spivak, Gayatri Chakravorty. "Can the Subaltern Speak?" In *Marxism and the Interpretation of Culture*, edited by Cary Nelson and Lawrence Grossberg, 271–313. Urbana: Univ. of Illinois Press, 1988.

Steinberger, Peter J. *The Idea of the State.* New York: Cambridge Univ. Press, 2004.

Stephens, Angharad Closs. "The Affective Atmospheres of Nationalism." *Cultural Geographies* 23, no. 2 (2016): 181–98.

Steunenberg, Bernard, Simay Petek, and Christiane Rüth. "Between Reason and Emotion: Popular Discourses on Turkey's Membership of the EU." In *Turkey and the EU: Accession and Reform*, edited by Gamze Avcı and Ali Çarkoğlu, 241–60. New York: Routledge, 2013.

Suny, Ronald Grigor, and Fatma Müge Göçek. "Introduction: Leaving It to the Historians." In *A Question of Genocide: Armenians and Turks at the End of the Ottoman Empire*, edited by Ronald Grigor Suny, Fatma Müge Göçek, and Norman M. Naimark, 3–12. New York: Oxford Univ. Press, 2011.

Suny, Ronald Grigor, Fatma Müge Göçek, and Norman M. Naimark, eds. *A Question of Genocide: Armenians and Turks at the End of the Ottoman Empire.* New York: Oxford Univ. Press, 2011.

Tachau, Frank, and Metin Heper. "The State, Politics, and the Military in Turkey." *Comparative Politics* 16, no. 1 (1983): 17–33.

Tambar, Kabir. "The Aesthetics of Public Visibility: Alevi *Semah* and the Paradoxes of Pluralism in Turkey." *Comparative Studies in Society and History* 52, no. 3 (2010): 652–79.

———. *The Reckoning of Pluralism: Political Belonging and the Demands of History in Turkey*. Stanford, CA: Stanford Univ. Press, 2014.

Tanyeri-Erdemir, Tuğba. "Archaeology as a Source of National Pride in the Early Years of the Turkish Republic." *Journal of Field Archaeology* 31, no. 4 (2006): 381–93.

Taş, Hakkı. "The 15 July Abortive Coup and Post-truth Politics in Turkey." *Southeast European and Black Sea Studies* 18, no. 1 (2018): 1–19.

Taylor, Charles. *Modern Social Imaginaries*. Durham, NC: Duke Univ. Press, 2004.

Tekinalp, Munis. *Kemalizm*. Translated by Çetin Yetkin. 1936. Reprint. Istanbul: Toplumsal Dünüşüm Yayınları, 2004.

Tell, Dave. "Rhetoric and Power: An Inquiry into Foucault's Critique of Confession." *Philosophy and Rhetoric* 43, no. 2 (2010): 95–117.

Tuğal, Cihan. *The Fall of the Turkish Model: How the Arab Uprisings Brought Down Islamic Liberalism*. New York: Verso, 2016.

Türkmen-Dervişoğlu, Gülay. "Coming to Terms with a Difficult Past: The Trauma of the Assassination of Hrant Dink and Its Repercussions on Turkish National Identity." *Nations and Nationalism* 19, no. 4 (2013): 674–92.

Turner, Bryan S., and Berna Zengin Arslan. "State and Turkish Secularism: The Case of the Diyanet." In Bryan S. Turner, *The Religious and the Political: A Comparative Sociology of Religion*, 206–24. New York: Cambridge Univ. Press, 2013.

Ulgen, Fatma. "'Sabiha Gökçen's 80-Year-Old Secret': Kemalist Nation Formation and the Ottoman Armenians." PhD diss., Univ. of California–San Diego, 2010.

Ulutaş, Ufuk. "Religion and Secularism in Turkey: The Dilemma of the Directorate of Religious Affairs." *Middle Eastern Studies* 46, no. 3 (2010): 389–99.

Üngör, Uğur Ümit. *The Making of Modern Turkey: Nation and State in Eastern Anatolia, 1913–1950*. New York: Oxford Univ. Press, 2011.

Ünver, H. Akin. "Turkey's 'Deep-State' and the Ergenekon Conundrum." *Middle East Institute Policy Brief* 23 (Apr. 2009). At https://www.mei.edu/publications/turkeys-deep-state-and-ergenekon-conundrum.

VanderLippe, John M. *The Politics of Turkish Democracy: İsmet İnönü and the Formation of the Multi-party System, 1938–1950.* Albany: State Univ. of New York Press, 2005.

Vaner, Semih. "The Army." Translated by Rezan Benatar and İrvin C. Schick. In *Turkey in Transition: New Perspectives*, edited by İrvin C. Schick and Ertuğrul Ahmet Tonak, 236–65. New York: Oxford Univ. Press, 1987.

Vardar, Deniz. "European Union–Turkish Relations and the Question of Citizenship." In *Citizenship in a Global World: European Questions and Turkish Experiences*, edited by E. Fuat Keyman and Ahmet İçduygu, 87–102. New York: Routledge, 2005.

Vickers, Brian. *In Defense of Rhetoric.* New York: Oxford Univ. Press, 1988.

Vryonis, Speros, Jr. *The Mechanism of Catastrophe: The Turkish Pogrom of September 6–7, 1955, and the Destruction of the Greek Community of Istanbul.* New York: Greekworks, 2005.

Warnick, Barbara. "Two Systems of Invention: The Topics in the *Rhetoric* and *The New Rhetoric*." In *Rereading Aristotle's* Rhetoric, edited by Alan G. Gross and Arthur E. Walzer, 107–29. Carbondale: Southern Illinois Univ. Press, 2000.

Weber, Eugen. *Peasants into Frenchmen: The Modernization of Rural France, 1870–1914.* Stanford, CA: Stanford Univ. Press, 1976.

Wedeen, Lisa. *Peripheral Visions: Publics, Power, and Performance in Yemen.* Chicago: Univ. of Chicago Press, 2008.

White, Hayden. *Metahistory: The Historical Imagination in Nineteenth-Century Europe.* Baltimore: Johns Hopkins Univ. Press, 1973.

———. "The Value of Narrativity in the Representation of Reality." *Critical Inquiry* 7, no. 1 (1980): 5–27.

White, Jenny. *Muslim Nationalism and the New Turks.* Princeton, NJ: Princeton Univ. Press, 2013.

White, Paul J. "The Debate on the Identity of 'Alevi Kurds.'" In *Turkey's Alevi Enigma: A Comprehensive Overview*, edited by Paul J. White and Joost Jongerden, 17–29. Leiden: Brill, 2003.

Worringer, Renée. "'Sick Man of Europe' or 'Japan of the Near East'? Constructing Ottoman Modernity in the Hamidian and Young Turk Eras." *International Journal of Middle East Studies* 36, no. 2 (2004): 207–30.

Yavuz, M. Hakan. "Cleansing Islam from the Public Sphere." *Journal of International Affairs* 54, no. 1 (2000): 21–42.

———. "Turkey's Fault Lines and the Crisis of Kemalism." *Current History* 99, no. 633 (2000): 33–38.

Yavuz, M. Hakan, and Nihat Ali Özcan. "The Kurdish Question and Turkey's Justice and Development Party." *Middle East Policy* 13, no. 1 (2006): 102–19.

Yeğen, Mesut. "The Kurdish Question in Turkey: Denial to Recognition." In *Nationalisms and Politics in Turkey: Political Islam, Kemalism, and the Kurdish Issue*, edited by Marlies Casier and Joost Jongerden, 67–84. New York: Routledge, 2011.

Yeşilada, Birol. *EU–Turkey Relations in the 21st Century.* New York: Routledge, 2013.

Yılmaz, Hale. *Becoming Turkish: Nationalist Reforms and Cultural Negotiations in Early Republican Turkey, 1923–1945*. Syracuse, NY: Syracuse Univ. Press, 2013.

Yilmaz, Ihsan, and Galib Bashirov. "The AKP after 15 Years: Emergence of Erdoğanism in Turkey." *Third World Quarterly* 39, no. 9 (2018): 1812–830.

Young, Robert J. C. *White Mythologies: Writing History and the West.* 2nd ed. New York: Routledge, 2004.

Zarefsky, David. "Four Senses of Rhetorical History." In *Doing Rhetorical History: Concepts and Cases*, edited by Kathleen J. Turner, 19–32. Tuscaloosa: Univ. of Alabama Press, 1998.

Žižek, Slavoj. *The Sublime Object of Ideology*. New York: Verso, 1989.

Zürcher, Erik J. [variously Erik-Jan or Erik Jan]. "The Ottoman Legacy of the Kemalist Republic." In *The Young Turk Legacy and Nation Building: From the Ottoman Empire to Atatürk's Turkey*, 136–50. London: I. B. Taurus, 2010.

———. "Ottoman Sources of Kemalist Thought." In *Late Ottoman Society: The Intellectual Legacy*, edited by Elisabeth Özdalga, 14–27. New York: Routledge, 2005.

———. *Political Opposition in the Early Turkish Republic: The Progressive Republican Party, 1924–1925*. New York: Brill, 1991.

———. "The Politician as Historian, Historians in Politics: On the *Nutuk* (Speech) of Mustafa Kemal Pasha." In *The Young Turk Legacy and Nation Building: From the Ottoman Empire to Atatürk's Turkey*, 6–16. London: I. B. Taurus, 2010.

———. "Renewal and Silence: Postwar Unionist and Kemalist Rhetoric on the Armenian Genocide." In *A Question of Genocide: Armenians and Turks at the End of the Ottoman Empire*, edited by Ronald Grigor Suny, Fatma Müge Göçek, and Norman M. Naimark, 306–16. New York: Oxford Univ. Press, 2011.

———. "The Rise and Fall of 'Modern' Turkey: Bernard Lewis's *Emergence* Fifty Years On." In *The Young Turk Legacy and Nation Building: From the Ottoman Empire to Atatürk's Turkey*, 41–53. London: I. B. Taurus, 2010.

———. *Turkey: A Modern History*. 3rd ed. New York: I. B. Tauris, 2004.

———. *The Unionist Factor: The Role of the Committee of Union and Progress in the Turkish Nationalist Movement 1905–1926*. Leiden, Netherlands: Brill, 1984.

———. "The Vocabulary of Muslim Nationalism." *International Journal of the Sociology of Language* 137 (1999): 81–92.

———. *The Young Turk Legacy and Nation Building: From the Ottoman Empire to Atatürk's Turkey*. London: I. B. Taurus, 2010.

———. "Young Turk Memoirs as a Historical Source: Kâzım Karabekir's *İstiklâl Harbimiz*." In *The Young Turk Legacy and Nation Building: From the Ottoman Empire to Atatürk's Turkey*, 17–25. London: I. B. Taurus, 2010.

Index

Matthew deTar is assistant professor of rhetoric and culture at Ohio University. He completed his PhD at Northwestern University. His work has appeared in *Communication and Critical/Cultural Studies*, *Rhetoric and Public Affairs*, *Journal of Contemporary Thought*, *Advances in the History of Rhetoric*, and *Departures in Critical Qualitative Inquiry*. His research has been supported by the Center for Religion, Law, and Democracy at Willamette University, the Institute for Turkish Studies at Georgetown University, and the Buffett Institute for Global Affairs at Northwestern University.